Building Java™ Enterprise Applications
Applications
Volume I: Architecture

Related titles from O'Reilly

Creating Effective JavaHelp™

Database Programming with JDBC and Java™

Developing JavaBeans™

Enterprise JavaBeans™

Java™ 2D Graphics

Java™ & XML

Java™ and XSLT

Java™ Cookbook

Java™ Cryptography

Java™ Distributed Computing

Java™ Enterprise in a Nutshell

Java™ Examples in a Nutshell

Java™ Foundation Classes in a Nutshell

Java™ I/O

Java™ in a Nutshell

Java™ Internationalization

Java™ Message Service

Java™ Network Programming

Java™ Performance Tuning

Java™ Programming with Oracle SQLJ

Java™ Security

JavaServer™ Pages

JavaServer™ Pages Pocket Reference

Java™ Servlet Programming

Java™ Swing

Java™ Threads

Jini™ in a Nutshell

Learning Java™

Also available

The Java™ Enterprise CD Bookshelf

Java™ Professional Library

Building Java™ Enterprise Applications

Applications

Volume I: Architecture

Brett McLaughlin

O'REILLY®

Beijing · Cambridge · Farnham · Köln · Paris · Sebastopol · Taipei · Tokyo

Building Java™ Enterprise Applications Volume I: Architecture
by Brett McLaughlin

Published by O'Reilly & Associates, Inc., 1005 Gravenstein Highway North, Sebastopol, CA 95472.

O'Reilly & Associates books may be purchased for educational, business, or sales promotional use. Online editions are also available for most titles (*safari.oreilly.com*). For more information contact our corporate/institutional sales department: (800) 998-9938 or *corporate@oreilly.com*.

Editor:	Mike Loukides
Production Editor:	Emily Quill
Cover Designer:	Hanna Dyer
Interior Designer:	Melanie Wang

Printing History:

March 2002:	First Edition.

ISBN: 0-596-00123-1

[M]

Table of Contents

Preface

If you're basing your livelihood on Java these days, you are going to run across at least one enterprise application programming project; if it hasn't come upon you already, it's just around the corner. I've been faced with more than twenty at this point in my career, and see many more in my future. Each time I get into these projects, I find myself paging through book after book and searching the Web, looking for the same information time after time. Additionally, I've developed a bit of a toolkit for handling common enterprise tasks.

What I have determined is that there are many terrific books on specific technologies like Enterprise JavaBeans, servlets, and the Java Message Service. These books cover the details of these APIs and explain how to use them. I have also found, though, that there is no resource in existence that describes connecting these components in an intelligent way. No coherent examples are documented and explained that tell how best to code façade patterns, attach entity beans to directory servers, use servlets and JSP with EJB without killing performance, or a host of other common tasks. At the same time, these very issues are the heart of my job description, and probably of many other programmers' as well.

Rather than simply write a short article or two and fall short of really addressing the topic (something I see lots of people doing), I convinced O'Reilly & Associates to put forth an exhaustive series on enterprise programming in Java. I'm proud to say that you have in your hands the first volume of that series. It covers the back-end of application programming and explains databases, entity beans, session beans, the Java Message Service, JNDI, RMI, LDAP, and a whole lot more.

The topic will be extended in the next two volumes, which are already planned. The second volume will cover traditional web applications, including HTTP, HTML, servlets, JSP, and XML presentation solutions. The third volume will detail the web services paradigm, demonstrating the use of UDDI, SOAP, WSDL, and other emerging technologies.

In each volume, you will find extensive code (the code listings in this book, without comments, total well over 100 pages, about 30% of the actual book), without needless instruction or banter. I've gotten straight to the point, and tried to let you see code, not discussion of code, whenever possible. I hope that you enjoy the series, and that it aids you in your own enterprise application programming.

Organization

This book starts from the back of an enterprise application, moves from introduction into design and planning, through the database and directory server, and into the code you'll need to use this data. Here are concise descriptions of each chapter.

Chapter 1, *Introduction*
> This chapter expands on the basic information in this Preface. It provides a blueprint for the series as well as the topics included in the chapters of this book.

Chapter 2, *Blueprints*
> As suggested by the title, this chapter presents the vital planning and requirements phase of enterprise programming. It explains how decisions are made and how business needs are mapped to technical requirements, and outlines the process of taking a vague description and converting it to a technical blueprint.

Chapter 3, *Foundation*
> This chapter starts to dig into technical details. It takes the blueprints from Chapter 2 and begins to implement these in terms of data storage. You'll learn how to handle issues surrounding relational databases, write the SQL to create the data store, and develop constraints for the database. You'll also learn about directory servers and create a directory for the book's sample application.

Chapter 4, *Entity Basics*
> This chapter details the basics of entity beans in terms of enterprise programming. You'll create your first entity bean for the sample application, learn about IDs and sequences, and set the groundwork for the rest of the application.

Chapter 5, *Advanced Entities*
> This chapter deals with more advanced concepts. IDs and sequences will be handled in a more generic fashion, and you'll mix session beans with entity beans, learn about information maps, and delve into more advanced CMP entity beans.

Chapter 6, *Managers*
> This chapter introduces the manager component, explaining how data can be abstracted into Java components. Specifically, you'll write code to provide access to the directory server created earlier, and tie this component in with already-developed entity beans and databases.

Chapter 7, *Completing the Data Layer*

> This chapter puts the finishing touches on the data access layer. You'll deal with threading and multiple directory server instances, as well as client applications. Finally, testing will be put in place to ensure that everything is working correctly to this point.

Chapter 8, *Business Logic*

> This chapter moves from the data layer into the business layer. It further explains using the manager component, specifically with session beans. You'll also find out the best approaches to connecting your session beans to the entities and managers already in place

Chapter 9, *Messaging and Packaging*

> This chapter completes the business layer with a discussion of using JMS and message-driven beans. You'll create a messaging layer in your application as well as clients that interact with it. Finally, basic packaging issues are detailed and related to the components already developed.

Chapter 10, *Beyond Architecture*

> This final chapter gives some general advice for moving beyond this first volume into web applications and web services. It also provides some practical information and resources for continuing in your application development.

Appendixes

> The appendixes cover deployment of SQL scripts, installation of directory servers, application server setup and configuration, and supplemental code listings. These are chock-full of technical details that didn't easily fit into the chapters.

Software and Versions

This book covers a variety of APIs, but all fall underneath the Java 2 Enterprise Edition (J2EE) umbrella. I've used the 1.3 version of this platform, which is the "latest and greatest" available. You can download J2EE 1.3 and find out more about it online at *http://java.sun.com/j2ee/*.

The nature of application programming in the enterprise requires an application server on which to deploy your components. This requires a lot of vendor-specific deployment and packaging details. I've avoided these paradigms throughout the book, instead focusing on the vendor-neutral code that you will need to write. However, the appendixes at the end of this book detail deployment of various vendors' tools, specifically BEA Weblogic, the most popular large-scale application server available. This is a J2EE 1.3 application server, so you will be set with it or any other 1.3-compatible server.

The source for the examples in this book is contained completely within the book itself. Both source and binary forms of all examples (including extensive Javadoc not necessarily included in the text) are available online at *http://www.newInstance.com*.

Conventions Used in This Book

I use the following font conventions in this book:

Italic is used for:

- Unix pathnames, filenames, and program names
- Internet addresses, such as domain names and URLs
- Object names and classes
- New terms where they are defined

`Constant width` is used for:

- Command lines and options that should be typed verbatim
- Names and keywords in Java programs, including method names, variable names, and class names
- XML element names and tags, attribute names, and other XML constructs that appear as they would within an XML document

`Constant width bold` is used for:

- Highlighting emphasized areas in code

EJB names are printed in roman. (An EJB name is not necessarily the name of a class or any other Java object.)

 This icon signifies a note relating to the nearby text.

 This icon signifies a warning relating to the nearby text.

Comments and Questions

Please address comments and questions concerning this book to the publisher:

O'Reilly & Associates, Inc.
1005 Gravenstein Highway North
Sebastopol, CA 95472
(800) 998-9938 (in the United States or Canada)
(707) 829-0515 (international or local)
(707) 829-0104 (fax)

There is a web page for this book, where we list errata, examples, or any additional information. You can access this page at:

http://www.oreilly.com/catalog/javentappsv1

To comment or ask technical questions about this book, send email to:

bookquestions@oreilly.com

For more information about books, conferences, Resource Centers, and the O'Reilly Network, see our web site at:

http://www.oreilly.com

Also visit the author's web site, *http://www.newInstance.com*.

Acknowledgments

I have to think Mike Loukides and Kyle Hart, my right-hand man and woman at O'Reilly, for helping guide a very difficult book to its end. The first words of this book were actually written in November of 1999 (yes, you read that right!), so it's been a long time coming. Thanks also to Diana Reid at BEA for support and much-needed help on getting things running with BEA Weblogic.

I'd be in a heap of trouble without the support of my extended family: Gary and Shirley Greathouse, Quinn and Joni Greathouse, Larry and Judy McLaughlin, Shannon McLaughlin, and Sarah Jane Burden. Also to Laura and Laura Jordan, who made me an uncle with the addition of little Nathan (Nate to those who he drools on), who provided much-needed laughs when things got tough. I love all of you.

Of course, the biggest debt of gratitude lies with my wife. She simply makes life worth getting up for, never complains (too much) when I work long hours, and is always excited when I finish even though she has no idea what all this Java stuff is about. And, as if all that isn't enough, in June she's giving me a baby boy! If I take longer to answer mail this summer (2002), it's only because I'm learning to be a daddy with little Dean, my upcoming first child. Can you tell I'm excited? I love you Leigh and Dean (one day he'll realize this was the first time his name was in print).

Again, to the Lord who got me this far: Even so, come Lord Jesus.

## CHAPTER 1

Introduction

Java has become a confusing world. Five years ago, there were few decisions to make once you started programming in Java—you used AWT for graphical user interfaces, sockets for network programming, and hacked together everything else you needed. Since then, though, the APIs available for the Java language have grown, and grown...and grown. Now you can dabble in Swing, servlets, Enterprise JavaBeans (EJB), JavaMail, and more. Additionally, there are now packages of APIs, like the Java 2 Micro Edition (J2ME) and Java 2 Enterprise Edition (J2EE). While these packages seem to be nicely wrapped bundles of useful APIs, they don't help the average developer figure out how to piece together the APIs contained in these packages. Though it's simple to find documentation on the individual APIs, getting the "big picture" is difficult, at best. One of the most interesting, but difficult, aspects of Java today is building Java enterprise applications using the J2EE package.

All of this has led the folks at O'Reilly to be interested in a book specifically focused on building enterprise applications with these APIs. Instead of small, piecemeal examples, we've found that readers want large applications built from the ground up, and explanations of design decisions. Additionally, readers have been adamant about seeing more than just the Java part of the picture; they want to know how to set up a database, and get an LDAP store running, and integrate these. How does a UDDI registry fit into the equation? I'm going to address all of these issues in this series (yes, I said series!) of books, *Building Java Enterprise Applications*. You hold Volume I in your hands.

So, this chapter is a true introduction. Not only will it introduce you to what I'll be covering in this book and the materials you'll need to follow along, but it will also tell you how this series is going to be put together. You'll see what's coming in Volumes II and III, how the examples are structured, and what topics will be covered in this book as well as future ones.

I'm glad you're willing to come along with me as we try something new. And, with that, let's get down to the details of building enterprise applications.

Building Java Enterprise Applications

From the first page of the first chapter to the last page of the last index, this series is going to focus on *building* applications. That probably sounds redundant, since you picked up this book knowing the title, but let me explain what I mean. First, I'm not going to explain the basics of the technologies used in this book. If you don't know what an entity bean is, or haven't ever written a SQL statement, or want to learn about JSPs, this book isn't for you. I'd recommend you pick up a copy of the O'Reilly book on the subject you want to learn about, and start there. The "Related Works" section at the end of this chapter is a good reference for linking a subject to the right O'Reilly book.

Second, this book is aimed squarely at the enterprise developer, and especially at someone who has an existing or upcoming project that uses all or part of the J2EE platform. I'll explain later what constitutes an enterprise application, but this book will be most helpful if you have some real business problems to solve and can apply the concepts in these chapters directly to them.

Third, I expect you to be comfortable with (and hopefully, desirous of) lots of code. I'm going to try to keep explanations to the bare minimum on basic concepts, and instead focus on tougher problems, real-world issues that aren't covered in other books, and typical mistakes I see in day-to-day programming. If you're not ready to wade through a lot of code (thousands of lines in this volume, for starters), you might want to set this down and pick it up again once you've had a little more experience (as if any real programmer would put something down because it's over their head!).

Fourth, this book focuses on writing applications from the ground up, using only Java as the programming language. While many enterprise applications do have to deal with legacy code or non-Java system integration, that is a topic well unto itself. To keep things clear and concise, this book deals with systems that are entirely based on the Java programming language. While the third volume on web services will certainly touch on integration with other languages, this architecture volume does not.

And finally, I'm hoping that you're willing to work through this volume, and even the rest of the series, chapter by chapter, example by example. I'll be taking you through the building of a non-trivial application in this book, and continue on with that example over the next two volumes. Although all the code covered will be available online, I've presented things in a manner that assumes you're going through the code with me. So even if you don't usually do this sort of thing, you might want to try it for this book, as it will really help you out. Also, the next two volumes will assume that you've got the code from this book working, as we'll be building on top of that infrastructure. To help you see how things will fit together, let's now walk through the three volumes that will make up this series.

Lest any of you go to the bank on the description of the series presented here, I should warn you that as with all plans, things may change. Additionally, the folks at O'Reilly have had lots of discussion about whether to first put out a volume on traditional web applications (servlets, JSP, HTML) or on web services (SOAP, UDDI, WSDL). So, if you've got an opinion, let us know! There are details on getting in touch with us in the Preface of this book, and I look forward to hearing your thoughts.

Volume I: Architecture

This first volume focuses on application architecture and serves as the foundation for the next two volumes. I'll dive a little further into the specifics of what this book covers in the next section.

Any enterprise application has two baseline components: design and data stores. The first of these components, design, turns out to be more about concepts and theory than about actual programming. In fact, most developers rush right through this step because they want to get to coding, and almost inevitably end up paying a price for that haste later on. In light of that, this book pays a lot of attention to design decisions involved in enterprise applications. Additionally, it lays out the process flow for database interaction, and sets up connectors for allowing our later work with web applications and web services to interact with the infrastructure set up in this book.

Additionally, this volume will spend a lot of time detailing how to develop data stores for use in these applications. Obviously, this involves databases, from designing tables and columns to dealing with database sequences and triggers. Since each database has its own unique features, appendixes are included to offer advice on vendor-specific variations in SQL and on how to optimize your code for specific databases. Additionally, I'll spend a good bit of time delving into directory services and explaining how authentication data should be handled differently from application data. This will set the stage for the EJBs discussed in this book, which are also used heavily in the second and third volumes.

Volume II: Web Applications

The second volume in the series will continue where Volume I leaves off, adding a web application front-end to the architecture designed in the first book. In this volume, *web application* means using J2EE technologies (servlets, JDBC, JSPs) and HTML to construct an HTTP-accessible application front-end. In addition to explaining how these APIs fit together, this volume will also connect these front-end components to the back-ends created in Volume I. RMI, EJBs, JDBC, and more will be explained in light of the web application.

I'll also explain how various XML-based solutions like XSL and XML transformations can provide alternatives to HTML user interfaces. Although not completely integrated into the J2EE platform, XML and related technologies are becoming a vital part of any large-scale application, especially one that serves both static and dynamic content. I'll also look at XML data binding, RSS, and other means of communicating content between application front-ends.

Finally, some of the satellite components of J2EE, such as JavaMail, will be explained and discussed in relation to a functioning web application. While not critical for typical applications, these APIs can be immensely helpful in implementing an additional layer of communication between your applications and the end user. By the end of this volume, you'll not only have a complete understanding of web applications, but you'll have built a front-to-back practical solution (using the example code of Volumes I and II).

Volume III: Web Services

The third volume in this series will focus specifically on web services. It takes the business components discussed in Volume I (EJBs and other Java classes) and explains how they can be converted into web services using technologies such as SOAP and WSDL. Issues related to security, communication, and service registration will be explored. This is presented as a contrast to the web application interface discussed in Volume II.

This volume will also discuss the considerations involved with transmitting data across a network. Custom data types, large amounts of information, and object serialization are all important considerations, and will be given detailed coverage. You'll also learn how UDDI registries and WSDL are important not only in allowing component access, but also in restricting that access to only those methods you want to expose. Finally, exposing EJBs will be covered in detail.

Architecture

Now that you have a good idea of how the volumes in this series progress, I want to focus on what will be covered in this book. This description follows the flow of the book itself, and lets you know where to turn if you're looking for something specific. I'll also give you a little more detail here than what is in the Preface.

Databases

After walking through some design issues, the first technical topic in this book is that of databases. Although almost every Java developer working on enterprise applications has used a database, very few are competent database developers. In other words, programmers know how to create rows and columns, but have very little

---

understanding of the best way to tune tables, of how to perform database normalization, or of making a database work in an efficient, useful way.

In the chapters on database design and setup, I'll show how to create a database structure via the Structured Query Language (SQL). More importantly, I'll focus on how to set up a good relational structure and examine how EJBs need to access the data. This discussion should allow you to move from using a database to mastering one, at least in the context of enterprise applications. Discussions will be applicable to any database vendor.

Directory Servers

While traditional relational databases are still the prevalent force for data storage in enterprise applications, alternative data mediums are becoming popular. XML-based databases and object-oriented databases are in direct competition with relational databases, and directory servers offer a complementary solution to existing databases. For data that is read far more often than it is written, directory servers excel in performance. Examples of this sort of data are authentication credentials, such as usernames and passwords, which tend to be performance-driven. In other words, the less time a user waits to log in, the better your application is perceived.

This book takes an extensive look at directory servers in order to show you how to develop systems that integrate multiple types of data stores. I'll explain how to set up the directory store schema (which is analogous to the tables and columns of a relational database) and how to populate the directory store. I'll also show you how the Java Naming and Directory Interface (JNDI) can provide fast access to a directory server. Finally, I'll cover the tricky issues that surround using multiple data stores: replication, data overlap, and keeping data in sync and uncorrupted.

Enterprise JavaBeans

Once you've got a data store (actually, a couple of them) in place, I'll finally move on to Java, and accessing that data through Java. In addition to the JNDI access for directory servers, you'll learn how to use Enterprise JavaBeans (EJB) to interact with a database. I'll cover setting up your EJB container, writing entity beans for data access, and using session beans to provide a layer between your entity beans and the rest of your application. Finally, I'll detail how message-driven beans can allow communication between components that was almost impossible in earlier versions of the EJB specification.

Of course, we'll quickly move beyond these basics. I'll demonstrate the impact that EJB 2.0 has on your enterprise applications, and cover more complex issues such as using database sequences, direct access to entity beans, and how the container affects your EJB design. I'll also detail the ins and outs of Remote Method Invocation (RMI) and how to make it perform at its best. Several chapters will be devoted to the EJB layer, so you'll have plenty of Java code to sink your teeth into: entity beans, session beans, and message-driven beans will all be explored in relation to the enterprise application.

What You'll Need

Before getting into the thick of things, let's take a moment to cover what you'll need to work through this book. Most crucial are the APIs involved, but also important are the application server, the tools I'll refer to, and all the support facilities for writing enterprise applications. You'll also probably have your own set of tools (code editors, HTML editors, etc.), and you should not have too much trouble adapting to any of the instructions for specific products that you use.

APIs

First and foremost, this book is focused on the 1.3 version of the J2EE specification. You can download the J2EE specification from Sun online at *http://java.sun.com/j2ee*. I also highly recommend that you download the J2EE SDK (essentially the reference implementation), which can be used for running the example code.

Let me say a word about application servers. There are as many application server vendors as there are colors, and picking one isn't always a trivial task. Additionally, trying to cover the nuances of each application server in a single book is simply impossible; you'll always find a vendor or version that doesn't fit the instructions, and in those cases a book's instructions can cause confusion instead of resolving it. To keep this to a minimum, I've taken two steps. First, the content in the chapters of this book is focused on APIs, code, and deployment descriptors, and will work on any J2EE 1.3 application server. In other words, the chapters are all vendor-neutral. However, this leaves a lot of vendor-specific detail up in the air, as most application servers have specific instructions for setup and deployment. To accommodate this, the appendixes in this book will show you how to get the examples to work using the BEA Weblogic application server.

If you work in an environment where another application server is in use, you can take your applications and deploy them to that application server, using the specific vendor's documentation. The result is an application that is as portable as it can be in today's world of too-many variations on the J2EE theme. Additionally, as demand and time dictate, instructions for working with other popular application servers will be posted online at this book's web site, *http://www.newInstance.com*. I'm going to handle this process much like an open source project, so if you go online and don't see your vendor covered, I welcome your help and will work with you to get instructions online for your application server. Hopefully, this will be the best compromise between getting you timely and accurate information, and not creating confusion throughout the book's text.

There is also specific software needed for chapters that go beyond Java; for example, you'll need a directory server for the LDAP chapters and a database for the data store chapters. I'll discuss specific alternatives in those chapters and explain what factors can influence your choices in these areas. I try to always recommend (at a minimum) an open source option and a popular commercial alternative. More often than not, one of these will result in a good match for your needs.

Tools and Utilities

I also recommend a few tools and utilities for this book. While you can certainly make your own choices here, I'll let you know what has worked for me. First, you'll want a Java Integrated Development Environment (IDE). While I often use word-pad, *vi*, or Emacs for editing code, large projects demand keeping up with three, four, or more active files. It's here that an IDE can really help out. I prefer jEdit, available for free at *http://www.jedit.org*. There are tons of helpful plug-ins, Java syntax highlighting is included, and it has good support with new versions coming out fast and often.

I also recommend that you have a tool for working with databases that allows fast SQL querying. Here, I am fond of a commercial tool, SQL Navigator, which is available for purchase at *http://www.quest.com/sql_navigator/*. This tool allows interactive querying, a nice interface for setting up your database schema, and a lot more. It's also particularly useful when dealing with Oracle, its preferred database, as it allows you to use PL/SQL, triggers, and other features specific to Oracle. Outside of SQL Navigator, there are many other free tools available for working with databases.

Finally, quite a bit of XML will be in play throughout the EJB chapters. It's needed to write deployment descriptors, and I'll also examine using XML for properties and configuration information. Additionally, many application servers add vendor-specific XML descriptors that you'll need at deployment time. I recommend an XML editor to make validation of these files easy. While you can (as I did until recently) write some command-line tools using an XML parser to handle this task, I again have recently taken up using an IDE. jEdit works well here, and I have also had some success with XMLSpy, available at *http://www.xmlspy.com*. All these tools are optional, and I won't dwell on them in the text, but they can really increase productivity and make life a little easier.

Related Works

In addition to everything I've said so far, I'm a big advocate of books as an aid in learning and programming. A famous preacher, Lester Roloff, once said, "The best memory is the pencil." I tend to agree, as I'm constantly making notes about this method or that class, trying to remember what they do. However, there are a lot of books already written with these notes categorized, indexed, and explained in detail, so I'll provide you a short list of books that may be helpful as you work through this volume.

Generally, these are books on the technologies that are detailed in this work, and will help you get up to speed on the basics of these technologies. Many times, I assume you have knowledge of the topics in these books, and they are all worthwhile additions to your library.

- *Enterprise JavaBeans*, by Richard Monson-Haefel
- *Database Programming with JDBC and Java*, by George Reese
- *Java Enterprise in a Nutshell*, by David Flanagan, Jim Farley, William Crawford, and Kris Magnusson
- *Java Message Service*, by Richard Monson-Haefel and David Chappell
- *MySQL and mSQL*, by Randy Jay Yarger, George Reese, and Tim King
- *Oracle Design*, by Dave Ensor and Ian Stevenson

All of these are published by O'Reilly. Obviously there are many other helpful books out there, but these should get you started. Armed with this information, you're ready to move beyond introduction into the world of enterprise application programming.

## CHAPTER 2

Blueprints

Let's begin to delve into enterprise applications. With some basic knowledge of the Java APIs and related technologies (such as XML) that are involved with these applications, you are as qualified as the next programmer to start building applications! This is a new frontier, even though it's been three or four years since the J2EE specification was released. That may sound a bit far-fetched, but technology is moving at an incredible rate, as are the APIs that support it. Just two years ago, applications had far fewer tools, technologies, and specifications upon which to build. For these reasons, you start with most other programmers on a generally level playing field. And as each phase of building an application is addressed, I discuss the principles that will guide you in your own applications, using any combination of APIs and tools.

However, discussing these complex applications in the abstract is like talking about music (which is like dancing about architecture, according to Miles Davis). In other words, trying to describe how to build an application without in fact building one is nearly impossible. For that reason, this entire series discusses the Java APIs and code within the context of a large, enterprise application that will be accessible through a web interface (in Volume II) and as a web service (in Volume III). Starting in this chapter, I will detail a fictional company, Forethought Brokerage, and discuss the application they are building (or rather, that *you* are building for them). Beginning with only a set of requirements, you will construct the Forethought application from the ground up, including data storage, API selection, and of course implementation. At the end of the series, the application will finally be ready to run, complete with several advanced features that are usable in your own applications. In this first volume, you'll build a data store that includes a database, a directory server, and numerous Enterprise JavaBeans.

This chapter begins the process by presenting a set of requirements. I will take these requirements and design blueprints for the application, "roughing out" each portion of the application and explaining each decision made. With this set of blueprints in hand, it's possible to detail each section of the application. Additionally, in a commercial environment, multiple teams could work on different portions of the application in parallel; this is possible only with a well-designed set of plans for the application, agreed upon before development begins. Although you are the only developer working on the example application, following this practice will teach you how to design your own applications so that multiple programmers can work on them. Once a general set of requirements is laid out and met, I'll run through a brief survey of the key technologies used throughout the rest of this book. If you are familiar with databases, directory servers, enterprise Java, and XML, you can probably skim these later sections of the chapter. However, if you're new to enterprise programming, these descriptions will help prepare you for the chapters that follow.

I will also go beyond just the data and business layers, which this book focuses on, and describe the presentation layer of the application. This will apply to the web interface detailed in Volume II, but will also give you perspective on how things fit together, and provide you with a good idea of how to proceed if you don't want to wait for the next volume in the series.

Forethought Brokerage

Like any good building, an application begins with a set of requirements, often having little to do with implementation details. The first challenge of constructing an application, then, is to translate these requirements into technological outlines and a plan for action. While this can be simple when the person or group defining these requirements is technical, it is far more often the case that this mapping of requirements to an application blueprint is the most difficult portion of architecting an application. A marketing or product management group explaining their needs rarely has an idea of what is technically feasible, or even possible, with today's programming languages. Additionally, these initial requirements have a way of changing during a project, resulting in a moving target for completing a "successful" application. In fact, this is the first lesson in building an application: an application that meets the initial set of requirements is not automatically a success! Instead, it must anticipate the changing of requirements and be able to adapt in kind. For this reason, a flexible architecture and well-designed set of blueprints can lead to customer sign-off, protecting the application designer from these changes, or at least providing a reasonable window of change when requirements do evolve. This is the kind of architecture and blueprint that must be developed for Forethought Brokerage.[*]

The Company

Forethought Brokerage has been serving their clients in a traditional investment brokerage sense for nearly 20 years. Specializing in long-term clients and customer service, the brokerage has until recently run their entire operation largely through a

---

[*] Forethought Brokerage is a completely fictional company, and any resemblance to an existing or future company is purely accidental and unintentional.

paper office, using carbon receipts, conference calls, and face-to-face meetings. They have monitored their clients' funds through frequent phone calls, monitoring the market, and by sweat and hard work. Although this has succeeded in building their client base and keeping them in business for almost 20 years, it has also caused some problems. They have had to remain a locally based business, as they have no facility to handle clients around the country and the world, and their established pattern of personal consultations begins to break down over distance. Additionally, monitoring funds in 24 time zones instead of one is a significant increase in workload.

Forethought has also had a longtime fear of problems related to the paper trail on which their office relies. Even though Forethought has an offsite storage location, searches through paperwork and misfiled receipts have caused many a late night for partners and immeasurable stress for clients. The company realizes that the computer age has taken over in business, and wants to move into an electronic form of communication and storage. This would also enable them to establish additional offices and expand geographically while using one unified computer system for their records, and would allow clients to access their profiles and investments online, as many have requested. With this recognition of their problems, Forethought has begun to define the desired functionality of the application they want built.

Identified Needs

Forethought's product management and marketing groups (usually made up of the proverbial "pointy-haired bosses") have determined their company's needs and are ready to supply these needs to you, the lead architect and developer of their new application. These needs must be met for the application to be any sort of success, and many of them must be mapped from a business requirement to a technical one. Let's take a look at what the application requires.

Online accessibility

First and foremost, Forethought wants to move to a web-based solution for their clients and employees (they won't make it to web services until Volume III). As offices open in new locations, these offices should be able to operate within the Forethought system through simple Internet access. Additionally, online accessibility means that agents away from the office can still access their clients' investments. Forethought also wants a means of securing access to the application, through a username and password, at a minimum. They also would like any other security appropriate for the privileged information that clients and brokers would view online.

Forethought has also determined that using a simple web browser should be sufficient to access the application. This enables easy rollout of the application, and avoids any costs of delivering disks or CDs with special software to clients wanting to access their accounts online. Since any user with a PC can be expected to have a web browser on their computer, Internet access to the application through a browser is ideal.

Supports wireless devices

As the company expands, agents need to travel more, both between offices and to clients that are geographically dispersed. With this travel comes a need to communicate, which of course is most common through mobile phones. Forethought wants to take advantage of today's wireless phones, and use Internet access as a means of supplying remote agents information about their clients quickly. An agent on the road should be able to use a WAP or HDML phone to connect to the Forethought web application and quickly gain basic information about a client and his or her accounts.

The same thinking applies to employees with Palm Pilot or other handheld devices. Delivering content to these Internet-capable devices should be possible with the application. Of course, like any company, Forethought wants to keep maintenance costs as low as possible, while still providing content to these varying devices. In other words, reusability of the application's content is important.

Handles scheduling

Scheduling is also an important aspect of Forethought's needs. As mentioned, employees (particularly brokers) will be traveling, so the tracking of meetings, appointments, and events will be critical to the company's success. Without the ability to determine where a broker must be at what time, that broker is useless to the company. Additionally, brokers shouldn't be tied to their calendar applications on a specific desktop computer. Laptops, multiple desktops, and wireless devices should all be able to access the same shared schedule, allowing the broker to check and maintain his schedule from anywhere he can access the Forethought application via the Internet.

Stores information about employees as well as clients

In addition to providing clients online access to their accounts, the application should also be able to serve Forethought as an information and intranet service. In other words, referencing details about other brokers could help an agent give referrals to clients who are moving, and could also help management monitor employees across the country and the world. This sort of dual-purpose application, where both clients and internal workers use the provided services, is becoming more and more common.

"Fast performance and standards compliance"

All too often, marketing and management groups toss a statement like "standards-based" or "performance-driven" into an application's requirements. It would seem that these types of statements are meant to appease the technical nature of the developers working on the application, but in fact these statements are nebulous at best, and often entirely useless. How fast must the application respond? Is a World Wide Web Consortium (W3C) recommendation a standard? Are de facto standards like the Simple API for XML (SAX) standard? What sort of benchmarks should be performed? All of these questions are left ambiguously defined with vague requirements like "fast performance and standards compliance."

While the knowledge of these issues by the marketing and product groups is often as indeterminate as the questions themselves, the points are worth noting. Choosing a technology or solution that is not supportable or that may be antiquated in several years will leave you having to explain your bad decisions to upper management. While this is not a blanket recommendation to accept all standards hook, line, and sinker, it is a good idea to justify all decisions made. As an example, using large portions of the J2EE specification makes a lot of sense, as Sun will certainly support Java and the J2EE platform for many years to come. However, if a part of this or any other specification doesn't stand up to the task it's designed for, other solutions should be examined, even if they are not "as standard." Just make sure you justify straying from the well-trodden path. At the end of the day, or week, or project, you are accountable for your decisions. Ensure that you can explain all of them.

Proposed Solutions

With the requirements set out by Forethought, it is time to look at solving each problem, and then turning the solutions into a single coherent application. However, the last task (creating one logical application design) is often much harder than solving the individual problems that requirements pose. While a database may be a better means of storing data in one case, a directory server may be more appropriate in another. Combining both data sources is the complex problem. The same goes for handling multiple presentation layers created from similar content. You should look at solving the specific problems first, and then design an overall application to incorporate the various solutions you decide upon.

You will also need to determine which technologies and APIs should be used. As this is a book on Java, the decisions recommended shouldn't come as a great surprise— of course we will use Java! However, in a company not already sold on Java, you would need to justify this decision just as you would justify using XML, or servlets, or EJB. If you aren't sure about Java or need an introductory text comparing the language with other popular programming languages, check out *Exploring Java*, by Patrick Niemeyer, or *Java in a Nutshell*, by David Flanagan (both from O'Reilly).

Java and J2EE for web delivery

Java has arguably become the language of choice for network programming. While Perl, PHP, and Python are becoming more common, Java still has a strong, solidified position in the enterprise application space. The language is also certainly more web-oriented than C, C++, or Microsoft's C#.

With the release of the Java 2 Enterprise Edition (J2EE), Sun gave many programmers a major missing piece of the Java puzzle: a guideline for developing enterprise applications. More than just a collection of APIs, the J2EE platform also comes with the Application Programming Model (APM), which specifies how applications should be built and pieces together many APIs that puzzled many developers for years. While parts of the APM are questionable or appear to be unfinished, the net effect is that more programmers than ever before have embraced Java, admitting that it has officially "matured." For these reasons, we will use the J2EE APIs and the APM as a starting point for our application. The J2EE APIs include servlets, JSP, EJB, and JMS. While we may use only parts of some of these APIs and discard others altogether, starting with this proven model allows us to deliver Forethought's application online to their clients and other employees, the first requirement of the application.

JSP, XML, and XSL for content and presentation

In addition to online accessibility, Forethought wanted to be able to deliver their new application to wireless devices, and particularly to brokers in the field. The decision to make here is how to separate content from presentation, and try to reuse the content with different presentations. Before going further, I should define my terms a little more concretely. *Content* is the business data that is viewed by an application client (a wireless phone, handheld organizer, web browser, and others). The key phrase in this definition is "business data": this is typically the balance of an account, a user's personal information, or an employee's scheduled meetings. However, this is raw data, without markup. In other words, the content of a page might consist of this information:

```
Brett Hund
Broker
2545550289
Waco
1212 City River Drive
Waco, Texas
76712
```

This is an entry for a broker. It contains the broker's name and title on the first two lines, his phone number on the third line, office on the fourth, and office address on the final three lines. In any Java enterprise application, servlets are usually the best choice for obtaining content from a data store or set of business components and then handing that content off to a presentation technology. Servlets are covered in greater detail in Volume II on web applications.

You'll also want to turn that content into *presentation*. Presentation here refers to a formatted HTML page, a WML deck for a wireless phone, or any other formatted data suitable for display to a user. Typically, using JSP, servlets, and now XML and XSL are all excellent choices for turning simple content into a fancier presentation. I'll focus on these concepts in Volume II as well.

Services architecture

With Forethought's requirement for scheduling, you will have to do your first bit of true creative work. Java, J2EE, XML, and XSL all require programming, but they are built upon proven concepts. However, there are no stock APIs for handling scheduling, and a set of tools and utilities for this aspect of the application will have to be created from scratch. This quickly turns into a complex problem: consider business logic that sets up introductory meetings with new clients, but must assure that a potential broker has no existing meetings already set up at the desired time.

Additionally, building the scheduling component into a more robust *services framework* can really pay off over the long term. By services framework, I mean a system that allows any component that corresponds to a specific set of guidelines (such as a particular Java interface) to be integrated into an application. Although this is not a book on component development and won't go too heavily into this framework, some groundwork to generalize how components interact with applications will be detailed and coded. Years down the line, all your components will mesh into a common system instead of existing piecemeal throughout the application. The business logic to handle appointments and client interaction is covered in Chapter 9, and scheduling and services are covered in Chapter 10.

Storing data

The requirement of storing information about clients and employees is one of the simplest to handle. It requires a decision about the medium for data storage. The two most prevalent options are relational databases (RDBMS) and directory servers (often using the Lightweight Directory Access Protocol, or LDAP). Although there are other options, such as object-oriented database management systems (OODBMS), they are not as well-accepted or proven technologies, and therefore are not the best solution for Forethought's traditional data needs.

In the case of the Forethought application, you don't necessarily have to choose one or the other—in fact, using both a database and a directory server makes a lot of sense. Pure data storage, such as handling employees' and clients' personal information, is definitely in the realm of the database. This sort of information, used often in both read (view) and write (update) operations, is best suited for storage in an RDBMS, which is optimized for general access. However, Forethought also needs security for their application, through a username and password combination. This information is read far more often than it is written, and authentication is typically expected to be a fast operation. The reasons that make a database ideal for general information make it poor for authentication data: its stability for writing results in slower reading. Here, a directory server tuned for fast searches and frequent reads is a perfect fit. Therefore, a combination approach is well suited in this case, and solves the problem of data storage for the application. Databases and directory servers are covered in Chapter 3.

As for accessing this data, proven solutions exist, all within the J2EE programming model. Enterprise JavaBeans (EJB) is perfect for database access and is covered in Chapters 4 and 5. Directory servers can be accessed most easily through the Java Naming and Directory Interface (JNDI). Usable within any Java code, beans could also be written to provide directory server access; however, for reasons discussed in Chapter 6, it is often better to use normal Java classes for this facet of an application.

Servlets, EJB, caching, and performance

The last requirement discussed, that of "fast performance and standards compliance," is a bit vague. However, all the solutions discussed so far are based on these very premises: Java, J2EE, XML, XSL, and all the rest are accepted standards. And using a directory server for authentication was a decision made for performance reasons. In other words, good design decisions generally involve these principles, even without marketing or product management reminding you of them. I'll also detail using caching and design patterns that can improve performance as we go along.

At this point, the individual requirements of the application have all been addressed, and you now face the difficult task of integrating these solutions into a larger, complete system. I've tried to discuss each component separately from those around it: the data storage is dealt with separately from the services and data access, which is separated from the business logic, which is then separated from content, which is in turn separated from presentation. Each portion of the application operates in isolation and supplies data to the next layer as needed. This architecture can allow easy updates and additions of functionality over time. It also makes debugging simple, since a problem can be quickly isolated to a specific application layer. With these concepts in mind, let's now look at designing our complete application, layer by layer. The rest of the book is split into sections that correspond to each of these layers.

The Data Layer

The foundation of any application is the data that it contains and utilizes. Without data, there is no need for an application! Unfortunately, designing a data layer does not produce immediate visible results—no screens appear, no business logic occurs, and management is rarely impressed with entity-relationship diagrams. Because of this, the data layer is often designed and implemented hastily, leaving the rest of the application to suffer and compensate for early mistakes. Instead of taking this precarious approach, this book covers the data layer first and attempts to design it soundly.

In addition to data storage, data access is typically part of the data layer. However, these different functions can be separated from each other; do not be tempted to model your data differently because of a product or technique used in the data access layer. More often than not, the data of an application outlasts the application itself. Data formatted for a specific product or application server may be completely unusable for other products that expect data in a standard format.* Only *after* the data has been modeled and the storage mediums designed should data access be considered. This section covers databases and directory servers as well as data access methods.

---

* I emphasize this point because there are several application servers out there that require modifications to the database in order to "perform optimally"; for example, the Persistence PowerTier EJB Server used to suggest adding columns in database tables for the OCA attribute, as well as modeling data in an OO rather than relational format. These types of changes may improve application performance over the short term but almost always cause problems in the long run, and should be avoided at all costs.

Databases

Once you decide to use a relational database, the number of decisions left decreases quite a bit. First, you must choose a database vendor. Second, the database must be accessible through a JDBC (Java Database Connectivity) driver.* Then, the data design must be determined, and finally, the data schema should be populated.

Determining what database to use can be very difficult; the data of an application often outlasts other parts of an application, or becomes used by other applications, over time. This means that your database vendor (and your resulting relationship with the vendor) will play a critical role. Often, though, this decision is taken out of the developer's hands; many large companies establish a standard vendor and simply purchase new licenses for additional database instances as needed. In these cases, you will simply need to become familiar with the selected vendor. However, in the case where no standard exists, there are numerous options. Trying to recommend a single option for all cases is impossible; instead, certain conditions favor specific vendors. On large systems, and particularly on Sun Solaris hardware, Oracle is an excellent choice. Linux servers and clusters often use Oracle as well, and open source solutions like MySQL, PostgreSQL, and InstantDB are also popular. Microsoft platforms tend to work best with the Microsoft database offering, MS SQL Server. And there are many, many other vendors to choose from, such as Sybase, Cloudscape, mSQL, and Interbase. While the example code shown in this book utilizes only standard ANSI SQL and should work on any of these databases, the appendixes cover various database-specific SQL idioms.

JDBC drivers are available for each of these vendors. Additionally, the JDBC-ODBC bridge driver can be used to access databases on Windows systems if a native JDBC driver is not available, but this situation is rare. In fact, Java has become so prevalent that almost all databases supply a JDBC driver with installation, and application servers (particularly EJB servers) provide JDBC drivers as well.

As for designing the data schema, I'll leave that for the next chapter. For now it is enough to know that aside from the usernames and passwords that will be stored in an LDAP directory server, we will house all application data in a single database instance. I'm also not going to deal with replication or high availability at the database level in this book; these topics are books unto themselves, and shouldn't affect the overall application design. However, this is by no means a recommendation against employing these techniques—data reliability is an important issue, and some sort of redundancy should be built into your application, especially at the data level.

---

* While these are portrayed as two independent decisions, it is possible that the second decision can affect the first. If you are writing a Java application and your database has no stable JDBC driver, you may have to rethink the database vendor. That said, with the prevalence of Java today, this is not as large a problem as it was years ago.

Directory Servers

Using a directory server is not quite as complex as using a database; while the techniques involved are less established, there are fewer options and chances for misuse. The most common problem is attempting to use a directory server as a wholesale replacement for a database. By deciding to store only authentication information in the directory server, that problem has already been avoided in the Forethought application. While there are certainly situations in which other information could be housed in a directory server, keeping things simple is usually a good idea, and this is what is being done for Forethought.

Since LDAP services were first created at the Universities of Michigan and Berkeley, there has been a well-established set of standard object types and structures defined for use.* Directory servers are structured like a tree, unlike the relational structure of an RDBMS, and usually come prepopulated with a top-level organization node, as well as groups and users (often called *People*) nodes. It's always a good idea to use these existing structures when possible and to extend them when new structures are needed, instead of creating brand-new object types. You'll get to look at this in a lot more detail in Chapters 3 and 6.

Unlike databases, there are not as many established choices for LDAP directory services. In the commercial space, Netscape's iPlanet Directory Server has been the dominant choice since its inception. Many application servers are now coming with bundled directory services, but as of this writing, those offerings were weak at best. The only commercial bundled server that seemed promising was Oracle's directory server, bundled as part of the Oracle 8*i* suite of servers. Excepting that case, if you need a commercial solution, Netscape remains the best option. For the open source fans out there (of which I'm one!), openLDAP is a great solution. Written in C, it's robust and proven, and has work in it from some of the original LDAP gurus at Michigan and Berkeley. As with the databases, the appendixes in the back of this book will cover vendor-specific idioms in directory server setup and deployment.

Data Access

The final part of the data layer is providing access to the data stores. While this decision is primarily specific to the application you are writing (in this case, the Forethought system), it is the one application component that may be used by other applications, sometimes without your foreknowledge. As three-tiered and n-tiered application architectures become more prevalent, companies become less willing to directly expose their data stores. In the past, other companies or applications that

---

* The longer story of directory servers is rooted in the history of X.509. However, that's pretty dry stuff, so I'm going to leave it to interested parties to research this information on their own. You can start by checking out *http://www.openldap.org/*.

needed to access data were given direct access to a company's database, usually through some particular port. By far the most common example of this is SQL*net, which provides an unencrypted channel for SQL queries to be executed, returning the results in the same fashion. Obviously, an unencrypted channel is not a very secure means of exposing data; it also requires any security restrictions or filtering to be implemented at the database level to protect sensitive data. Attempts to rectify this deficiency (such as Oracle's Secure Networking product, which encrypts the SQL*net communication) have proven to be extremely sensitive, and not always easy to configure and use.

With the ability to create a pure data access layer through coded modules in an application, direct access can be turned off, or completely disallowed from the start. Instead, other companies and applications can make requests of the data access layer just as the original application's business layer would (this is discussed in the next section). Because this is code, it can be customized for the specific needs of the company; for instance, only users who authenticate through the data access layer could be allowed to query the database. Any other filtering could also be done at this level, rather than involving the data storage mechanism itself. Let's look at some potential access layers for the application now.

Java Database Connectivity (JDBC)

The most common method of interacting with a database is through JDBC, the Java Database Connectivity API. This API, part of the J2EE platform, allows programmatic interaction with any SQL-based database. As already mentioned, any database used in an enterprise application should have a suitable JDBC driver (or else you may want to select another database vendor!). JDBC also allows security to be used, as any connection requires a username and password. A single Java class using JDBC can connect to a database with multiple sets of permissions, allowing user-specific data access.

JDBC is most commonly used for accessing data directly from servlets or from standalone Java classes. While it is often more complicated to write *good* JDBC code than to use EJB entity beans, particularly container-managed persistence beans (discussed next), the resulting code is very fast and flexible. Another advantage of using JDBC directly, as opposed to an EJB solution, is that you can explicitly control caching, allowing rapid access to commonly used data. In the Forethought application, certain components, such as the scheduler, can really benefit from this caching. It is in this portion of the Forethought application that JDBC could be used directly. Additionally, using JDBC in this way does not require the overhead of an EJB server handling data requests. It is also worth mentioning that most other solutions for accessing databases (particularly EJB entity beans) actually use JDBC, wrapping it in an abstraction layer. In other words, JDBC and EJB are not competing APIs; EJB actually allows encapsulation of JDBC. For more on JDBC, you can pick up a copy of *Database Programming with JDBC and Java*, by George Reese (O'Reilly).

EJB entity beans

Another solution for accessing databases is Enterprise JavaBeans (EJB). EJB is built just for this type of task, particularly entity beans. Entity beans are intended to represent data in Java, without any business logic wrapping the data. In fact, the business layer (using servlets or EJB session beans, discussed later) would use data from entity beans to perform business logic computations. Used as a pure-Java data representation, entity beans can be extremely useful.

Entity beans in EJB 2.0 come in two flavors: bean-managed persistence (BMP) and container-managed persistence (CMP). BMP beans essentially allow the developers to do whatever they want within the EJB framework. BMP beans are usually made up almost entirely of JDBC code, and simply take advantage of the EJB container for access to data sources, performance, and passivation and activation. CMP beans, however, are quite a different story. A CMP bean only allows the developer to write the mapping of a database's data to Java variables. All interaction with the database (through JDBC) is handled by the container. Usually tools are provided with an EJB server or container to take a CMP bean and generate the container classes that handle database communication. The container then deploys both the developer's code and the generated classes, allowing the bean to behave (at runtime) identically to a BMP bean.

Much of the basic database access for the Forethought application, such as obtaining employee records and updating client accounts, can be handled through simple CMP beans. In addition to avoiding a lot of tedious JDBC code, this solution cuts down on the pure volume of code that has to be developed and maintained, which is always a win for upper management: more work in less time! Only when you need to perform queries and operations that are too complex for simple CMP access would you need to look at using BMP beans. For more information on Enterprise JavaBeans, you can pick up *Enterprise JavaBeans* by Richard Monson-Haefel (O'Reilly).

Java Naming and Directory Interface (JNDI)

So far, I've discussed only database access. We still need to deal with data access to the directory server, which contains authentication information for the application. JDBC obviously doesn't help here, since LDAP directory servers are *not* databases, and thus are not accessible with JDBC. As I mentioned earlier, JNDI is the solution to this problem. Like JDBC, it provides a means of writing code that is vendor-neutral[*]

---

[*] This is a small oversimplification. In fact, JNDI services require information about the services it connects to, usually a hostname and port, and sometimes a username and password. These values would change across products, assuming the products were not running on the exact same machine and port number. However, using property files, even this bit of vendor-specific code can be removed.

and that works across all types of a service.* In the Forethought case, this provides the perfect analog to JDBC for directory service access. As JNDI is also part of the J2EE platform, it is also available to you (since we already decided to use J2EE). You can find out more about JNDI in *Java Enterprise in a Nutshell*, by David Flanagan et al. (O'Reilly).

With data access APIs established, all communication to the Forethought data can be funneled through either JDBC classes, EJB entity beans, or JNDI. Making this decision at this point in application design prevents you from having to backtrack, or worry about loopholes in security to the database and directory server. With that structure in place, the data layer is finalized; Figure 2-1 shows the completed data layer architecture.

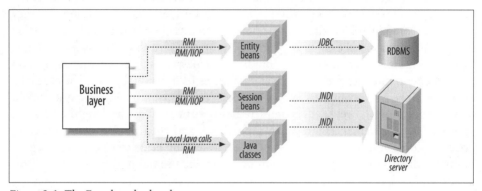

Figure 2-1. The Forethought data layer

The Business Layer

Next in the design process is the task of creating a business layer. This portion of the application is wedged between presentation (what the user sees) and data (what the application depends on). The business layer, then, does just what it implies: it performs business (logic). Data on its own is rarely relevant, and often makes no sense without some context applied to it. In the same fashion, the presentation layer must have something to present (no rocket science here!). In this business layer, then, data is manipulated, transformed, and converted into content suitable for presentation.

The core of this layer is the code that actually executes business logic. This code maps to a company's business processes; in the best case, a single module of code represents a single business process. These modules can then be called to obtain a

---

* In this case, I am referring to LDAP, or RMI, or a filesystem as a type of service. While JNDI code should work with all vendors' products in one type (such as any LDAP server), it will not work across types; in other words, the same code won't function for access to LDAP, flat files, and RMI, but it will work for Netscape, Oracle, and openLDAP.

client's outstanding balance, for example. This figure is rarely stored in the database, but instead is calculated from the client's purchases subtracted from his or her assets. This allows the raw data to be masked from the presentation layer of an application; instead of asking for data and performing calculations, the application needs to request only the business process that results in a client's account balance, and format the result.

Business Logic

With entity beans in place for handling data access to most of our application, it makes sense to continue to leverage EJB for the business logic in our application. In this case, EJB session beans are a good fit. Session beans are complementary to entity beans and are designed specifically for handling business tasks. Additionally, they can be easily modularized, allowing mapping from a single business task to a session bean (as mentioned earlier, this is optimal). In this way, session beans can be "strung together" in logical ways, creating complete business processes. In this case, I am using the term *business process* to refer to a series of individual tasks. For example, obtaining a client's account balance or checking for availability of a new stock might be a business task; however, the complete business process of checking the balance, ensuring that enough is left to make a purchase, and then buying the stock comprises multiple individual tasks. Because each session bean can access the entity beans for the data it needs, one session bean may be used in multiple business processes without having to modify the single business task.

The biggest decision to be made regarding session beans is the type of bean to use for each task; session beans come in two flavors, stateful and stateless. *Stateful* session beans reside in memory once they are created and maintain information across requests. *Stateless* session beans, on the other hand, are "fire-and-forget" beans, which execute a request and are then disposed of until requested again. All information in the bean is trashed between requests. While stateful beans can be helpful for processes or tasks that span multiple requests, they are often slower and obviously require more memory in the virtual machine. Stateless session beans, though, are very fast, and often only a few instances are needed to serve hundreds of requests. These qualities make them ideal for most business tasks, and preferable for better application performance.

Stateless session beans

We have not yet identified all the business processes, so determining exactly what business tasks should be modeled in stateless session beans is a bit difficult at this point. However, I will go ahead and set out some general guidelines for the use of stateless session beans.

First, unless there is a reason *not* to use stateless session beans, you should use them. Using stateless beans over stateful ones in the general case can drastically increase application performance. Because the EJB container can share stateless session bean instances across all EJB clients, it can maximize performance, as well as cache the instances in some cases.

Second, stateless session beans should rarely be used for accessing the directory server. While entity beans are used for database access, session beans would have to use JNDI for LDAP access. In this situation, connecting to the LDAP service is often more time-consuming than the actual operations once connected. This is a perfect example of a good case for using stateful session beans—connecting once and holding the connection open across requests can help avoid the initial delay of connecting to the LDAP service for each request. Another option (which I'll lay out in Chapter 5) is simply to use a standalone Java class for LDAP access, avoiding the overhead of EJB altogether.

Finally, when using stateless session beans, similar operations should be combined into one bean. Although the bean doesn't persist data across requests, it can be used multiple times over one request and bean lookup. For this reason, multiple methods that operate on the same logical data can be consolidated into a single bean. This can really clean up code and clarify what different components are used for.

Stateful session beans

I've emphasized this quite a bit, but I'll say once more that you don't want to use stateful session beans for many of our business processes. However, there are times when the persistent nature of these beans, the very facet that makes them dangerous to overuse, is very helpful. One case is as a connector to LDAP for other components, as previously mentioned. Another case is when you are handling large data sets that require paging. Consider that a broker needs to list clients who meet a certain set of criteria, such as living in Chicago and having positive account balances. If the number of results is fairly large, it makes sense to show only a few matches at a time (say, 20) and allow the broker to move through pages of results. In this case, performing the query each time wastes time and resources; instead, a stateful session bean could obtain all results from the query, and then supply methods (getNextPage( ), getPreviousPage( ), etc.) for moving through the results. Storing the complete data set allows this to occur quickly, as the application needs to pause only at the initial search (a wait that users are accustomed to when performing searches), while functioning quickly on the paging commands. As we delve into the implementation of the Forethought application, we will watch for these situations and use stateful session beans where appropriate.

Messaging

The last portion of the business layer is the messaging required for a scheduler component. For this part of the application, we will use EJB 2.0's message-driven beans. Like session beans, these services may use entity beans for data access. It is also likely that many services will interact directly with the data layer through JDBC, which allows a different server than the one containing the EJB container to house these services and cuts down on RMI traffic required for EJB utilization. It also allows the EJB server to devote most of its resources to serving application clients; clients waiting for search results are much more impatient than an employee checking her next meeting. This correctly distributes the processing of the application in accordance with the user patterns. Communication between components that are interdependent, or that trigger the starting or stopping of tasks, is based on messaging. Using the Java Message Service, alone or through message-driven beans, provides a means of handling this communication without getting hung up on network and latency issues.

With the session beans and messaging architecture in place, the business layer is complete. You may have noticed that it was much simpler to design this layer than the data access layer, where many more decisions had to be made. While this observation holds true at this early stage of overall architecture, when the implementation occurs, defining business logic modules will later consume much more time than creating database tables and relationships. However, at this point, there is simply a large "black box" of business logic wedged between presentation and data, and we will flesh it out later. Figure 2-2 shows the business layer, separating the various technologies discussed.

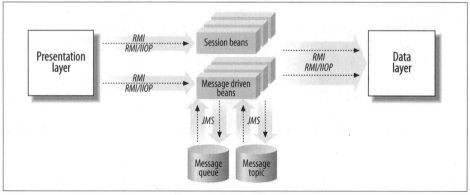

Figure 2-2. The Forethought business layer

The Presentation Layer

Last, but not least, is the presentation layer. As with the data layer, creating the presentation layer is another difficult task, as there are many decisions to be made. Additionally, this layer often has the most constraints upon it: clients have a variety of browsers and versions of browsers, as well as other Internet-capable devices; output may need to be in a specific format; speed of display may be a factor; and so on. In the Forethought application, the presentation layer must be able to serve multiple types of clients, and do it in a way that doesn't force a lot of duplication of content. JSP, XML, and XSL are all part of the solutions that will be examined for solving this problem.

As I'll be spending Volume II on the subject of presentation, I'll leave these details for a later discussion. However, this is not entirely for the sake of another book; it is also to show you that the details of the data and business layers are often completely isolated from the presentation layer. This means that two groups could design these at different times, or you could even develop a set of data stores and business rules without worrying about presentation until later (the approach taken by this book). This method forces you to uncouple these layers, which is critical to good application design. It also allows an easy conversion of an application to a set of web services; since your business layer is not specifically aimed at a web application, it is easy to expose beans and other business components as web services down the line. So I'll leave this area intentionally open for interpretation. Of course, this doesn't prevent a basic diagramming of how the presentation layer (be it servlets, web services, Java Swing, or anything else) interacts with the other layers in the application. Figure 2-3 shows this basic interaction.

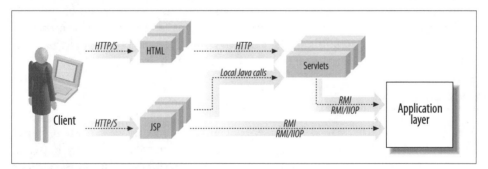

Figure 2-3. The Forethought presentation layer

Finalizing the Plans

By now it may seem that I have spent an eternity doing nothing but talking about the Forethought application. In reality, I have barely scratched the surface of a complete application design. Most companies require functional specifications, detailing what an application will do and the business needs it should serve. Often, technical design documents that specify the details in even more depth are required before a development team can begin work on a project. In some cases, an appropriate team might have to be assembled, which may involve contracting and consulting resources hired to supplement full-time employees. In other words, enjoy that I spent only a chapter on this subject, rather than a whole book! It's a luxury you would have only with a fictional company.

In any case, I have outlined the Forethought application well enough to give you an idea of the technologies and general techniques that will be used. Additionally, minimal architecture diagrams have been taking shape. With the data, business, and presentation layers all sketched out, the three separate layers can be combined into a single, overall application architecture. This complete picture is shown in Figure 2-4.

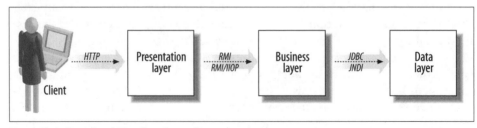

Figure 2-4. Completed Forethought application architecture

You can see that because of the separation between the layers, there is really no work to be done to "connect" these layers together. Java RMI and EJB services connect the business layer to the data layer, running through EJB and JNDI data access code. Connections between the presentation layer and the business layer can happen via RMI, normal Java network communication, or perhaps SOAP and similar protocols for web services interfaces. It's finally time, then, to close the book (proverbially of course!) on the application design for now, and move on to implementation.

What's Next?

With the application designed and blueprints in place, you are now ready to begin filling in the details. The foundation is always the most critical portion of a house, as all other construction must be supported by it. In enterprise applications, particularly those on the Web, data itself is this fundamental layer. Data is the focus of the next chapter, and databases and directory servers are discussed as two options for storing this critical substance. Then, the data schema will be designed, the tables created, and preparations will be put in place for the rest of the application code.

Additionally, I will highlight how designing a data store is often almost completely unrelated to the specific application itself. By remaining general in the storage design and implementation, the foundation can be used and reused without having to be altered for different applications of the data, even for those applications you have yet to consider. This is key to the ever-changing landscape of web applications.

CHAPTER 3

Foundation

Enough talk—it's finally time to get on with some implementation. If you're much of a developer this is probably exciting news; all developers must take part in application design, and may even grow to enjoy it, but there's nothing like getting your hands dirty with some actual code. However, it isn't quite time to open your favorite IDE or editor and start punching out Java code. In fact, we'll get through this entire chapter without looking at a single line of Java. Instead, this chapter focuses on the data stores, creating the medium for holding the application's data. There's plenty of technical material, though, so don't get too worried just yet.

As mentioned in the first two chapters, the design of an application is its blueprint, and is crucial to its success. Now that you have this blueprint, you need to lay the foundation of the application with the data storage. Literally everything else in the application (as well as in other applications that may potentially use the Forethought data) depends on the decisions made here. I'll begin by discussing the overall design of the data. This involves defining the schema for the data without worrying about whether the data will be stored in a database, directory server, or any other specific technology.

Once you've determined how the information for the entire application will be laid out, you can begin to decide where specific data needs to be stored. In the case of the Forethought application, it has already been decided that data will be stored in one database (ignoring replication issues) and one directory server (ignoring failover instances). This simplifies the decision-making process quite a bit. The authentication data should be stored in the directory server, and the rest of the data housed within a database. All that is left, then, is designing the actual physical layout of the database and LDAP store, and implementing these designs. This will be detailed in the last part of the chapter.

Designing the Data Stores

The first step in the actual design of the data store is to identify each major section that we need to think about. Like the rest of the application design so far, good design is more about breaking up large pieces into small pieces than performing any mystical process. In the last chapter, the application was broken up into layers (data, business, and presentation); this chapter concentrates on the first of those, the data layer. That layer was broken up into the data itself, and data access; now the data can be broken up even *further*, into database tables and directory server objects. Through this process, a complex application becomes a series of small, manageable tasks that when put together make up a lot more than the sum of their parts.

So with that in mind, let's segregate the data. The first division is probably the easiest to handle: user data. Only basic information is required, so it's simple to determine that users should have their names and basic contact information stored in the database. In addition to user data, authentication data is a necessity. While authentication data will reside in a directory server, it still must contain a unique key that can be related back to the users in the database. This authentication data must also define permissions as well as simple username and password combinations.

Once this basic information about application users is in place, you can move on to the business details that Forethought is so concerned about. This is the account information that Forethought's clients are interested in, as well. There is a need to store accounts of the company's clients, transactions that involve those accounts, and investments the clients make. I'm distinguishing between *transactions*, where clients either deposit or withdraw funds, and *investments*, where clients invest money and yield either a profit or a loss. Then, like the authentication information, this information must have a tie to the user data store.

Finally, the application must be able to store information about events for scheduling purposes. For the sake of the example, this information will contain only a basic description of the meeting, the meeting time, and the attendees. It's worth noting that in many cases, you could easily add a much richer set of details for the data objects, such as users' email addresses and preferences, account histories, and complex event tracking such as departments and locations. However, you get the idea, and keeping the example simple enables you to carry this book under your arm instead of in a wheelbarrow.

Users

The first portion of the data store is the easiest to design. Storing information about users is generally not a difficult task; the most complex part of the job is determining what information needs to be stored. For the purposes of the example application, this information is fairly limited. Here's a list of this basic information and how it could be logically grouped:

- Username for application
- User's "real" name
  —First name
  —Last name
- User's home office
  —City
  —State

Even this simple list contains enough information to distinguish users from each other. While an application client might have the same first and last name as another client, you should build rules into the application to ensure the uniqueness of their usernames. For now we'll simply assume that the mechanism that creates usernames, either programmatically or by letting the user select one, can be coded to utilize this sort of constraint and inform the user if errors occur.

Data constraints

With this basic step complete, it's time to make some decisions about constraints set upon the data. For example, usernames should be unique. The issue, then, is whether this constraint belongs at the application level or at the data layer. Your initial impulse may be to place the constraint at the database (or directory server) level, rather than in Java code.

However, this type of constraint can often result in error messages returned to Java programs that are difficult to deal with at runtime. Additionally, the error message returned is often vendor-specific. While Oracle may supply an ORA-1302 error code, PostgreSQL may return the string "Uniqueness constraint: duplicate data." And a directory server might use an entirely different format for error reporting. As you can see, although the data is protected from invalidity, the corresponding Java code still needs to perform some checks of its own. The code that creates users will need to specifically check for and handle this error condition. This is something I'll explain later.

At the same time, usernames may need to be at least four characters long (for example). This is another, similar constraint, but must be handled completely differently. First, the mechanism for length checking is not as standardized as the check for uniqueness. Some databases allow a data length (both minimum and maximum) to be directly defined. Other databases provide for triggers to be coded that perform these checks and generate errors, if needed. And still other databases provide no means for this sort of check at all. In these cases, where generic means are either nonexistent or insufficient, the answer is to code, code, code.

So, the answer to where data constraints belong is a mixed message. In almost all cases, if a constraint is set on data, it should be at least checked for specifically, if not completely handled, at the application level. And in the cases where a database offers a general way (preferably across databases) to enforce constraints at a lower level, those means should be used in addition to application code.

User types

Another requirement of the Forethought application is the ability to represent both clients and employees in a similar fashion. While there is certainly a temptation to store these users in two separate areas of the data store, you should not give in; the information being stored about employees and clients is exactly the same (username, first name, and last name). In fact, there is rarely a time when the core information about disparate groups of people is significantly different. The only difference here is that an employee has an associated office record, but simply adding a separate structure for office data takes care of that requirement and still allows the use of a single structure for both clients and employees.

Records, Structures, and Other Database Terms

As you've probably noticed, quite a few terms get thrown around when talking about databases. First, the entire database can be referred to as a *data store*. This is actually a generic term that can refer to any form of data storage, such as a relational database, object-oriented database, LDAP directory server, or even a set of flat files. Then, you have a *data structure* (or just *structure*). This refers to a physical structure within the data store that can hold compound data. In relational databases, a data structure almost always refers to a table. This table defines the way that data is stored; it gives it structure. Finally, you have *data records*. These records exist within a structure; in the context of a relational database, these are the rows in a database table. Keep these terms in mind as you continue on through the chapter, and things will make a lot more sense to you.

Using one structure for both types of users is not only simple, it also makes more advanced reporting possible. For example, you can find all employees and clients with the same last name without having to perform time-consuming unions or joins of data in multiple areas of the data store. Additionally, each constraint set on a table or LDAP object is generally limited to that structure, and trying to maintain constraints such as the uniqueness of usernames becomes much more difficult across multiple data structures. Overall, using a single structure for similar data will almost always result in better code and faster processing.

As for the process of differentiating between clients and employees, it is trivial to break up users using established data design techniques. It makes sense to create a new data structure and populate it with user types (clients and employees), and have each entry in the user structure reference the appropriate entry for that user. In addition to allowing a single structure for users, this technique also makes it simple to later add additional user types (for example, leads or potential clients). It's also easy to find out if an office reference should be examined: if a user is an employee, there will be an entry in the offices structure; if the user is a client, there won't.

Unique keys, characters, and IDs

As a final design note, I need to address unique keys in data structures. A fairly well understood rule in database design, and one that also applies to directory services, is that data can be organized more efficiently when there is a unique piece of data for each row or entry in a structure. In addition to providing a simple way to ensure that the same set of data is not entered twice, the unique identifier allows most data stores to index the data in the structure. Indexing generally improves performance of the data store, and can drastically improve the speed of searches and queries using those structures. Finally, a unique identifier for each entry allows that identifier to be used in other structures that reference the original.

In databases, this unique piece of data is usually known as a *primary key*, and when used in a referencing structure, a *foreign key*. For example, in the users structure, you could use the username as the primary key, since it has already been established that this piece of data should be unique for each user. The username could then be used to associate data in other tables to a particular user. The end result is a set of relations between the structures, thus the term *relational database*.

However, many structures will not have data that must be unique. In the offices structure, assume that all that is being stored is the city and state where the office is located. It is reasonable to think that two offices might be in the same city and state (consider huge cities like Dallas, New York City, and San Francisco). In these cases, there needs to be an additional piece of data for the primary key. Best practice is to call this piece of data XXX_ID where XXX is the name of the data being represented. For the offices data, this results in OFFICE_ID. Most databases provide an auto-numbering facility for these sorts of columns, allowing the database to handle assignment of the ID whenever data is inserted. Other databases, like Oracle, allow a sequence or counter to be created to handle these numbers, and the next value of the sequence can be obtained and then used for the new piece of data being inserted.

The result is two types of primary keys: the first, applicable to users, is a character value, and the second, applicable to user types and offices, is numeric. As already mentioned, these values are used heavily for indexing, and a numeric value is always easier to index on than a textual one. Additionally, numeric values usually require less space than textual ones (consider that even high-precision numbers will take less storage than an eight-character username). This observation results in another best practice: when possible, numeric primary keys are preferred over character-based ones. In the users table, you can either stay with using the username, or add another piece of data, called simply USER_ID, to hold a numeric ID for each user and serve as the primary key. Because the user information store will be used more often than any other piece of data, it makes sense to choose the latter and provide a numeric primary key for the table.

With all these decisions made, we have touched on several important topics in data design. In fact, designing the rest of the data storage will be simpler with these principles under your belt. Before moving on to user permissions, though, take a look at Figure 3-1, which shows the user data without any database- or LDAP-specific structures.

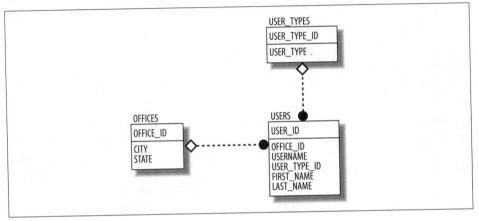

Figure 3-1. The Forethought user store

Permissions

The next segment of data to look at is the authentication system. Again, there are quite a few traditional best practices that can help out here. Generally, authentication can be broken up into permissions, with each permission specifying access rights to a resource or group of resources. A user's authentication rights, then, are determined by the permissions assigned to that user. What is left is the simpler task of designing storage for these permissions.

Simple names can be used for the permissions. These should be self-describing and somewhat representative of the permission's purpose. However, there is a fine line here; if these names become "too" readable, they can cause application performance to deteriorate. A name like EMPLOYEE_LOGIN works well, but can easily get out of hand: NEW_EMPLOYEE_APPLICATION_LOGIN. Moderation is the key here. Additionally, to avoid having to index on these character values, it makes sense to have a PERMISSION_ ID column that allows building of references and can keep performance high.

Granularity

The biggest decision to make in the area of permissions is not directly related to the storage of the data at all, but to the *meaning* of the data. It's usually best to consider data as neutral, or application-independent. In other words, while data is certainly used by various applications, it stands on its own. It is only when the data is given context by the application that it has meaning. This is precisely the reason that until now, I have not made any reference to the application using the data, or to optimizing data for a specific business task. These sorts of optimizations, or any decisions made at the data layer based on the business logic of an application, usually result in an application that performs well only in a specific context, and can also make sharing the data with other applications very difficult. Data that is tuned for a specific use may cause problems when used in ways not originally intended; since these unexpected uses almost always arise, preparing for these contingencies is a good idea.

However, we have to break that rule in permission handling (the first thing you do upon learning a good rule is to break it, right?). This deviation occurs for two reasons. First, the way in which permissions are used at the application level directly affects how they are stored, as you will see in a moment. Second, it is slightly less onerous to make decisions about permissions based on the application they are used within. This is because permissions are an intrinsic part of an application, and generally are not used by other applications. And when they *are* used by other applications, it tends to be in the same fashion; certainly permissions are worthless except for authentication purposes!

In this case, the decision to make is about the granularity of permissions. *Granularity* refers to how specific the permissions are; the more precise a permission's use, the more granular it is. For example, a permission called EMPLOYEE, which allows a user to log into the application, view client records, run reports, update accounts, and add clients, is not very granular: it is broad and sweeping in nature. However, if that permission were broken into LOGIN, VIEW_CLIENTS, RUN_REPORTS, UPDATE_ACCOUNTS, and ADD_CLIENTS, you would have a much more granular set of permissions. This latter method is generally a better one; too often, coarse-grained permissions like EMPLOYEE become umbrellas for lots of things that shouldn't be lumped together. For example, someone in the accounting department may find that he needs to delete accounts. Because the authentication structure has only the EMPLOYEE permission, the ability to delete records is then added to that permission. However, now *every* employee has that right, which was not intended: certainly not everyone should be able to delete client accounts! In this application, then, I will assume that a single permission applies to a specific resource, such as accounts. Further, most permissions will apply to a specific use of that resources, such as deletion. Thus, you can expect to see permission names like DELETE_ACCOUNTS, MODIFY_CLIENTS, and ADD_OFFICES.

Groups, roles, and permissions

This added granularity introduces some complexity into the maintenance of a user's permissions. As mentioned previously, sets of permissions are often assigned together; the EMPLOYEE permission was an example of such a set. With the more granular approach, adding an employee would result in the need to assign five, ten, or even more permissions to that employee. It would be preferable is to add the entire set of permissions and be able to maintain the set as a whole, rather than as individual permissions. We can accomplish this result with the introduction of groups, or roles.

A *group* (often called a *role*) is used to define a logical set of permissions. Users then have these groups or roles assigned to them. In addition to allowing administrators to manage sets of permissions, the use of roles makes the task of removing a user's permissions much simpler. Consider the case where no roles are used. An employee is hired and given ten permissions that all employees receive, including ADD_CLIENTS and RUN_REPORTS. The new employee is also a broker, and is given five more permissions associated with brokers. Among these, one is RUN_REPORTS. This is the same permission already granted to the user (through her entry as an employee), and is a part of both the broker and the employee permission sets. This causes no problems when creating the user, since the duplicate permission is already found and is not duplicated. The problem, though, arises in removal. Let's say that the employee does well, and is promoted from broker to manager. The broker permissions are removed at this point, and the employee is given manager permissions. What is the problem? The employee can no longer run reports! Removing individual permissions results in the RUN_REPORTS permission being removed, because it was present in both the employee and broker sets of permissions. This is, of course, incorrect, as the manager is certainly still an employee and should be able to run reports. However, in the case where roles are used, the permissions are assigned to the roles, and the roles to the user. Then, when the BROKER role is removed, the EMPLOYEE role remains, ensuring that the manager still has all permissions associated with employees. Here, roles (or groups) save us a tremendous amount of administrative headaches.

The only difference between a group and a role is that *group* is usually used when discussing directory servers, and *role* is usually referenced in regards to databases. I'll use the term *role* for now; when a determination is made later about which type of storage to use at the physical data layer, I'll use the term appropriate for that data structure. For now, though, it's possible to complete the permissions data storage by having a structure for permissions, a structure for roles, and by joining structures that connect permissions to roles and roles to users. Figure 3-2 shows this scheme (although without the users table that would be joined in, as that was shown in Figure 3-1).

Accounts

All that's left now is to define data storage for client accounts. First, let's assume that for any single client, there may be multiple accounts. Thus, in the accounts structure, you can define an account ID and then relate that structure to the users structure defined earlier (see Figure 3-1). You can also decide to allow for different types of accounts: money market, stock-based, interest-bearing, and so on. In the same way that a structure was created for user types, you can create one for account types.

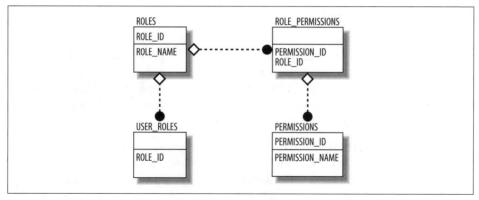

Figure 3-2. Authentication data for the Forethought application

The same referential schema can be set up, as well. Now you just need to add a field for storing the account balance to the accounts data structure.

There are two basic operations involved with these accounts: transactions and investments. Transactions represent clients depositing and withdrawing funds. These are fairly static processes, as no interest is involved; money is simply added to or removed from the account balance. Investments are not quite as simple. First, you need to store information about the funds that clients can invest in. These aren't tied to any specific client, so are stored separately, with an ID, name, and description. Those funds are then used in investments. Investments consist of an ID (as always, used in indexing), the fund invested in, the initial amount invested, the yield on that fund, and then a reference to the client's account (through the account ID). Putting all this information together results in a robust way of tracking each client's investments while allowing funds to be stored separately and reused across clients. The complete account structure is shown in Figure 3-3.

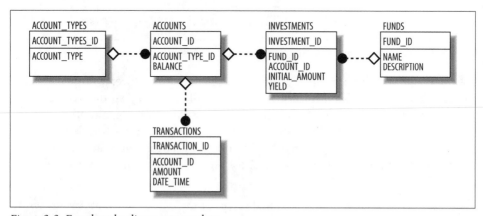

Figure 3-3. Forethought clients account data

Scheduling and Events

When it comes to dealing with storage for scheduling and events, things get much easier. First of all, an event can be represented as a single object. The description, location, purpose, time, and other details can all be defined as properties (rows in a database table, or attributes in an LDAP object class) of the event. Once the event object is in place, all that's left is to relate the event to various users, the attendees of the event. In other words, this is the simplest task yet.

To handle the relationship between an event and users, an attendee object needs to be created. This object will not hold any additional details about the event or contact numbers for the attendee—this information is all stored in other places within the data store. Instead, it will provide the link between an event (identified by the event ID, a primary key) and a user (identified by the user ID, a primary key). The table is completely meaningless on its own, as it is simply a series of numeric IDs, but it is integral to the overall scheduling process. Figure 3-4 shows this structure isolated from the USERS object. Although it seems to make even less sense without the link to that table, it's helpful to isolate the different portions of the application. In just a moment, the complete picture will be examined and the relations filled in between the various portions of the data store.

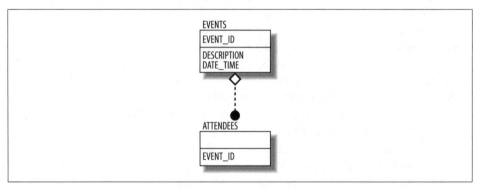

Figure 3-4. Forethought events scheduling

You may have noticed that there is no SCHEDULER table or object within the Forethought data store. As a practical matter, a schedule is simply an ordered series of events. But the ordering and the criteria for which events to contain are business-driven. So while events should be stored within the data store, a schedule is actually a derived object that will be created by the code, as I'll detail later on. For now, it's enough to say that no table needs to exist for schedules; the simple events table and attendees relations will suffice.

This completes our look at the individual pieces of the data schema, at least in terms of the Forethought example. There are some other things you may need to add for practical applications; I'll look briefly at these before continuing to the physical design.

Odds and Ends

When it comes to reality, a book can only give you part of the picture. However, I'll now try to point out some of the things that I won't be able to completely cover in this book. If any of these apply to your specific application, you can add them to the data model.

First, most applications need to capture additional information about users. Addresses, phone numbers, pager numbers, places of work, and social security numbers are often optional or required information. This data can either be added to the users structure or broken out into multiple structures. Usually, data like a social security number is tied to the user structure itself; however, data like an address is often broken into a separate structure. Using a separate structure for an address is common, as people often have different addresses for home and work. In these cases, a table with address types is probably appropriate.

The storage of office information is also rather poorly designed. In the example, the city and state of each office is stored with the office data. This means that states are probably duplicated (for offices in the same state), and possibly cities are as well. This isn't such a good idea, as this duplicated data can add up over the life of an application. Adding addresses causes even more duplication. A better idea is to create a states table, and then possibly a location or city structure, with a city and a reference to the states structure. Finally, using the ID of the city in the offices and addresses structure completes the picture. In this way, data redundancy is minimized. It also eases management; a change to the name of a city or even state (it happens; just ask Russia) can be made in one data structure, and that change will affect all related records.

These are only a few items that were glossed over; you can probably think of 10 or 15 more that are related to your application or your background. Feel free to modify, add, and delete as needed. For now, though, it's time to move on to physical data design. Figure 3-5 shows the completed logical design, with all the references I discussed in place, linking all of the structures together.

Databases

With the general data model done, we can now begin to cover the implementation details. In other words, we are finally through all the high-level talk and into the meat! In this section, you'll pick apart the data model and determine what portions belong in a database. You can then look at actually creating the tables, rows, columns, and keys that you'll need in the database to represent the data. Once you've accomplished that, we'll spend the next section looking at directory servers and performing the same task for the data that belongs in that physical medium.

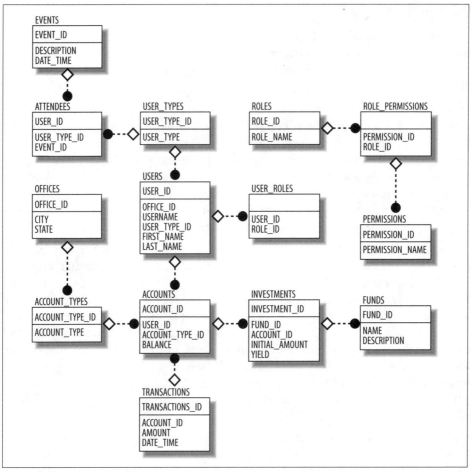

Figure 3-5. Complete Forethought data layout

Of course, the language of choice for databases is the Structured Query Language (SQL), and we'll use it to deal with databases here. Most databases now come with tools to make the creation of data structures simple; these are usually graphical and present a visual means of creating data structures. Additionally, a number of third-party tools are good for this sort of task (like SQL Navigator, already mentioned in Chapter 1). I'll focus on using pure SQL in this section, so the code will work on any database, on any platform, without you having to learn or buy a specific vendor's tool.

User Storage

Now that you've made it through all the preliminary steps, you can start creating tables. The first group of data schema that I focused on in the design was the user store. This consisted of a structure for users, the offices that the users worked in, and

Vendor-Specific SQL

The acronym SQL is used fairly generically in the text. When referenced, this implies the use of ANSI-92 SQL. However, most database vendors provide extensions to SQL, and often even additional data types. While these additional constructs can improve performance on a specific database, it makes the resulting SQL vendor-dependent. While that may be good for databases, it isn't so good for authors.

An example of this sort of extension is Oracle's VARCHAR2 data type. ANSI SQL provides CHAR and VARCHAR data types. CHARs always take up a precise length; for example, a field declared as CHAR(12) would always result in 12 characters. The text "Modano" would actually be stored as "Modano   " (note the extra 6 spaces): the padding ensures a 12-character length. This of course results in a lot of wasted space. So VARCHAR was defined to allow dynamic length. "Modano" would stay "Modano" in a field of length 6, 12, or 20. Oracle, though, adds a VARCHAR2 data type that is optimized even further than the standard SQL type VARCHAR. In the text, when VARCHAR is used, Oracle users would be wise to convert to VARCHAR2. These types of optimizations are almost endlessly varied from database to database, however, and can't all be covered here.

As if that weren't enough, some databases do *not* support certain data types and constructs. These features are often important in ensuring data integrity, so think twice before using those databases for any purpose other than testing or prototyping. Additionally, there is no common symbol or convention for adding comments into your SQL scripts across databases; many (Oracle, Cloudscape, etc.) allow the use of a double hyphen (--), but there are other variations, such as InstantDB, that allow the use of a semicolon (;).

All SQL statements here will work on any database that accepts standard ANSI SQL. However, when vendor-specific optimizations can dramatically affect performance, they will be noted in the text, and examples of SQL for a specific database will be shown if appropriate. Additionally, you should check Appendix A and your database's documentation for additional enhancements that can be made. Finally, the examples that can be obtained from *http://www.newInstance.com* contain different SQL scripts that will run on a variety of different databases.

---

a related table for representing the types of users, employees and clients. As you have almost certainly guessed, each of these structures maps to a table in the database we will use. Beyond that, there is little complexity left in designing the data storage.

First, you need to map each column to the appropriate data type. The ID columns all can become integers, as they should simply be numeric values without decimal places. All the columns that contain textual values (the type of user, the city where an office is located, the user's first name, and so on) can become VARCHAR columns. This allows them to contain text, but by avoiding the CHAR type, no unnecessary spaces are added to the columns' contents. The one exception to this is in the state column for offices. I'd recommend using two-letter abbreviations for all 50 states within the U.S., and since two characters are *always* needed, using the CHAR data type is appropriate.

Another simple decision is which columns can have null values and which cannot. In the case of the user store, every single column should be required (you will see some optional columns when I get to the accounts store). The user's name, information about offices and user types, and relations between the tables are all required pieces of information.

We have already discussed and diagrammed the relationships between the various tables, and primary and foreign key constraints will put these relationships into action. The scripts in Examples 3-1 and 3-2 include these constraints. Be sure that your database supports referential integrity; if it doesn't, make the changes indicated in Appendix A. In the case of the Forethought database, referential integrity will ensure that users are not assigned to nonexistent user types, for example. It also will help when deleting an office if it was relocated or the company was downsized. You can easily make changes to the employees affected by this change (those in the deleted office) when referential integrity is in place. On the other hand, if this feature is not supported by your database, costly searches through all users in the database have to be performed in such cases. While databases that do not support foreign key constraints are great for debugging, prototyping, and in particular for experimenting (for example, on a laptop in an airplane), they are rarely suitable for production applications.

The final detail to point out is that I do *not* recommend creating a column for the user's username. Remember that I discussed storing usernames, passwords, and authentication data in the Forethought directory server, instead of the database. However, the rest of the user information is stored in the database. What you need, then, is a way to relate user information in the database with the same user's data in the directory server. While there is nothing to be done at a physical level, some programmatic constraints can be put in place with a little planning.* To facilitate implementing these constraints, you can add a column to your USERS table in the database called USER_DN. This will store the *distinguished name* (DN) of the user in the LDAP directory server. The user's DN in this arena serves as a unique identifier, and can be used to bridge the information gap between the database and directory server. Java code can then locate a user in the database by using the LDAP DN, or locate a user in the directory server by using the USER_DN column of the USERS table in the database.

With data types, relationships, and a link between the database and directory server decided upon, you're ready to create the database schema. Example 3-1 shows the completed SQL script for creating the discussed tables and relationships.

---

* Although there is no way to relate databases to directory servers yet, companies like Oracle may provide this means soon. Because Oracle 8/9i and other "all-in-one" products of that nature often contain a database and directory server in the same package, it would not be surprising to see these relationships between differing physical data stores become available.

Example 3-1. SQL Script to Create the User Store

```sql
-- USER_TYPES table
CREATE TABLE USER_TYPES (
      USER_TYPE_ID          INT PRIMARY KEY NOT NULL,
      USER_TYPE             VARCHAR(20) NOT NULL
);

-- OFFICES table
CREATE TABLE OFFICES (
      OFFICE_ID             INT PRIMARY KEY NOT NULL,
      CITY                  VARCHAR(20) NOT NULL,
      STATE                 CHAR(2) NOT NULL
);

-- USERS table
CREATE TABLE USERS (
      USER_ID               INT PRIMARY KEY NOT NULL,
      OFFICE_ID             INT,
      USER_DN               VARCHAR(100) NOT NULL,
      USER_TYPE_ID          INT NOT NULL,
      FIRST_NAME            VARCHAR(20) NOT NULL,
      LAST_NAME             VARCHAR(30) NOT NULL,
      CONSTRAINT OFFICE_ID_FK FOREIGN KEY (OFFICE_ID)
        REFERENCES OFFICES (OFFICE_ID),
      CONSTRAINT USER_TYPE_ID_FK FOREIGN KEY (USER_TYPE_ID)
        REFERENCES USER_TYPES (USER_TYPE_ID)
);
```

If you are watching closely, you may note something a little odd here, at least if you are familiar with SQL. The OFFICE_ID column in the USERS table does not have the NOT NULL clause, as you might expect:

```sql
CREATE TABLE USERS (
      USER_ID               INT PRIMARY KEY NOT NULL,
      OFFICE_ID             INT,
-- and so on...
```

Omitting the NOT NULL clause is somewhat unusual, as you generally would want to require users to be related to an entry in the OFFICES table. However, this table will also store Forethought clients, which do not have associated offices. To allow for this, the NOT NULL clause is removed, so that clients (without offices) can leave a null value in the OFFICE_ID column. At the same time, the foreign key constraint will ensure that if a value is present, it must refer to an existing entry in the OFFICES table. This issue is fairly typical; although you want to require data when appropriate, be sure not to add in constraints that will cause you trouble later on.

With that minor problem handled, you can get back to the table design and database-specific optimizations. As already mentioned, Oracle adds a data type, VARCHAR2, that can greatly improve the performance of a database when that type is used instead of the standard ANSI SQL VARCHAR data type. Additionally, Oracle's integer type is called INTEGER, not INT. Example 3-2 shows the original SQL script shown in Example 3-1 converted over to use these updated data types. Of course, this version of the script will work only on Oracle databases.[*]

Example 3-2. Oracle Version of Script to Create the User Store

```
-- USER_TYPES table
CREATE TABLE USER_TYPES (
        USER_TYPE_ID          INTEGER PRIMARY KEY NOT NULL,
        USER_TYPE             VARCHAR2(20) NOT NULL
);

-- OFFICES table
CREATE TABLE OFFICES (
        OFFICE_ID             INTEGER PRIMARY KEY NOT NULL,
        CITY                  VARCHAR2(20) NOT NULL,
        STATE                 CHAR(2) NOT NULL
);

-- USERS table
CREATE TABLE USERS (
        USER_ID               INTEGER PRIMARY KEY NOT NULL,
        OFFICE_ID             INTEGER,
        USER_DN               VARCHAR2(100) NOT NULL,
        USER_TYPE_ID          INTEGER NOT NULL,
        FIRST_NAME            VARCHAR2(20) NOT NULL,
        LAST_NAME             VARCHAR2(30) NOT NULL,
        CONSTRAINT OFFICE_ID_FK FOREIGN KEY (OFFICE_ID)
          REFERENCES OFFICES (OFFICE_ID),
        CONSTRAINT USER_TYPE_ID_FK FOREIGN KEY (USER_TYPE_ID)
          REFERENCES USER_TYPES (USER_TYPE_ID)
);
```

Once you've run the appropriate script against your database, the complete user store should be set up and ready for use.

 If you had any errors when running the SQL scripts or are unsure of how to execute these scripts against your database, consult the appendixes of this book. Appendix A contains the contents of the SQL scripts optimized for a variety of different databases. These scripts, as mentioned earlier, are also all available online at this book's web site, *http://www.newInstance.com*. As for deployment of the script, your database should have documentation on the tools and steps to execute a SQL script against your particular database. Additionally, Appendix B has a concise set of instructions for a variety of databases, and may allow you to get up and running quickly. If you are still receiving errors after using the scripts in the appendix and following the deployment instructions, consult your database vendor.

---

[*] The VARCHAR2 data type is allowed by all versions of the Oracle database. This includes not only 8*i* and 9*i*, but Oracle WebDB and Oracle Lite as well.

A data model diagram (also called an *entity-relationship* or *ER* diagram) detailing the result of the work so far is shown in Figure 3-6. It notes the tables, primary keys, and relationships between tables. The abbreviation FK is used to represent a foreign key, a column that references a value in another table. If you have vendor-specific tools to view your database schema graphically, it should resemble this figure.*

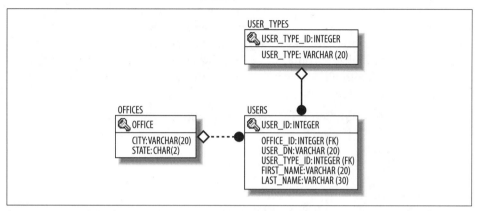

Figure 3-6. Database diagram for the user store

Accounts Storage

It's time to move on and look at building the accounts store. You may have noticed that I skipped over user permissions and the rest of the application's authentication data; that information will reside in the directory server instead of the database layer, so I'll discuss it later in the chapter. For now, let's move on to dealing with accounts, funds, investments, and the rest within the database.

As with the user store, relatively few decisions are left after the extensive design discussions, and the remaining decisions are fairly simple. First, you must determine the data type for each column. Again, you can use integers for all of the ID columns. The character-based columns in this case are all VARCHAR data types, as none are fixed width (as the STATE column in the OFFICES table was). There are also several columns to which you should assign the SQL FLOAT data type, such as the balance of an account, the amount of a transaction, and the yield on an investment. These are all decimal numbers that will be used in calculations within the application's business logic. Finally, assign the DATE data type to the column that stores the time a transaction occurs.

Unlike the user store, though, several columns within the accounts store can have null values, and therefore do not need the NOT NULL keywords added to their definitions

---

* Most databases come with simple tools for this sort of graphical database browsing, and additional tools can usually be downloaded for free or purchased commercially. If you don't have a tool that gives you this capability, look into obtaining one. The resulting view is helpful in seeing relationships between various tables and the data that they contain.

within the SQL script. The description of a fund and the yield of an account are two examples. A fund may be entered into the system without additional description, and an investment, at least initially, probably does not have any yield. Later in the life of the investment, the yield can be added in.*

The various ID columns on each table are made the primary keys for those tables. Then foreign keys are set up to relate the various tables to each other, as the diagram in Figure 3-4 details. Also note that a relationship is set up between the ACCOUNTS table and the USERS table that essentially "bridges" the user store with the accounts store. It also ensures that accounts are deleted when users are removed, and that no account is created without a user who "owns" the account. Similar constraints are enforced for funds and investments.

Example 3-3 is the SQL script that will create the accounts storage for the Forethought application.

Example 3-3. SQL Script to Create the Accounts Store

```
-- ACCOUNT_TYPES table
CREATE TABLE ACCOUNT_TYPES (
        ACCOUNT_TYPE_ID     INT PRIMARY KEY NOT NULL,
        ACCOUNT_TYPE        VARCHAR(20) NOT NULL
);

-- ACCOUNTS table
CREATE TABLE ACCOUNTS (
        ACCOUNT_ID          INT PRIMARY KEY NOT NULL,
        USER_ID             INT NOT NULL,
        ACCOUNT_TYPE_ID     INT NOT NULL,
        BALANCE             FLOAT NOT NULL,
        CONSTRAINT USER_ID_FK FOREIGN KEY (USER_ID)
          REFERENCES USERS (USER_ID),
        CONSTRAINT ACCOUNT_TYPE_ID_FK FOREIGN KEY (ACCOUNT_TYPE_ID)
          REFERENCES ACCOUNT_TYPES (ACCOUNT_TYPE_ID)
);

-- TRANSACTIONS table
CREATE TABLE TRANSACTIONS (
        TRANSACTION_ID      INT PRIMARY KEY NOT NULL,
        ACCOUNT_ID          INT NOT NULL,
        AMOUNT              FLOAT NOT NULL,
        DATE_TIME           DATE NOT NULL,
        CONSTRAINT ACCOUNT_ID_FK FOREIGN KEY (ACCOUNT_ID)
          REFERENCES ACCOUNTS (ACCOUNT_ID)
);
```

---

* Another option here would be to require the YIELD column and assign it a default value of 1.00, which essentially means that all calculations simply return the value of the initial amount invested. However, this removes the ability to differentiate between new investments (without a yield) and investments that truly do have a yield of 1.00. It also results in a column having dual meanings, which isn't a very good idea.

Example 3-3. SQL Script to Create the Accounts Store (continued)

```
-- FUNDS table
CREATE TABLE FUNDS (
        FUND_ID            INT PRIMARY KEY NOT NULL,
        NAME               VARCHAR(20) NOT NULL,
        DESCRIPTION        VARCHAR(200)
);

-- INVESTMENTS table
CREATE TABLE INVESTMENTS (
        INVESTMENT_ID      INT PRIMARY KEY NOT NULL,
        FUND_ID            INT NOT NULL,
        ACCOUNT_ID         INT NOT NULL,
        INITIAL_AMOUNT     FLOAT NOT NULL,
        YIELD              FLOAT,
        CONSTRAINT FUND_ID_FK FOREIGN KEY (FUND_ID)
          REFERENCES FUNDS (FUND_ID),
        CONSTRAINT ACCOUNT_ID_FK2 FOREIGN KEY (ACCOUNT_ID)
          REFERENCES ACCOUNTS (ACCOUNT_ID)
);
```

The data diagram in Figure 3-7 shows the tables and relationships created by the script detailed in Example 3-3 (as well as those in Appendix A).

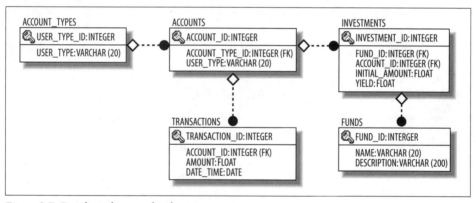

Figure 3-7. Database diagram for the accounts store

Scheduling and Events Storage

Handling the creation of the events store turns out to be a piece of cake; there are only two tables involved, both of which are very basic. The first, the EVENTS table, simply needs an ID for the primary key and a couple of columns for details. The first column will store the event description, and the second the date and time of the event. As mentioned in the "Odds and Ends" section earlier, you may want to add additional columns, such as an event name, information about the location, or any other relevant information. The table here is kept simple for the sake of example.

With that table in place, all that's left is to relate an event to a group of attendees, which should relate to the USERS table. For this, you need a *many-to-many* relationship, where an event may have many users attending, and a user may attend many events. To facilitate this type of relationship, a *join table*, which simply connects an event to a user, can be used. It does not have a primary key column;* instead, it has foreign keys relating to the EVENTS table and the USERS table. In this way, two one-to-many relationships create a many-to-many relationship and join the two tables desired. Example 3-4 shows a SQL script that creates the two tables and shows the relationships described between the other application tables.

Example 3-4. SQL Script to Create Events Store

```
-- EVENTS table
CREATE TABLE EVENTS (
        EVENT_ID              INT PRIMARY KEY NOT NULL,
        DESCRIPTION           VARCHAR(50) NOT NULL,
        DATE_TIME             DATE NOT NULL
);

-- ATTENDEES table
CREATE TABLE ATTENDEES (
        USER_ID            INT NOT NULL,
        EVENT_ID           INT NOT NULL,
        CONSTRAINT AT_USER_ID_FK FOREIGN KEY (USER_ID)
          REFERENCES USERS (USER_ID),
        CONSTRAINT EVENT_ID_FK FOREIGN KEY (EVENT_ID)
          REFERENCES EVENTS (EVENT_ID)
);
```

Figure 3-8 is the result of the script in Example 3-4.

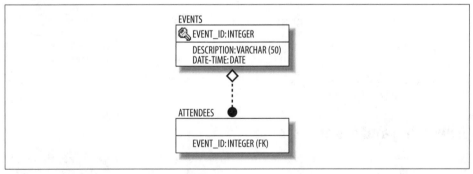

Figure 3-8. Database diagram for the events store

---

* It isn't uncommon to create a compound primary key out of all foreign keys in the table. However, in most databases this neither improves nor degrades performance, so I'm generally agnostic on the practice.

Note that this figure, like Figures 3-6 and 3-7, doesn't include relationships with other tables. For example, the USER_ID column and the relationship with the USERS table are omitted. Instead, the figure shows only the specific data related to the events store. For a complete schema diagram, refer to Figure 3-9.

Connecting the Dots

Once you have executed all three SQL scripts against your database, the physical database model should be complete. Again, I recommend that you use some type of visual tool to confirm that all the relationships between tables are in place, and that the columns are of the correct data types and sizes. Figure 3-9 shows a diagram that represents the completed data model for the Forethought application.

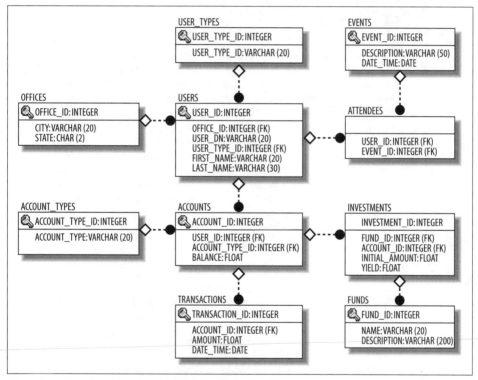

Figure 3-9. Completed data model for Forethought database

Seed Data

Although you'll add most of the data for your application through the entity beans and LDAP components detailed in the following chapters, some data will need to be seeded manually. This is necessary because some tables will not be accessible to bean clients. In the Forethought application, the two examples of this are the USER_TYPES and ACCOUNT_TYPES tables. The entity beans for these tables (detailed in Chapter 4 and Appendix E) provide only local interfaces, so a client can't use them from an application. Example 3-5 shows a simple SQL script to add some initial data for these tables.

Example 3-5. Seeding Data in the Type Tables

```
INSERT INTO USER_TYPES VALUES (1, 'Client');
INSERT INTO USER_TYPES VALUES (2, 'Employee');

INSERT INTO ACCOUNT_TYPES VALUES (1, 'Everyday');
INSERT INTO ACCOUNT_TYPES VALUES (2, 'Investment');
INSERT INTO ACCOUNT_TYPES VALUES (3, 'Investment Plus');
INSERT INTO ACCOUNT_TYPES VALUES (4, 'Money Market');
INSERT INTO ACCOUNT_TYPES VALUES (5, 'Savings');
```

In any production system, a process should be put in place for backing up data. I don't cover this sort of operation, as the process differs for various database vendors. However, you should consult your documentation for a means to back up your data schema, or at least take some type of snapshot of the data.

While details of accomplishing this task are beyond the scope of this book, it is assumed you will perform backup-related operations with your own applications. At this point in the Forethought application, backup should occur. While no data has yet been entered, recovering the database's structure while it is clean can be a real timesaver, especially if the steps to execute SQL against your database are complex or require specific tools to be installed. Even if you don't back up your work on the Forethought sample application, you should realize that this is one point where a backup should occur.

Cleaning Up

As a final bit of aid in database design, you should always develop SQL scripts for clearing out the structures in your database. This is not only to clear out the data, but the actual tables, rows, and constraints as well. Often in development, you will work, re-work, and re-work again; being able to easily clear out your database schema and re-create it becomes a handy tool in these situations. Finally, a common tendency in design is to add a table, add another table, remove the first table, make some changes, and add again. This back-and-forth method of design often results in a non-repeatable creation process; in other words, you have no scripts that can re-create the final database schema from scratch. The lack of scripts to re-create the database makes deployment onto testing and production systems very difficult. By cleaning out your schema and testing your scripts from an empty start, you can ensure these problems don't occur in your applications. Example 3-6, then, is a SQL script for dropping all tables[*] in the Forethought database schema.

 Be aware that dropping a table will dispose of all the data within that table. If you are re-creating the structure after inserting data into it (either yourself or by following the examples throughout this book), that data will be lost upon running these scripts. If you do need to preserve existing data, be sure to back up or export that data before running the example SQL scripts.

Example 3-6. Cleaning Out the Forethought Database Schema

```
-- Drop all tables
DROP TABLE ATTENDEES;
DROP TABLE EVENTS;
DROP TABLE INVESTMENTS;
DROP TABLE FUNDS;
DROP TABLE TRANSACTIONS;
DROP TABLE ACCOUNTS;
DROP TABLE ACCOUNT_TYPES;
DROP TABLE ATTENDEES;
DROP TABLE EVENTS;
DROP TABLE USERS;
DROP TABLE USER_TYPES;
DROP TABLE OFFICES;
```

Directory Servers

Now that the database is ready to go, it's time to round out the data storage by working with a directory server, which at least in this case is much simpler than working with a database. Almost all directory servers come with several predefined data structures; in this example application, these structures are almost completely sufficient for our needs. In this section I'll discuss what information you'll need to store in the directory and how you can use pre-built and custom structures to handle these data needs.

Briefly, though, let me discuss directory servers at a high level. This is by no means a complete overview of directory servers or LDAP, but it should at least get you through this chapter. First, you should realize that a directory server is laid out hierarchically, instead of in the relational manner of a database. Here is where all of those tree structures you studied in college finally start to pay off. An instance of a directory server is identified uniquely by its organization. The *organization* in a directory server is analogous to a database schema in an RDBMS. So if you named your

---

[*] Realize that dropping tables results in the constraints and relationships between those tables also being dropped. Additionally, the *order* of the drops is relevant, as tables without foreign keys must be deleted before the tables that depend on them.

database schema "Forethought" (for you Oracle users, the SID might be "FTHT"), your directory server would have an organization of "Forethought" as well.

Database Schema, LDAP Schema

I've spent most of this chapter talking about database schemas, which you are probably familiar with. However, in this section, I am referring to LDAP schemas. The word *schema* in this context has a subtly different meaning that you should be aware of. A database schema consists of a specific set of tables, relationships, triggers, and other constructs, and deals with the way information can be stored. However, there is no change to the actual rules of the database itself; tables, rows, and columns are well-defined database features. An LDAP schema, however, refers to the actual structure of object types in the database. For example, the default LDAP schema contains a user object called *inetOrgPerson* (mentioned in the upcoming "Users and Passwords" section), which inherits from organizationalPerson, and on up the object chain. But if additional information storage was needed, such as a *yearsEmployed* field, a new object could be created. I'll call this object *applicationOrgPerson*, and presumably it would extend *inetOrgPerson*. In this case, I have changed the LDAP structure available, otherwise known as the LDAP schema. The difference is that instead of creating instances of existing objects, as in a database schema, I am creating actual objects themselves. Understanding this difference will help in your comprehension of the LDAP and directory server discussions in this chapter and the rest of the book.

As if that weren't enough, terminology also differs from directory server to database server. A table in a database is an *object class* in a directory server. A field, or column, in the table becomes an *attribute* of the object class. And rows in the table become *objects* in the directory server. In each section, the appropriate terms are being used; as a rule of thumb, think of the directory server as Java-centric, and you'll do just fine, while the database section follows the terms you are familiar with from RDBMS systems.

Second, directory servers do not have tables and rows; they have objects and object instances. This should seem quite simple to you as a Java developer, and makes directory servers easy to deal with from Java. You define object types and then populate those types, using attributes (similar to database table columns). These objects are then placed under organizational units. An *organizational unit* is a group of like objects and is analogous to a database table. The object instances under this organizational unit are then similar to the rows in a database table. Finally, these units are connected to an organization, giving identity to the objects that they contain.

The result is a partitioned data store that can store quite a bit of data while still maintaining a good amount of organization and structure. Of course, when you connect these objects, groups, units, and the directory server organization itself, you get a nice hierarchical data structure, which is of course what a directory server is. When used to complement the relational structure of a database, you end up with a nice strong data storage facility. It's helpful to use your knowledge about databases, and their relationship to a directory server, to understand how all these pieces fit together. Figure 3-10 shows this relationship pictorially, and should help you get an idea of how the two data store structures relate.

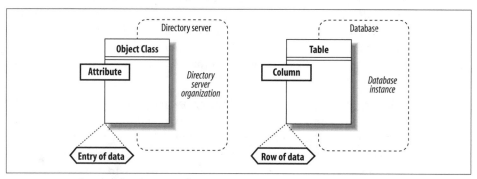

Figure 3-10. Relating a database to a directory server

Finally, there must be a way to navigate through this structure; since the hierarchy is the key part of the structure, each object can be defined by the object's path to the root of the tree. In other words, each object has an identifier, as does its group, organizational unit, organization, and every other directory service structure. Piecing these together can result in a pathway leading from an object in the tree back to the top-level organization. This path, when strung together into a string, is called a *distinguished name*; it is unique within the tree (which is why it's called distinguished). Figure 3-11 shows how an object's distinguished name is built, starting with the object and moving to the root of the tree.

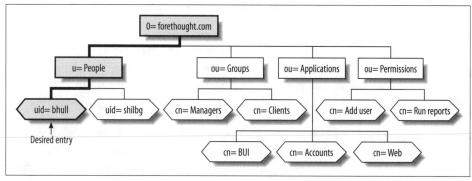

Figure 3-11. Building a distinguished name

The result is similar to referencing a database table by the schema name, table name, and primary key of a particular row in that table. It also looks and behaves a lot like a Unix path or a URL. I know this is all a bit sketchy, so let's look at some application to help you understand how this all fits together.

Users and Passwords

In any enterprise application, you'll end up spending a lot of time dealing with users. Of course, an application without users is about as useful as one of those plastic "spork" things (remember those? The little fork/spoon combinations that never did either job very well?). In the "Databases" section, we came up with tables to hold data about the user type, the offices a user could work in, and the user himself. However, I left the username out, and mentioned a decision to store that piece of information in the directory server. I also stated that the user's password should be stored in the directory as well.

In the database, every piece of data required the creation of a storage facility (a table) for the data. In directory servers, the same holds true, and you need an organizational unit to hold users. However, you can use the default organizational unit of *People* for this task.* Each user will then have a user ID (UID) stored as a property of the user object. This UID becomes the key for the user, and is part of each user's distinguished name (DN). So, for a user with a UID of *bhull*, the corresponding DN would be *uid=bhull,ou=People,o=forethought.com*. Here, the "uid" refers to "user ID", "ou" refers to "organizational unit", and "o" refers to the "organization". Figure 3-12 shows how this DN relates to the overall directory structure.

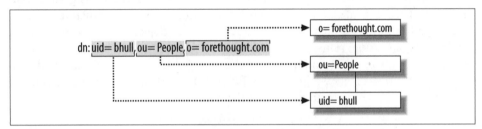

Figure 3-12. A user entry in the directory server

All the application users can then "hang" off the *People* organizational unit. This also allows you to take advantage of your directory server for other applications by using this same organizational unit for those applications' users as well. For this reason, creating an organizational unit specifically for this application (for example, *ou=Online Brokerage,o=forethought.com*) and then adding users to that structure isn't a very good idea; the directory tree would likely end up cluttered with various applications, with user information stored under each. This method of storing all users under a generic *People* branch allows you to use the same user information for a variety of applications.

The default object used to store a person, *inetOrgPerson*, contains attributes for all the information you'll need to record for users: a username, a password, and the ability to

---

* Almost every directory server's default installation will have a pre-built *People* organizational unit, with a DN of *ou=People,o=forethought.com*. If your server does not, consult Appendix C for details on creating that unit.

reference the user object from groups (which I'll talk about next). In this case, then, the default LDAP schema suits our needs perfectly. You can use the uid attribute for the username, and the userpassword attribute for the password. All other fields can be left unused, as they aren't really relevant to the Forethought application.

However, the *inetOrgPerson* object isn't quite perfect for this application's needs; while it has attributes for all the information you need to store, the attributes we want to use (for user ID and user password) are not required attributes. The only required attributes for the *inetOrgPerson* object class are sn (the surname or last name of the user), cn (the common name or first name of the user), and objectclass (filled in automatically by the directory server). You need to add the username and password attributes to the set of required information to ensure no users are created without at least a username and password.

Structural constraints versus programmatic constraints

At this point, you can either add constraints to your LDAP schema at a physical level (like the constraints in the "Databases" section) or decide to enforce the constraints later at a programmatic level. As in the database design, it is preferable to add these constraints into the LDAP schema. This approach ensures that no invalid data gets into the directory server and makes programming tasks easier down the line. However, you don't have much control over this particular design. First, it is a bad idea to actually change the default *inetOrgPerson* object class itself. I will talk a bit more about this in the next section, but for now suffice it to say that changing the default object classes is a bad idea, and that extending these object classes and creating new ones is much better. Doing so also keeps the core directory server compatible with other standard directory server schemas.

However, I already mentioned that the proposed parent class, the *inetOrgPerson* object class, has the uid and userpassword attributes as allowed attributes. Extending this object does *not* allow us to change those from optional to required attributes, as that would essentially break the inheritance chain. This rule is similar to the Java rule that doesn't allow member variables in a parent class to be made more accessible in a derivative class (such as moving from private to protected, or protected to public). Its consequence is that extending the *inetOrgPerson* object class and then adding additional constraints on existing attributes impossible. So in this case, you have to use programmatic constraints instead of physical ones. This means that the default *inetOrgPerson* object class will suffice as-is for our needs. Next, I will look at extending object classes and creating new ones in order to handle users' authentication data.

Permissions and Roles

With the user object class in place, you can now tackle permissions and roles that determine how users can interact with the Forethought application and what portions of the application they can access. As in the case of storing users, it is a good idea to see if any existing structures map well to the application requirements. In this case, we need an object class to store a single permission, and then another object class that represents a role, which should be able to reference multiple permissions. Finally, a role should be assignable to multiple users, creating the last link between users and their individual access rights.

Default LDAP schemas do not provide any sort of permissions object class, but the default object class *groupOfUniqueNames* seems to be a close match for a role. This object can be given a name and can hold references to one or more users (under the *ou=People,o=forethought.com* branch of the LDAP tree). Additionally, most directory servers come preconfigured with an organizational unit called *Groups*, resulting in a branch whose DN would be *ou=Groups,o=forethought.com*. The ability to both reference users and have default storage makes using an LDAP group to represent roles possible. However, you still need to handle permissions, and then build a link to them from the *groupOfUniqueNames* object class or a derivative of that class.

The task, then, is to create an object class from scratch. This is actually not as big a deal as it might seem. You can use a simple name; in this case the name *forethoughtPermission* works well. It would be possible to simply use *permission*, as that is descriptive enough, but prefacing it with "forethought" ensures that there is no ambiguity about the role of the new object class. If another application using this directory server needed a different type of permission, it could create another class with the same purpose and assign it the name *<applicationName>Permission*, keeping the two object classes distinct.[*] You also need to decide on the parent class for the new object class. Since you are not extending any existing functionality, the default base class *top* can be used as a parent. You should always try to extend the existing object class hierarchy and avoid creating new top-level objects. This is the very reason that the *top* object class is named what it is: it should be the single top-level class. The required attributes for this new class should simply be a name and the `objectClass` attribute that all objects must have (inherited from the *top* object class). You can now create a new object class in your directory server called *forethoughtPermission*. Assign the *top* object class as its parent, and add the `cn` attribute to its set of required attributes. While `cn` (common name) is used for a user's first name, it is used for naming other objects as well. In this application, it will be used for naming the groups later on. You should also add the `description` attribute to the list of optional attributes for the new object class so that a lengthier description of the permission's purpose can be added to instances of the class. Save the new object class, and you are ready to move back to looking at groups that will represent user roles.

---

[*] If this doesn't seem like a common case, think again: directory servers are often used across entire companies, and applications often share data. Additionally, many applications do have different criteria they must store for a permission, such as to whom the permission can be granted. Therefore, keeping object class names *succinct* is not as important as keeping them *distinct*.

While directory servers and LDAP are more standardized than data-bases are, the process of making changes to the LDAP schema is different for each vendor. In some, like the iPlanet directory server, a handy GUI is provided to make changes easy. In others, like OpenLDAP, *ldif* files must be used. Appendix C covers two of the most important directory servers, and includes details on installation, configuration, and modifying the LDAP schema. Refer to this appendix for instructions related to your specific product.

Since the *groupOfUniqueNames* object class already has an attribute to store user references (in the form of holding each user's DN), all that's needed to make it suitable for use is a similar facility for referencing permissions. This facility effectively makes the *groupOfUniqueNames* object class a "many-to-many join table" between users and permissions in the data scheme. To create the link between a group and the new permissions object class, you need to add an attribute to the group. Creating an attribute is similar to creating an object class; you just need to specify the attribute type. The LDAP type "'case-ignore string" should be chosen here,* as this allows DNs for permission object class instances to be used as values for the attribute. This, then, is the link between the groups in the application (roles) and permissions (*forethoughtPermission* object instances). If your directory server has a means to specify that the attribute can occur multiple times within an object class, select this option as well; these groups will usually have references to more than one permission instance. Name the new attribute uniquePermission. While permission would be descriptive, prepending it with the word "unique" indicates that permissions are not duplicated within the same group.

With this attribute added, you can now deal with the group object class. As discussed, the default object, *groupOfUniqueNames*, is a good starting point, but not sufficient for our needs. You'll need to add to the object class the ability to have the uniquePermission attribute as part of the object class's definition. However, adding an attribute to an existing object class brings up an important design issue related to directory servers.

Addition versus extension

At this point, there is a design decision to make. The directory server allows you either to add the uniquePermission attribute to the set of allowed attributes for *groupOfUniqueNames*, or to extend the *groupOfUniqueNames* class and create a new descendant object class where you can make the desired change. The latter choice, extension, is *always* preferred; this is one of the very few design principles that is

---

* Some directory servers, most notably iPlanet, offer a "Distinguished Name" LDAP type, which should be used. This will ensure that only valid DNs are supplied as values for the attribute. For more details on specific directory servers, check out Appendix C.

absolute. Changing a default LDAP object class is very dangerous, as it causes your directory server's schema to immediately become incompatible with all other directory servers. While you could certainly make the changes in these other directory servers, you lose the ability to communicate through common structures, and communication between a modified directory server and an unmodified one, perhaps for sharing groups (*groupOfUniqueNames* objects), would be made impossible.* So instead, you need to extend your directory server schema. Create a new object class and call it *groupOfForethoughtNames*, with the parent object *groupOfUniqueNames*. You then need to add the custom attribute, `uniquePermission`, to the set of required attributes for the new object class. Once you have added this attribute, the groups object class is ready to use. The object class hierarchy for these new object classes is shown in Figure 3-13 (note that only relevant attributes are shown for each class). Attributes above the line in each object class are required, and those below are optional. The connecting lines represent potential references between object class instances.

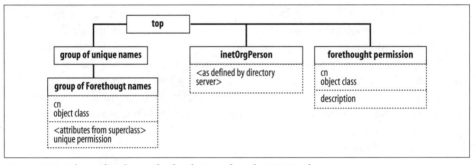

Figure 3-13. Object class hierarchy for the Forethought LDAP schema

Directory Hierarchy

Now that all of your object classes are in place and the LDAP schema is complete, you can create the object instances needed for storing Forethought data. Depending on the directory server you are using, some of these may already exist in your directory hierarchy. At the top of your tree, you should have an organization called "forethought.com" where the DN is *o=forethought.com*.† Underneath this top level, you want to be able to store users, permissions, and groups. As discussed earlier, most servers come with a preconfigured organizational unit for users called *People*; if it

---

* I'm exaggerating slightly here; good programmers can program for these sorts of aberrant solutions and allow communication across heterogeneous object classes. However, it is still bad practice, and cannot be discouraged enough.

† If you are using an internationally aware directory server, the DN may be a little longer. A country reference is sometimes present, resulting in the DN looking more like *o=forethought.com, c=US* (for the United States). You can substitute your country code as appropriate.

Object Class Hierarchy, Directory Hierarchy

Like the difference between an LDAP schema and a database schema, distinguishing between object class hierarchies and directory hierarchies is a subtle thing. The *object class hierarchy* of a directory server is the set of physical objects that are allowed to exist within the schema. There are almost always many more of these physical objects, the object classes, than actual object instances in use. However, the object instances and the treelike structure of data that they make up comprise the actual *directory hierarchy*, sometimes called (even more confusingly) simply the *object hierarchy*. The best analogy here is to closely relate a directory server to the Java language. Each object class is some compiled Java object, sitting around in byte code available for use in an application. However, most applications don't use every available class; instead they use a subset of these classes and create instances. There are multiple instances of some classes, and only single instances of others. This same principle applies in a directory server.

In the case of the Forethought application, then, you first modified the default LDAP schema, adding additional attributes and object classes. This completed the work on the object class hierarchy. In this section, you added additional organizational units and prepared a place for instances of the *inetOrgPerson*, *forethoughtPermission*, and *groupOfForethoughtNames* to reside. The result is a complete directory hierarchy. It is important to understand the difference, as reading through this chapter can be quite confusing without that distinction. The figures in these sections can help you grasp these differences.

doesn't exist, you should create this unit. The end result is a unit with a DN of *ou=People, o=forethought.com*. All the users (instances of the *inetOrgPerson* object class) will then reside under this unit. We've already discussed user DNs, identified by their user ID, the uid attribute.

When storing permissions and groups, you can use the same model. Create two additional organizational units directly under the forethought.com organization, *Permissions* and *Groups* (for many directory servers, the *Groups* unit is already configured for you, like the *People* unit was). Instances of the *groupOfForethoughtNames* object class, identified by a name (the cn attribute), will then have DNs similar to *cn=Administrators,ou=Groups,o=forethought.com*. In the same manner, permissions will have DNs like *cn=Add Users,ou=Permissions,o=forethought.com*. Again, consult Appendix C for specific details on creating these additional organizational units. Figure 3-14 shows the completed Forethought directory hierarchy, ready to use in your application. Note that the entries for users, permissions, and groups are for example purposes only, and shouldn't be in your directory server; they seek to show where data will be added (in the next chapters).

With this hierarchy in place, you are ready to move on. It's been a long ride, but it's finally time to move on to some actual code.

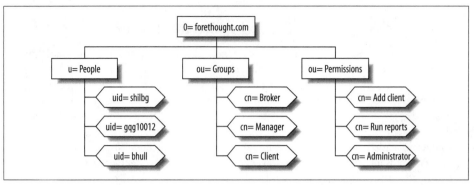

Figure 3-14. Completed Forethought directory hierarchy, with illustrative entries

What's Next?

You've made it through the creation of the data storage mediums, a major milestone in application design. As I have said several times, this portion of the framework will govern much of the rest of the application. Most notably, the data access layer is purely a reflection of the work already done here. We'll discuss this access in the next chapter, and work on allowing programmatic access to the data stores discussed here. This access will serve the rest of the application as well as components from other applications that may need data from the Forethought application.

Also in the next chapter, you'll get your first look at Enterprise JavaBeans, and in particular entity beans. We'll also examine the role of JNDI for allowing access to the directory server structures created in this chapter. In other words, we'll be running the gamut of Java approaches to accessing data in databases and directory servers. Once finished, you will have a functioning data layer for the application, with both a solid foundation and a set of sturdy beams, struts, and scaffolding upon which to build. Let's go onto this additional structure now (or at least after you've refilled your coffee and taken a deep breath).

## CHAPTER 4

Entity Basics

This chapter will look at entity beans as a means of accessing the Forethought application's data storage. I'll begin with simple entity beans to provide application entry points to the database, and address many questions common to entity bean development. Should you pass around the entity bean? Should you access the data exclusively through session beans, or directly through the entity beans? What are details objects, façade patterns, and good principles of entity bean design? All these questions will be answered, as I discuss not just writing EJB code, but writing *effective* EJB code.

At the end of this chapter, you will have the first entity bean created and deployed, ready for use. More importantly, you will have a good understanding of basic entity bean programming practices; you'll have looked at using container-managed persistence, package and class naming, handling method exposure through the remote interface, and more. In other words, you'll be ready for any basic entity bean problem that comes along, as well as for the advanced topics I'll address in Chapter 5.

Basic Design Patterns

To access the data that will be stored in the database, you can use EJB's entity bean functionality. Keep in mind, however, that this is not by any means a book on how to write Enterprise JavaBeans; for that I recommend Richard Monson-Haefel's excellent book, *Enterprise JavaBeans* (O'Reilly). Here, I'll simply focus on using EJBs correctly, and detail some useful design patterns.

In addition to looking at some design patterns and actual code, you must be familiar with two technologies that are intrinsic to EJBs: RMI and JNDI. Remote Method Invocation, or RMI, is the basis of all Enterprise JavaBeans calls. In a nutshell, RMI causes a remote call to a Java object over the network[*] to behave exactly like a local

---

[*] In reality, EJB servers are often on the same physical hardware as the servlet engine making the RMI calls, especially in development. On the other hand, production environments often have EJB servers on multiple machines, requiring RMI calls between session and entity beans as well as from the servlet engine to the EJB layer. In either case, I use the generic term "network communication" to refer to any communication to the EJB layer; I'll spend more time on this in the later section "The Local Interface."

call. The Java Naming and Directory Interface, or JNDI, allows objects to be bound into a namespace and then referenced by other objects. The namespace in this case is purely an abstract concept, but organization of Java objects and information in this manner does work well; all components of an application can use this single means of storage. Of course, like any other technology, RMI and JNDI require resources. JNDI requires memory in which to store the objects bound into its contexts, and both require runtime resources to operate. For example, looking up an object in the JNDI registry is more time-consuming than referencing a local object, and executing an RMI call is more expensive in terms of resources than executing a local method invocation. As always, you must focus on logical tradeoffs, and use both technologies only when needed. As usual, you should have a good reason for everything. And now, assuming that you are comfortable with these technologies, let's look at entity beans in detail.

First, you need to address access to entity beans (yes, I'm getting to the code; just be patient!). This might seem like a simple topic, but debates have been raging for years on various email lists concerning the means of accessing entity beans. The arguments center over whether entity beans should be accessed directly by an application (be it a servlet, Java application, or some other code fragment), or whether these calls should pass through a session bean, which then "proxies" the call to the entity bean. In the latter case, more RMI communication is involved, more JNDI lookups occur, and serialization may be necessary in passing returned values. However, accessing entity beans through some sort of proxy is still the preferred means of access.

While it might seem that I am jumping the gun, this topic will affect the way you code entity beans. First, the proxy method of accessing beans allows the entity beans to be more "basic" in nature. In other words, an entity bean can assume that the preparatory work in dealing with data, such as validation, type checking, and so forth, is done by the time it gets that data. The bean also doesn't have to worry about data conversion, such as from a Java `String` into a data type appropriate for that bean. These sorts of situations are common when a servlet communicates directly with data entities, but if you assume that session beans play an intermediary role, these are not problems for entity beans. I won't look at implementing this design pattern (called the *façade* design pattern) with session beans right now, but I will in later chapters. For now, it is enough to know that the application's entity beans only need to read and write data, and that the data is appropriate for use by the time it is handed off to these beans.

Coding the Bean

It's finally time to write some code. If you are new to EJB, you should pick up the aforementioned *Enterprise JavaBeans* and skim through Chapter 4 before continuing on. That should give you enough of a basic foundation to understand this chapter, as I'm going to move through the basic entity bean code pretty quickly.

I'll start the entity bean work with the office data structure. Remember the OFFICES table from last chapter? The table structure is shown again in Figure 4-1 for reference.

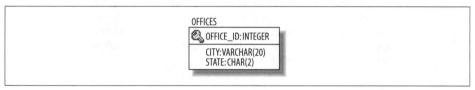

Figure 4-1. The office data structure

I'll use this structure for the first entity bean, as it has a very simple structure. It also does not depend on any other objects (i.e., it has no foreign keys), a subject I will address in the next chapter. Dependent objects introduce some additional considerations, but I will look at those when we start to code beans for tables with foreign keys, like the USERS table. For the time being, it's enough to know that this office structure is as simple as it gets. You need to store the ID (an int), the city (a String), and the state (another String).

As this bean is simple in nature, it is a perfect candidate for *container-managed persistence* (CMP). There are no special JDBC calls that need to be made, no multiple-table queries, and no explicit data caching that needs to be performed. In the absence of these special cases, CMP is almost always a better choice than *bean-managed persistence* (BMP). While CMP beans are not truly portable yet, as each container generates specific implementation classes for that product, the basic classes I'll look at in a CMP bean *are* portable. In other words, you won't be able to take a complete JAR file (with implementation classes) from BEA Weblogic and deploy it on Lutris Enhydra, but you will be able to take the user-coded classes from this chapter and use them to generate classes for both BEA Weblogic and Lutris Enhydra. The resultant JARs can then be deployed on the respective application servers. This adds a bit of work, but is as close to complete portability as is possible in today's EJB containers. It does allow us to write vendor-neutral code and not have to focus on a specific application server in this chapter.

All these reasons add up to a good case for using CMP instead of BMP. Additionally, the EJB 2.0 specification makes CMP an even more attractive solution, offering almost complete portability in all aspects of CMP entity beans.

While the process of creating the "skeleton" classes for a CMP entity bean (the home and remote interfaces, the primary key, and the implementation class) is vendor-neutral, the means of generating container classes and deploying into a specific application server varies widely from product to product. In this book, I focus on BEA Weblogic, the most prevalent application server in use today, as it would be impossible to cover the ever-growing number of application servers. However, it should be fairly trivial to take the instructions for the Weblogic server and relate them to your own application server.

I've moved any steps specific to Weblogic to the appendixes, leaving only vendor-neutral code in the chapters' content. This should make it easier to see what is general code, and what is platform-specific. Appendix D, then, covers installation and setup of the Weblogic application server for this book.

Adapters and Entity Beans

In preparing to code CMP entity beans, it turns out that most of the EJB callbacks that must be implemented are empty in almost all cases; the container will generate the code for these callbacks at deployment time. Instead of coding these methods into each entity bean implementation, wasting time and space in these beans and generally adding a lot of clutter, you can create an adapter class to handle this task for you. This concept, initially presented in Richard Monson-Haefel's book, is used here for the clarity it provides in later code. Example 4-1 is a slightly modified version of Richard's EntityAdapter class, which provides default, empty implementations of the required entity bean callbacks. The entity bean implementation classes in this chapter will extend this class, rather than implementing the javax.ejb.EntityBean interface directly.

Example 4-1. The EntityAdapter Helper Class

```
package com.forethought.ejb.util;

import javax.ejb.EntityBean;
import javax.ejb.EntityContext;

public class EntityAdapter implements EntityBean {

    protected EntityContext entityContext;

    public void ejbActivate() {
    }

    public void ejbPassivate() {
    }

    public void ejbLoad() {
    }
```

Example 4-1. The EntityAdapter Helper Class (continued)

```
    public void ejbStore( ) {
    }

    public void ejbRemove( ) {
    }

    public void setEntityContext(EntityContext entityContext) {
        this.entityContext = entityContext;
    }

    public void unsetEntityContext( ) {
        entityContext = null;
    }

    public EntityContext getEntityContext( ) {
        return entityContext;
    }
}
```

If you have any implementation classes that need to provide special behavior for a callback, you can override the adapter class; overriding still allows you to leave out any callbacks that are not implemented, keeping code clean. In addition, I've introduced the com.forethought.ejb package in this class. All the entity beans created for the example can be put into this base package, in a subpackage using the bean's name (for example, office or user), with the EntityAdapter class in the util subpackage of the same structure. So entity and session beans end up prefaced with com. forethought.ejb.office or com.forethought.ejb.shoppingCart. This is the same naming scheme you'll see in Sun's PetStore and most other enterprise applications.

In addition to package naming, I follow standard practices for the actual bean class names. This entails using the actual name of the data object as the name of an entity bean's remote interface. In the case of an office, the interface name simply becomes Office. The home interface has "Home" appended to it, resulting in OfficeHome, and the bean implementation itself gets the word "Bean" added to it, resulting in OfficeBean. And with this last detail covered, you're ready to move to the bean code for the office classes.

The Remote Interface

Once the naming has been determined, it is simple to code the remote interface, which is always a good starting point in EJB coding. In this case, coding the remote interface is a matter of simply providing a few accessors and mutators* for the data

---

* Throughout this book, the terms *accessor* and *mutator* are used; you may be more familiar with the terms *getter* and *setter*. However, as I'm a dog person, and my wife is a veterinary technician, we both realize that a *setter* is an animal, not a Java term. So an accessor provides access to a variable (the getXXX( ) style methods), and a mutator modifies a variable (the setXXX( ) style methods).

fields in the office structure. Additionally, you should notice that no methods are provided to modify the ID of an office. That data is intrinsic to the database and is used in indexing, but has no business meaning; as a result, it should never be modified by an application. The only time this information is ever fed to an entity bean is in the finder methods, where an office is located by its primary key (findByPrimaryKey( ) in the home interface), and in the creation of an office, where it is required for row creation (the create( ) method in the remote interface). I'll look at this in Chapter 5 and discuss how you can avoid even these situations of directly dealing with a database-specific value.

Additionally, you will notice that the ID of the office is returned as an Integer, instead of the Java primitive int type. An Integer is returned for two important reasons. First, CMP 2.0 introduces container-managed relationships (sometimes called CMR, or CMP relationships). This is a way of letting an EJB container manage relationships between entity beans (like the Office bean here, and the User bean in Appendix E). When these relationships are used, the container is responsible for generating additional classes to handle them, similar to a container generating implementation classes for your CMP beans. When these classes are generated, though, most containers make several assumptions; the first is that the primary key value on an entity bean is stored as a Java object (java.lang.Integer), and not as a primitive type (int). While this is not true in all EJB containers, it is in most. For this reason alone, it is better to use Integer instead of int when dealing with primary key types.

Using an Integer with primary keys also has a nice side effect. Because Java programmers are almost always more accustomed to working with the int data type, using Integer makes the primary key value stand out. The result is that developers think a little bit more about working with the value, resulting in primary keys being handled with care, as they should be. Therefore, you will note that the getId( ) method in the remote interface of the Office bean returns an Integer, not an int, and the create( ) method in the bean's home interface requires an Integer as well.

Something else to note is the apparent naming discrepancy between the database columns and the entity bean. You can see from Figure 4-1 that the primary key column in the database is OFFICE_ID, and the field name, as well as related methods, in the Java class is simply ID (or id as a method variable). This discrepancy may seem a little odd, but turns out to be perfectly natural. In the database layer, simply using ID as the column name can result in some very unclear SQL statements. For example, consider this SQL selecting all users and their offices:

```
SELECT FIRST_NAME, LAST_NAME, CITY, STATE
  FROM USERS u, OFFICES o
 WHERE u.OFFICE_ID = o.OFFICE_ID
```

There is no ambiguity; the join occurs between the OFFICE_ID columns of each table. However, consider the following SQL, which would produce the equivalent results when the OFFICES table's primary key column was named ID:

```
SELECT FIRST_NAME, LAST_NAME, CITY, STATE
  FROM USERS u, OFFICES o
  WHERE u.OFFICE_ID = o.ID
```

This is certainly not as clear; add to this statement joins with five, ten, or even more additional tables (something quite common even in medium-size systems), and the joins between columns in different tables can become a nightmare. In the example's naming system, columns in one table are always joined to columns in other tables with the same name; there is no room left for mistakes.

However, using this same naming in Java results in some odd code. Consider that it is common to use the lowercased name of a class as the name of an object class. For example, an instance of the class Office is often called office. If the ID method variable is named officeId, this practice can result in the rather strange code fragment shown here:

```
// Get an instance of the Office class
Integer keyValue = office.getOfficeId( );
```

It seems a bit redundant to call getOfficeID( ) on an office; while this might be a meaningful method on an instance of the User class, it doesn't make a lot of sense on the Office class. Here, this is only a minor annoyance, but it could occur hundreds of times in hundreds of classes in a complete application, becoming quite a nuisance. There are enough annoyances in programming without adding to the list, so you should stick to using database conventions in the database, and Java conventions in the application. It takes a little extra concentration during implementation, but is well worth it in the long run.

So, with no further talk, Example 4-2 is the remote interface for the Office bean.

Example 4-2. The Remote Interface for the Office Bean

```
package com.forethought.ejb.office;

import java.rmi.RemoteException;
import javax.ejb.EJBObject;

public interface Office extends EJBObject {

    public Integer getId( ) throws RemoteException;

    public String getCity( ) throws RemoteException;
    public void setCity(String city) throws RemoteException;

    public String getState( ) throws RemoteException;
    public void setState(String state) throws RemoteException;
}
```

Lest you fall into an ugly trap, be sure not to use a capital "D" in the getId( ) method (calling it getID( ) is incorrect). This rule holds true when looking at the bean implementation class, as well. While you may prefer this style (as I do), it will cause problems in your container's CMP process. The container converts the first letter of the variable (the "I" in "Id") to lowercase, takes the resultant name ("id"), and matches that to a member variable. If you use getID( ), you'll then be forced to use a member variable called "iD", which is obviously not what you want. So stick with the uppercase-lowercase convention, and save yourself some trouble.

There's also a growing trend to name remote interfaces <Bean-Name>Remote, so that the remote interface for our office entity bean would be called OfficeRemote. This convention is a response to the local interfaces introduced in EJB 2.0 (which I'll discuss in the next chapter). However, I'm not a big fan of this, for a couple of reasons. First and foremost, I like to make the most common case the simplest; since beans most commonly have a remote interface, I make the naming of the remote interface the simplest for a client to work with. Why type "OfficeRemote" when 99 out of 100 cases, you can just type "Office"? Then, if a local interface is needed, the name of that class can be OfficeLocal. The one time this name is used instead of the remote interface, the name change is a clear indication of the use of a local interface. So stick with the bean name for your remote interfaces; programmers writing bean clients will thank you for the simplicity later.

The Local Interface

At this point, you need to stop a minute and think about how your bean is going to be used. It's clear that any application clients that need to work with offices will require the remote interface you just coded. However, because offices are related to users (refer back to Figure 3-9 if you're unsure of why this is so), you will also have some entity bean–to–entity bean communication. In this case, the overhead of RMI communication becomes unnecessary, and a local interface can improve performance drastically. It's important to understand that there is nothing to prevent a bean from providing both local interfaces (for inter-bean communication) and remote interfaces (for client-to-bean communication).

It's also trivial to code the local interface of a bean once you have the remote interface. Example 4-3 shows this interface, and it's remarkably similar to the remote interface from the previous section. You'll use this local interface later, in the User bean, which will have a persistence relationship with the Office bean.

Example 4-3. The Office Bean Local Interface

```
package com.forethought.ejb.office;

import javax.ejb.EJBException;
```

Example 4-3. The Office Bean Local Interface (continued)

```
import javax.ejb.EJBLocalObject;

public interface OfficeLocal extends EJBLocalObject {

    public Integer getId( ) throws EJBException;

    public String getCity( ) throws EJBException;
    public void setCity(String city) throws EJBException;

    public String getState( ) throws EJBException;
    public void setState(String state) throws EJBException;
}
```

The Primary Key

Primary keys in beans where only one value is used are a piece of cake. In the case of the Office bean, the primary key is the OFFICE_ID column, named simply id in the Java code you've seen so far. All you need to do is identify the field used for the primary key in the *ejb-jar.xml* deployment descriptor (I'll detail this more fully in a moment). Your entry will look something like this:

```
<ejb-name>OfficeBean</ejb-name>
<home>com.forethought.ejb.office.OfficeHome</home>
<remote>com.forethought.ejb.office.Office</remote>
<local-home>com.forethought.ejb.office.OfficeLocalHome</local-home>
<local>com.forethought.ejb.office.OfficeLocal</local>
<ejb-class>com.forethought.ejb.office.OfficeBean</ejb-class>
<persistence-type>Container</persistence-type>
<prim-key-class>java.lang.Integer</prim-key-class>
<reentrant>False</reentrant>

<abstract-schema-name>OFFICES</abstract-schema-name>
<cmp-field><field-name>id</field-name></cmp-field>
<cmp-field><field-name>city</field-name></cmp-field>
<cmp-field><field-name>state</field-name></cmp-field>
<primkey-field>id</primkey-field>
```

If you do come across a case where more than one value is used for a primary key, you can code an actual Java class. However, this situation is fairly rare, so I won't cover it here. The majority of cases require you to simply add to your deployment descriptor for handling primary keys. You'll also notice (again) that the java.lang. Integer type is used; as already discussed, EJB containers generally must work in Java object types, rather than in primitives.

The Home Interface

The home interface is also simple to code. For now, the ID of the office to create is passed directly to the create( ) method. Later, you'll remove that dependency, and the ID will be determined independently of the application client. You also can add the basic finder, findByPrimaryKey( ), which takes in the Integer primary key type. Example 4-4 shows this code listing.

Example 4-4. The Home Interface for the Office Bean

```
package com.forethought.ejb.office;

import java.rmi.RemoteException;
import javax.ejb.CreateException;
import javax.ejb.EJBHome;
import javax.ejb.FinderException;

public interface OfficeHome extends EJBHome {

    public Office create(Integer id, String city, String state)
        throws CreateException, RemoteException;

    public Office findByPrimaryKey(Integer officeID)
        throws FinderException, RemoteException;
}
```

Like the remote interface, many folks have taken to calling the remote home interface <Bean-Name>HomeRemote (in this case OfficeHomeRemote), again in deference to local interfaces. And in the same vein, I recommend against it for the same reasons as the remote interface. It's best to leave the remote home interface as-is, and use OfficeLocalHome as needed.

The Local Home Interface

Just as you coded up a local interface for persistence relationships and bean-to-bean communication, you should create a corresponding local home interface. This is extremely similar to the remote home interface, and bears little discussion. Example 4-5 is the Office bean's local home interface.

Example 4-5. The Local Home Interface for the Office Bean

```
package com.forethought.ejb.office;

import javax.ejb.CreateException;
import javax.ejb.EJBException;
import javax.ejb.EJBLocalHome;
import javax.ejb.FinderException;

public interface OfficeLocalHome extends EJBLocalHome {

    public OfficeLocal create(Integer id, String city, String state)
        throws CreateException, EJBException;

    public OfficeLocal findByPrimaryKey(Integer officeID)
        throws FinderException, EJBException;
}
```

The Bean Implementation

Last, but not least, Example 4-6 is the bean implementation class. Notice that it extends the `EntityAdapter` class instead of directly implementing `EntityBean`, like other examples you may find. Because the bean's persistence is container-managed, the accessor and mutator methods are declared abstract. The container will handle the method implementations that make these updates affect the underlying data store.

Example 4-6. The Implementation for the Office Bean

```
package com.forethought.ejb.office;

// EJB imports
import javax.ejb.CreateException;

import com.forethought.ejb.util.EntityAdapter;

public abstract class OfficeBean extends EntityAdapter {

    public Integer ejbCreate(Integer id, String city, String state)
        throws CreateException {

        setId(id);
        setCity(city);
        setState(state);

        return null;
    }

    public void ejbPostCreate(int id, String city, String state)
        throws CreateException {

        // Empty implementation
    }

    public abstract Integer getId( );
    public abstract void setId(Integer id);

    public abstract String getCity( );
    public abstract void setCity(String city);

    public abstract String getState( );
    public abstract void setState(String state);
}
```

Take special note of the `throws CreateException` clause on the `ejbCreate( )` and `ejbPostCreate( )` methods. I have several books on EJB 2.0 on my desk right now that omit this clause; however, leaving it out causes several application servers, including the J2EE reference implementation, to fail on deployment. Therefore, be sure to have your bean creation methods throw this exception. It also makes sense in that the subclasses of the Office class that the container creates need to be able to report errors during bean creation, and a CreateException gives them that ability. Since a subclass can't add new exceptions to the method declaration, the throws clause must exist in your bean class.

Also, be sure that your creation methods use the other methods in the class for assignment. A common mistake is to code the ejbCreate( ) method like this:

```
public Integer ejbCreate(Integer id, String city, String state)
    throws CreateException {

    this.id = id;
    this.city = city;
    this.state = state;

    return null;
}
```

This was common in EJB 1.1, but doesn't work so well in EJB 2.0. You want to be sure that you invoke the container-generated methods, which will handle database access. Invoking the container-generated methods also means you don't have to explicitly define member variables for the class, so that's one less detail to worry about. Also note that the creation method invokes setId( ), which I earlier said wouldn't be made available to clients. That remains true, because even though it's in the bean's implementation class, the remote interface does not expose the method, keeping it hidden from the client.

One final note before moving on: you should notice in this book's source code (downloadable from *http://www.newInstance.com*) that the methods in the bean implementation are not commented, as they are in the remote interface. This is a fairly standard practice; methods are commented (and therefore available in Javadoc) in interfaces, but these comments are not duplicated in the implementation, which generally makes implementation classes simpler to move through. If there are details specific to the implementation that need to be documented, they are suitable for commenting; however, such comments usually are made in the code and are preceded with the double-slash (//), rather than being Javadoc-style comments. Such practices are followed in all the EJBs in this chapter and the rest of the book.

Deploying the Bean

At this point, you've completed the code for your entity bean, and now you need to deploy the bean. This involves creating a deployment descriptor for the bean and then wrapping the entire bean into a deployable unit. I'll cover each of these steps in the following sections.

Deployment Descriptors

To wrap all these classes into a coherent unit, you must create an XML deployment descriptor. These descriptors replace the horrible serialized deployment descriptors from EJB 1.0. XML deployment descriptors eliminate one vendor-dependent detail: the descriptor is standardized across all application servers. Notice that the document type definition (DTD) referred to in the DOCTYPE declaration refers to a Sun file, ensuring that no vendors add their own tags or extensions to the descriptor. If your server requires you to use a different DTD, you may have a serious problem on your hands; you may want to consider switching to a standards-based application server immediately. And if DTDs, elements, tags, and these other XML terms are Greek to you, pick up *Java and XML* (O'Reilly), by yours truly, to get answers to your XML-related questions.

Example 4-7, the deployment descriptor for the office entity bean, contains entries only for that bean, detailing its home, remote, implementation, and primary key classes. These are all required elements for an entity bean, as is specifying that the bean is not reentrant and specifying the persistence type, which in our case is container-managed. Later on, we'll add entries for numerous other entity beans that we will code and add to the application. Because we are deploying a CMP bean, the fields that must be handled by the container are listed; in this case, these are all the fields in the OfficeBean class. We also give the bean a name to be used, OfficeBean.

If you are familiar with EJB deployment descriptors, you might notice that I have left out the assembly-descriptor element and related subelements that allow permission specification for beans and their methods. That's so you can focus on the bean right now, and deal with security later. Don't worry, though; I'll get to all of this before we're done with our application. Leaving it out for now will allow the container to generate default permissions.

Example 4-7. The Office Entity Bean Deployment Descriptor

```
<?xml version="1.0"?>

<!DOCTYPE ejb-jar
    PUBLIC "-//Sun Microsystems, Inc.//DTD Enterprise JavaBeans 2.0//EN"
    "http://java.sun.com/dtd/ejb-jar_2_0.dtd">

<ejb-jar>
  <enterprise-beans>
    <entity>
      <description>
        This Office bean represents a Forethought office,
          including its location.
      </description>
      <display-name>OfficeBean</display-name>
      <ejb-name>OfficeBean</ejb-name>
```

Example 4-7. The Office Entity Bean Deployment Descriptor (continued)

```
      <home>com.forethought.ejb.office.OfficeHome</home>
      <remote>com.forethought.ejb.office.Office</remote>
      <local-home>com.forethought.ejb.office.OfficeLocalHome</local-home>
      <local>com.forethought.ejb.office.OfficeLocal</local>
      <ejb-class>com.forethought.ejb.office.OfficeBean</ejb-class>
      <persistence-type>Container</persistence-type>
      <prim-key-class>java.lang.Integer</prim-key-class>
      <reentrant>False</reentrant>

      <abstract-schema-name>OFFICES</abstract-schema-name>
      <cmp-field><field-name>id</field-name></cmp-field>
      <cmp-field><field-name>city</field-name></cmp-field>
      <cmp-field><field-name>state</field-name></cmp-field>
      <primkey-field>id</primkey-field>
    </entity>
  </enterprise-beans>
</ejb-jar>
```

 A word to the wise here: it might seem that the XML would be clearer with some reorganization. For example, the prim-key-class element might be easier to find if it were right below the other class entries (home, remote, and ejb-class). However, moving it will cause an error in deployment! The *ejb-jar_2_0.dtd* file specifies the order of elements, and is completely inflexible in this respect. This is a typical limitation of DTDs, as opposed to other constraint representations in XML such as XML Schemas. If these elements not in the correct order shown in the example, you will encounter errors in deployment.

Wrapping It Up

The process of creating the Office entity bean is finally complete (at least in its current form). You now need to create a deployable JAR file, and then create the container classes to add implementation details to your bean, such as SQL and JDBC code. First, ensure that your directory structure is set up correctly. The Java source files can all be in a top-level directory. You should then create a directory called *META-INF/*, and place the *ejb-jar.xml* deployment descriptor inside it. Next, compile your source files:

```
galadriel:/dev/javaentI $ javac -d build \
                  ch04/src/java/com/forethought/ejb/util/*.java \
                  ch04/src/java/com/forethought/ejb/office/*.java
```

Setting up your classpath for these compilations can be either really simple or really difficult. Many application servers provide a script that can be run to set up all the environment variables. Running this script takes care of all the classpath issues for you, and your compilations will be a piece of cake (refer to Appendixes D and E for these details for the Sun J2EE reference implementation). Or, you may have to manually add the entries needed to your classpath. You should consider creating your own script in these cases, and then bothering your server vendor until they provide you with a prebuilt script. Unfortunately, the libraries are packaged differently with every server (for example, in Weblogic there is one giant JAR, and in jBoss there are individual JARs for each API), so I can't tell you exactly what to type. Just look for a script; it's almost always there.

Correct any errors you receive by referring to the text. Once you've compiled the source, you should have the directory structure shown in Figure 4-2. Notice that I have *build/* and *deploy/* directories in place before compilation and deployment to segregate my files. You should create these as well (or use your own structure, of course).

Next, you need to create a JAR file of these classes and the deployment descriptor. Create it with the name *forethoughtEntities.jar*, as shown:

```
galadriel:/dev/javaentI $ cd build

galadriel:/dev/javaentI/build $ jar cvf ../deploy/forethoughtEntities.jar com \
                           META-INF/ejb-jar.xml
added manifest
adding: com/(in = 0) (out= 0)(stored 0%)
adding: com/forethought/(in = 0) (out= 0)(stored 0%)
adding: com/forethought/ejb/(in = 0) (out= 0)(stored 0%)
adding: com/forethought/ejb/office/(in = 0) (out= 0)(stored 0%)
adding: com/forethought/ejb/office/Office.class(in = 439) (out= 280)(deflated
36%)
adding: com/forethought/ejb/office/OfficeBean.class(in = 805) (out= 445)
(deflated 44%)
adding: com/forethought/ejb/office/OfficeHome.class(in = 480) (out= 260)
(deflated 45%)
adding: com/forethought/ejb/util/(in = 0) (out= 0)(stored 0%)
adding: com/forethought/ejb/util/EntityAdapter.class(in = 831) (out= 388)
(deflated 53%)
adding: META-INF/ejb-jar.xml(in = 1038) (out= 430)(deflated 58%)
```

With this archive ready for use, you can refer to Appendix D for instructions on taking the JAR from its current state to a deployable, CMP entity bean and descriptor.

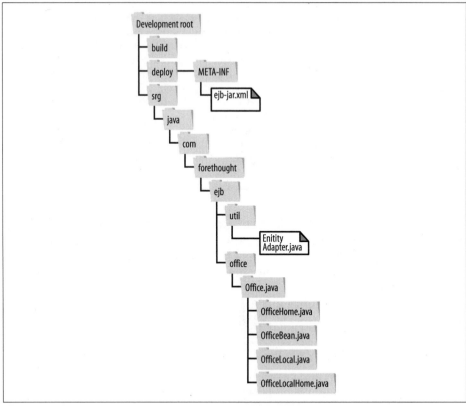

Figure 4-2. Directory structure for office entity bean

What's Next?

You should now have a good idea of common architectural problems related to basic entity beans. Primary keys, package naming, deployment descriptors, and more should all be at your fingertips. Once you've mastered these concepts, you're ready to look at some more interesting subjects. In the next chapter, I'll cover handling primary key values, detail objects, and more. So make sure that you understand the basics in this chapter, and keep reading.

## CHAPTER 5

Advanced Entities

In this chapter, we'll dig into some more interesting entity bean topics. I'll start by looking at how entity beans can and should abstract database IDs and sequences from business-oriented clients. You'll see how session beans can be used for these sorts of tasks, learn about database access through JDBC in beans, and put all these pieces into a coherent whole. From there I'll move on to discussing entity bean value objects, serialization of these objects, and decreasing RMI traffic.

I'll also discuss when to use container-managed persistence (CMP) and when to use bean-managed persistence (BMP). This leads you from accessing the database to accessing the directory server set up for usernames and authentication data. I'll also cover the variety of ways you can access a directory server. At this point, the Java Naming and Directory Interface (JNDI) will enter the picture, too. By the end of this chapter, you'll have several new entity beans, a session bean, a more advanced Office bean, and a thorough understanding of entity bean architecture.

IDs, Sequences, and CMP

The most common problem in working with entity beans is dealing with primary keys. The underlying principle is that EJB components should represent business objects and business entities. In other words, if something isn't used in the business of an application, it shouldn't be visible to the bean developer. What that means in terms of the entity beans so far is that you need to hide the details of offices' ID fields: they have no business meaning, and are useful only at the database level. Therefore, you don't want a user to pass in a value when creating a new office. Instead, the bean implementation (hidden to the bean client) should assign a viable ID at office creation. Straying from this principle will result in session beans and servlets having to deal with IDs that have no meaning outside of the database layer. The only use for an office's ID is in locating the office or in tying in the office to a related structure, like a user. For this reason, it is OK to allow a bean client to find out an office's ID, but it's not OK for that client to create the office by specifying an

ID. This is in contrast to the current OfficeHome interface, which has a create( ) method that looks like this:

```
public Office create(Integer id, String city, String state)
    throws CreateException, RemoteException;
```

The most common (and unfortunately, the worst) way to create an ID has been for developers to code logic into their entity bean's ejbCreate( ) method that directly interfaces with the database. This logic varies from selecting a random number to obtaining the next number from a database sequence (particularly common in Oracle databases) or retrieving the highest value in use and adding 1. There are so many different problems with this approach, though, that it should immediately be thrown out as an option in your bean programming. The first and most important problem is that this method is not vendor-neutral or database-neutral, and leaves your code working only on the specific setup you are using. Additionally, going to the database for a sequence value or the highest existing value results in additional JDBC calls, slowing the entire application. And the logic of picking a random or semi-random number is unreliable, at best.

Another solution is based on a popular white paper on persistence by Scott Ambler, available at *http://www.sdmagazine.com/documents/s=751/sdm9912p/9912p.htm*. In this excellent paper, Ambler details a solution using a HIGH and LOW pair of variables and creating a surrogate key. Basically, this uses a guaranteed approach: instead of getting the next available value for a key, it gets a variable that is guaranteed to be safe for the key value. This can result in lots of gaps in primary key values, which in extremely large databases may cause problems by running out of usable keys in the data type's range (but only in *very* large databases!). The biggest problem with this approach is not in implementation of the pattern, but in converting it into a bean. Should it be an entity bean? A stateless session bean? A simple Java class? It becomes tricky. In any case, this solution, where the HIGH and LOW values are stored in the database, does provide a vendor-neutral means of handling the ID problem. Connections to the database are obtained through the container instead of in a database-specific way. I won't use this complex solution here; check out Ambler's white paper if you are interested in his approach. Instead, we will look at some simpler ways to solve the problem in an EJB-based application

A slightly more popular approach is to take the same concept of storing allowed key values in a database, but using exact values instead of guaranteed values. That is, instead of storing a safe value, a single table (I'll call it PRIMARY_KEYS) stores the next available value for the primary key of each table. Getting a key value, then, simply involves requesting the value for a specific table name. For example, sequence. getNextValue("OFFICES") would return the next viable primary key value for the OFFICES table. Like Ambler's solution, the concept is not overly difficult to grasp, but the details surrounding an implementation are. The biggest issue is ensuring that stale data is never returned; two JDBC calls requesting a new key value for the same table must *never* overlap and return identical values. For this reason, using a bean makes a lot of sense; EJB transaction isolations can protect you from this unwanted situation by locking the database at each request. This ensures that each request is serviced one at a time. The bean would then obtain a value and immediately update the database by incrementing the available value; only then could other requests be serviced.

The last question is whether to use an entity or session bean. As you've been working with entity beans to this point, it might seem natural to use one; you would make it a bean-managed persistence entity bean, as each method call should trigger an update, something that normally happens only on an EJB's ejbLoad( ) call. Most containers hold onto entity beans, so this call usually does not occur on every method invocation. However, there is no real advantage in using an entity bean, as the callbacks it receives become meaningless in this context. Additionally, problems can occur when the same entity bean is loaded into two containers (common in a load-balanced situation); since the normal EJB callbacks aren't used, you can end up playing with fire when trying to manage instances in the bean pool, in passivation, or waiting to be created. All this leads to a good case for using a session bean, and a stateless one, at that. Most memory-efficient, stateless session beans can be brought into and out of existence quickly, and caching issues become irrelevant. Each call to a stateless session bean's method results in an instance being created and then thrown away;* no conflicts should arise, even across servers in a clustered environment. It's also possible to use transaction levels to make sure that the database is effectively locked, ensuring that no two requests get the same primary key value.

In addition to offering complete vendor-independence, this solution won't cause your database to have the gaps that the high/low approach results in. And by using session beans and isolation levels, you avoid concurrency issues, which solves the problem of hiding IDs from clients. It's now time to implement the idea. We first need to create a new table, and allow storage of a table name or key name, and the next available primary key value. We need to create a session bean that provides a method to get a valid ID given a key name, and then implement the bean in a way that uses JDBC to connect to the table, get the next value, and update the table. Add this bean to our deployment descriptor, modify our entity bean code to use it, and we're in business. So let's put some code to our talk.

Making It Work

The starting point to this solution is a new table in the database. This table is probably the simplest yet: it has only two columns, no ID, and does not need to reference any other tables. Example 5-1 shows the SQL used to create this table. All the PRIMARY_KEYS table needs is a KEY_NAME column to hold the table name that the key is

---

* This is a bit of an oversimplification. In actuality, the container often keeps pools of stateless beans around to service requests, and rarely throws them away.

for, and a NEXT_VALUE column to hold the next valid primary key for that table. Finally, there is some Forethought-specific work to do by adding entries for all the tables in the application, starting each value off at 1. Create this table in your database, using the SQL in Example 5-1.

The script in Example 5-1 assumes that you have no existing data; therefore the counters for all tables start at 1. If you need to use this structure for an application with existing data, you will need to make some small modifications. For each table, find the highest existing value in use, and start with a number at least 1 greater than that value. So if your table has primary keys ranging as high as 2012, you want to start that table's primary key value at 2013.

Additionally, this script drops any existing PRIMARY_KEYS table. If you already use this structure, and then run this script, you run the risk of duplicating primary key values. Be careful!

Example 5-1. SQL Script for Primary Keys Storage

```sql
-- Drop any existing PRIMARY_KEYS table
DROP TABLE PRIMARY_KEYS;

-- PRIMARY_KEYS table
CREATE TABLE PRIMARY_KEYS (
      KEY_NAME        VARCHAR(20) PRIMARY KEY NOT NULL,
      NEXT_VALUE      INT NOT NULL
);

-- Add initial values for each table
INSERT INTO PRIMARY_KEYS VALUES ('USER_TYPES', 1);
INSERT INTO PRIMARY_KEYS VALUES ('OFFICES', 1);
INSERT INTO PRIMARY_KEYS VALUES ('USERS', 1);
INSERT INTO PRIMARY_KEYS VALUES ('ACCOUNT_TYPES', 1);
INSERT INTO PRIMARY_KEYS VALUES ('ACCOUNTS', 1);
INSERT INTO PRIMARY_KEYS VALUES ('TRANSACTIONS', 1);
INSERT INTO PRIMARY_KEYS VALUES ('FUNDS', 1);
INSERT INTO PRIMARY_KEYS VALUES ('INVESTMENTS', 1);
```

With this table created, we can start writing the session bean to access the data in the table, ensuring that it is usable by the various entity beans in the application.

Before getting too carried away, realize that this scenario assumes that all the applications accessing your database will use this sequencing facility. If you are going to have concurrent access from other Java (or non-Java) components, the IDs in the PRIMARY_KEYS table can become stale. In this case, you will need to take a different approach.

Adapters and session beans

First, it's time to save some time and effort by writing another utility class. Like entity beans, session beans have several callback methods that often are never coded in standard beans. Although there aren't as many methods for session beans, it is still a pain to write empty method implementations for tens or even hundreds of session beans in an application. Writing a SessionAdapter class, similar to the EntityAdapter class, allows us to avoid this hassle and keep session bean code clean and concise. Example 5-2 shows this class; there is nothing new here, just a session bean version of Example 4-1.

Example 5-2. The SessionAdapter Utility Class

```
package com.forethought.ejb.util;

import javax.ejb.SessionBean;
import javax.ejb.SessionContext;

public class SessionAdapter implements SessionBean {

    protected SessionContext sessionContext;

    public void ejbActivate( ) {
    }

    public void ejbPassivate( ) {
    }

    public void ejbRemove( ) {
    }

    public void setSessionContext(SessionContext sessionContext) {
        this.sessionContext = sessionContext;
    }

    public void unsetSessionContext( ) {
        sessionContext = null;
    }

    public SessionContext getSessionContext( ) {
        return sessionContext;
    }
}
```

All of your session bean implementations can then extend the SessionAdapter utility class, allowing them to ignore any callbacks that are not explicitly used in the implementation. This paves the way for building the actual bean used in sequence retrieval.

The application exception

Before writing the session bean itself, you should take a moment to define a new application exception. In EJB-land, application exceptions are used to report problems that are not directly caused by RMI, network communication, and container-related issues. Since the sequence bean will need to perform SQL calls, JNDI lookups, and other subsystem work, it should be able to report problems with these operations in a way that distinguishes them from more generic errors. Example 5-3 is a very simple example of an appropriate application exception.

Example 5-3. The Sequence Application Exception

```
package com.forethought.ejb.sequence;

public class SequenceException extends Exception {

    public SequenceException(String message) {
        super("Sequence Bean Exception: " + message);
    }
}
```

This is about as simple an application exception as you will find; however, it does serve to distinguish exceptions related to the sequence bean's actions from network and EJB problems. This results in better error handling for clients (i.e., other entity beans) of this bean.

Still, this application is pretty simplistic, and doesn't offer much in the way of error reporting. Although you don't want to have to write sophisticated exception code for every application exception you need to write, you should sense a base exception class on the horizon. Example 5-4 is just that, and will be used as the superclass of all the Forethought application exceptions.

Example 5-4. The ForethoughtException Class

```
package com.forethought;

import java.io.PrintStream;
import java.io.PrintWriter;

public class ForethoughtException extends Exception {

    /** The root cause generating this exception */
    private Throwable cause;

    public ForethoughtException(String msg) {
        super(msg);
    }

    public ForethoughtException(String msg, Throwable cause) {
        super(msg);
        this.cause = cause;
```

Example 5-4. The ForethoughtException Class (continued)

```
    }

    public String getMessage( ) {
        if (cause != null) {
            return super.getMessage( ) + ": " + cause.getMessage( );
        } else {
            return super.getMessage( );
        }
    }

    public void printStackTrace( ) {
        super.printStackTrace( );
        if (cause != null) {
            System.err.print("Root cause: ");
            cause.printStackTrace( );
        }
    }

    public void printStackTrace(PrintStream s) {
        super.printStackTrace(s);
        if (cause != null) {
            s.print("Root cause: ");
            cause.printStackTrace(s);
        }
    }

    public void printStackTrace(PrintWriter w) {
        super.printStackTrace(w);
        if (cause != null) {
            w.print("Root cause: ");
            cause.printStackTrace(w);
        }
    }

    public Throwable getCause( )  {
        return cause;
    }
}
```

You can now make a few slight modifications to the SequenceException to take advantage of these new facilities:

```
package com.forethought.ejb.sequence;

import com.forethought.ForethoughtException;

public class SequenceException extends ForethoughtException {

    public SequenceException(String message) {
        super("Sequence Bean Exception: " + message);
    }
```

```
    public SequenceException(String message, Throwable cause) {
        super("Sequence Bean Exception: " + message, cause);
    }
}
```

By extending this base exception, it is possible to take in a root cause exception, as the ForethoughtException handles printing out the stack trace and message of the root cause exception. You now have a good facility in place for reporting errors.

The local interface

Next, code the local interface. Notice that I said *local* interface, not *remote* interface. By now you should realize that the Sequence bean being developed here is of use only to entity beans; it has no business meaning. Because of that, it needs to be accessible only to entity beans. Furthermore, because entity beans are already process-intensive, you should look to cut down on processing whenever possible. It therefore makes sense to locate the Sequence bean within the same container as your entity beans. Session beans may be put into other containers, and servlets and JSP beans may be spread out over multiple machines, but your entity beans should all have local (and therefore the fastest) access to the Sequence bean. To accommodate this, you should use local interfaces for the bean, as detailed in this section.

In this particular session bean, coding the actual local interface is a trivial task. You need only one method, which takes in a key name (generally a table name) and returns the next primary key value for that key. You can call this method getNextValue( ), and the bean itself Sequence, as it provides sequence values for entity beans. Example 5-5 shows the local interface for the Sequence session bean. Notice that it throws the new SequenceException when things related to the sequencing logic go wrong.

Example 5-5. The Sequence Local Interface

```
package com.forethought.ejb.sequence;

import javax.ejb.EJBException;
import javax.ejb.EJBLocalObject;

public interface SequenceLocal extends EJBLocalObject {

    public Integer getNextValue(String keyName)
        throws EJBException, SequenceException;

}
```

As you would expect, this method returns an Integer (not an int), which is the correct type for the primary key values used in the Forethought bean classes. This avoids constantly having to convert from ints to Integers and back.

The home interface

The local home interface for the Sequence bean is equally simple; remember that session beans do not have finder methods (findByXXX( ) methods), and that stateless session beans must have a create( ) method that takes no parameters. This single create( ) method is the only one needed by the bean. As in the previous section, this will be a local interface, albeit a home one, which allows the bean to be located in the same container as the entity beans in the application. Example 5-6 is this local home interface for the Sequence bean.

Example 5-6. The Sequence Local Home Interface

```
package com.forethought.ejb.sequence;

import javax.ejb.CreateException;
import javax.ejb.EJBLocalHome;

public interface SequenceLocalHome extends EJBLocalHome {

    public SequenceLocal create( ) throws CreateException;
}
```

With both local interfaces for the bean complete, you can move on to the implementation. Remember that session beans do not have primary key classes or fields, so you don't need to worry about those things for the Sequence session bean.

The bean

The real work is done in the implementation of the bean class, which is shown in Example 5-7. The ejbCreate( ) method stays empty, and doesn't perform any specific action. The getNextValue( ) method, though, has quite a bit of database interaction and logic within it.

First, the method declares an int, called returnValue, that will store the key value to return to the calling program. Then it constructs the two queries, to be used as prepared statements, for getting the current value and then updating it. Then the work begins. First, an InitialContext is obtained from the container.

 The example code in this and other chapters obtains the InitialContext by directly instantiating the object. This assumes that you are using an application server that supports this facility, which involves a *jndi.properties* file being in the application server classpath and generally requires Java 2. Most recent releases from vendors provide this functionality. However, if you have problems with this or your server does not support obtaining an InitialContext in this way, consult your vendor documentation for another means of obtaining the object in your application server.

The JNDI context is used to look up a JDBC `javax.sql.DataSource`.* I'll discuss binding the `DataSource` into JNDI in a minute; for now, assume that it's there and bound to the name *jdbc/forethoughtDB*. You should use the ENC context to obtain the JDNI context, a feature introduced in EJB 1.1. Adding to the power of JNDI, the *comp/env* name and all names bound below it (like *comp/env/jdbc/forethoughtDB*) are intended for application use, as we are doing here. Once we have the `DataSource`, it is trivial to obtain a JDBC `Connection` object. The ease of getting a connection this way, as opposed to using the JDBC `DriverManager` facility, is evident in the code sample; therefore, binding resources to JNDI in this manner is highly recommended.

The ENC What?

The ENC context, or environment context, is a utility introduced in EJB 1.1 and available in all EJB 2.0 implementations. It defines a common means for objects to be bound into the JNDI registry, specifically for use by Enterprise JavaBeans. The ENC context reserves the JNDI name *java:comp/env* for use by beans, and allows objects to be bound in that context or subcontexts. For example, by binding an object to the name *myObject* through the EJB deployment descriptor, the object is made available (by the application server) as *java:comp/env/myObject*. Any object that can be bound into JNDI can be bound into this context; it is simply a specific application of JNDI.

While constants can be wired into JNDI this way, it is most common to bind references to other beans or database connections and resources to the ENC context. Application servers generally provide tools for binding these special objects into JNDI. Most common are URLs (`java.net.URL`), JDBC database sources (`javax.sql.DataSource`), Java-Mail connections (`javax.mail.Session`), and JMS connections (`javax.jms.QueueConnectionFactory` and `javax.jms.TopicConnectionFactory`). These bindings allow the server or container to use factories to generate these objects and tie them in with other server resources more efficiently than developers can code them themselves. Using the ENC context to obtain resources is always preferable to manually obtaining handles to these resources.

With a database connection available, it's simple to turn these query strings into JDBC `PreparedStatement` objects. The first is executed, and the value saved for returning to the caller program. The second is then executed to update the database with the next available primary key value. At this point, it's important to note why the key value isn't returned directly, and is instead assigned to the `returnValue` variable created earlier. Returning immediately would leave both the `PreparedStatement`

---

* As you can see by the `javax.sql` instead of the `java.sql` package prefix, this is part of the JDBC standard extension. All J2EE-compliant application servers should support this, and make it available to your applications.

and Connection objects open. While some containers and databases happily take care of closing these objects, many do not, and the result is that after five or ten invocations, all the available connections to a database are used up and errors start occurring. Always be sure to close any open database connection objects.

Example 5-7. The Sequence Implementation

```
package com.forethought.ejb.sequence;

import java.sql.Connection;
import java.sql.DriverManager;
import java.sql.ResultSet;
import java.sql.SQLException;
import java.sql.PreparedStatement;
import javax.ejb.CreateException;
import javax.ejb.EJBException;
import javax.ejb.SessionBean;
import javax.naming.Context;
import javax.naming.InitialContext;
import javax.naming.NamingException;
import javax.sql.DataSource;

import com.forethought.ejb.util.SessionAdapter;

public class SequenceBean extends SessionAdapter {

    /** The query to get the next value from the keys table */
    private static final String selectQuery =
            new StringBuffer("SELECT NEXT_VALUE ")
                    .append("  FROM PRIMARY_KEYS ")
                    .append(" WHERE KEY_NAME = ?")
                    .toString();

    /** The query to update the next value in the keys table */
    private static final String updateQuery =
            new StringBuffer("UPDATE PRIMARY_KEYS ")
                    .append("   SET NEXT_VALUE = ? ")
                    .append(" WHERE KEY_NAME = ?")
                    .toString();

    public void ejbCreate() throws CreateException {
        // No action required for stateless session beans
    }

    public int getNextValue(String keyName) throws SequenceException {
        int returnValue;

        Connection con = null;
        PreparedStatement pstmt = null;
        ResultSet rs = null;
        try {
            Context context = new InitialContext();
            DataSource ds =
```

Example 5-7. The Sequence Implementation (continued)

```
                    (DataSource)
                        context.lookup("java:comp/env/jdbc/forethoughtDB");
            con = ds.getConnection( );

            pstmt = con.prepareStatement(selectQuery);
            pstmt.setString(1, keyName);
            rs = pstmt.executeQuery( );

            if (rs.next( )) {
                returnValue = rs.getInt("NEXT_VALUE");

                pstmt = con.prepareStatement(updateQuery);
                pstmt.setInt(1, returnValue + 1);
                pstmt.setString(2, keyName);
                pstmt.executeUpdate( );
            } else {
                // Close connections before throwing the exception
                try {
                    rs.close( );
                } catch (Exception ignored) { }
                try {
                    pstmt.close( );
                } catch (Exception ignored) { }
                try {
                    con.close( );
                } catch (Exception ignored) { }

                throw new SequenceException("Could not obtain a key " +
                    "value for the key name " + keyName);
            }
        } catch (NamingException e) {
            throw new SequenceException("Error getting JNDI " +
                "resources: " + e.getMessage( ), e);
        } catch (SQLException e) {
            throw new SequenceException("Error in SQL: " +
                e.getMessage( ), e);
        } finally {
            try {
                rs.close( );
            } catch (Exception ignored) { }
            try {
                pstmt.close( );
            } catch (Exception ignored) { }
            try {
                con.close( );
            } catch (Exception ignored) { }
        }

        return new Integer(returnValue);
    }
}
```

Any problems that occur are handled by the SequenceException. In this simple case, a message indicates what happened. However, you could easily add the ability to nest exceptions (and pass the originating exception into the SequenceException constructor), type-specific error messages, and any other information you wanted to make available for clients.

 I earlier mentioned that the approach described here works only if you have all access for primary keys moving through the Sequence bean. If you do not, there are still some simple (albeit less efficient) approaches to solving the problem of primary keys. The simplest is to change the getNextValue( ) method to take in a database table name, rather than a key:

```
public Integer getNextValue(String tableName);
```

Then, instead of using the PRIMARY_KEYS table, you could simply get the highest ID value in the supplied table. The following SQL statement takes care of this:

```
SELECT MAX(ID) FROM [tableName];
```

Returning this value with 1 added would retrieve a viable primary key. However, this approach requires entity bean knowledge of database table names (which is not great design), and also requires the MAX function for each getNextValue( ) method invocation, which is expensive. However, it is still preferable to a vendor-specific solution that is not portable across databases.

At this point, don't feel bad if you need to take a deep breath. I've flown through more EJB, JNDI, and JDBC in the last code listing than in the first few chapters combined. If you were hazy on any of the concepts, it would be a good idea to refresh your EJB skills with the aforementioned *Enterprise JavaBeans* or *Java Enterprise in a Nutshell*. It only gets thicker from here, as we dive further into EJB and deployment, RMI, and JNDI.

Deploying the Sequence Bean

If you're ready to move on, take a look at modifying your deployment descriptor to include an entry for the new session bean. Example 5-8 shows the modified descriptor. You should declare the bean as stateless, and of course enclose it within the session element to indicate the type of bean. Also be sure to use the localized versions of the home and remote tags.

Example 5-8. Updating the Deployment Descriptor

```
<?xml version="1.0"?>

<!DOCTYPE ejb-jar
    PUBLIC "-//Sun Microsystems, Inc.//DTD Enterprise JavaBeans 2.0//EN"
```

Example 5-8. Updating the Deployment Descriptor (continued)

```
    "http://java.sun.com/dtd/ejb-jar_2_0.dtd">

<ejb-jar>
  <enterprise-beans>
    <!-- Office bean definition -->

    <session>
      <description>
        This Sequence bean allows entity beans to obtain primary key
          values as if from a sequence.
      </description>
      <ejb-name>SequenceBean</ejb-name>
      <local-home>com.forethought.ejb.sequence.SequenceLocalHome</local-home>
      <local>com.forethought.ejb.sequence.SequenceLocal</local>
      <ejb-class>com.forethought.ejb.sequence.SequenceBean</ejb-class>
      <session-type>Stateless</session-type>
      <transaction-type>Container</transaction-type>
      <resource-ref>
        <description>Connection to the Forethought database.</description>
        <res-ref-name>jdbc/forethoughtDB</res-ref-name>
        <res-type>javax.sql.DataSource</res-type>
        <res-auth>Container</res-auth>
      </resource-ref>
    </session>
  </enterprise-beans>
</ejb-jar>
```

Perhaps the most important portion of the Sequence bean addition is the resource-ref entry. This allows resources, like the JDBC `DataSource` used in the implementation, to be bound into the JNDI ENC context. The object is bound to the JNDI name *jdbc/forethoughtDB*, which in turn is made available through the JNDI context *java: comp/env/jdbc/forethoughtDB*. Finally, the descriptor indicates that the container should handle authentication, allowing security principals to be used normally (something I'll get to later). At this point, the bean is ready to deploy, although the entity bean doesn't take advantage of it yet.

It is a good idea at this point to actually deploy the Sequence session bean, along with the Office entity bean. You can compile these classes, wrap them up in the JAR archive (as I talked about in the previous chapter), and deploy the JAR into your container (as described in Appendix D). Although you haven't added any functionality to your entity bean or taken advantage of the new session bean, you can head off any errors here. Choosing not to do this widens the window of errors that may occur. It's better to catch small mistakes and typos in your code or descriptor now, by deploying the beans before continuing.

Integrating the Changes

Now that the sequencing functionality is available to the application, you just need to take advantage of it. With the need for an ID eliminated from entity beans' clients, you first need to change the home interface's create( ) method, as I talked about earlier. This simply involves removing the id variable from the method signature. That change results in the following create( ) signature in the OfficeHome class:

```
public Office create(String city, String state)
    throws CreateException, RemoteException;
```

You should make the same change to the OfficeLocalHome interface:

```
public OfficeLocal create(String city, String state)
    throws CreateException, EJBException;
```

The next change in the code is the bean implementation itself. The ejbCreate( ) and ejbPostCreate( ) methods both should have the id variable removed from their method signatures. Be sure you change both of these, as it's easy to forget the ejbPostCreate( ) method. Finally, this bean needs to access the new Sequence bean and use it to obtain an ID value for a new office. This is a replacement for accepting the value from a bean client. Modify your bean's ejbCreate( ) method as shown in Example 5-9. Once you've added the necessary import statements to deal with JNDI, RMI, and the Sequence bean, you are ready to access the next primary key value through the functionality just provided.

Example 5-9. The OfficeBean Using the Sequence Bean for ID Values

```
package com.forethought.ejb.office;

import javax.ejb.CreateException;
import javax.naming.Context;
import javax.naming.InitialContext;
import javax.naming.NamingException;

import com.forethought.ejb.sequence.SequenceException;
import com.forethought.ejb.sequence.SequenceLocal;
import com.forethought.ejb.sequence.SequenceLocalHome;
import com.forethought.ejb.util.EntityAdapter;

public class OfficeBean extends EntityAdapter {

    public Integer ejbCreate(String city, String state)
        throws CreateException {

        // Get the next primary key value
        try {
            Context context = new InitialContext( );

            // Note that RMI-IIOP narrowing is not required
            SequenceLocalHome home = (SequenceLocalHome)
                context.lookup("java:comp/env/ejb/SequenceLocalHome");
```

```
        SequenceLocal sequence = home.create( );
        String officeKey =
            (String)context.lookup("java:comp/env/constants/OfficeKey");
        Integer id = sequence.getNextValue(officeKey);

        // Set values
        setId(id);
        setCity(city);
        setState(state);

        return null;
    } catch (NamingException e) {
        throw new CreateException("Could not obtain an " +
            "InitialContext.");
    } catch (SequenceException e) {
        throw new CreateException("Error getting primary key value: " +
            e.getMessage( ));
    }
}

public void ejbPostCreate(String city, String state) {
    // Empty implementation
}

public abstract Integer getId( );
public abstract void setId(Integer id);

public abstract String getCity( );
public abstract void setCity(String city);

public abstract String getState( );
public abstract void setState(String state);
}
```

Notice that you had to explicitly add a throws CreateException clause to the modified ejbCreate( ) method; although the Office home interface already has this (and therefore, no changes are needed in that respect), you must add it to the bean to allow it to throw the Exception* within the method. You'll also notice that the code relies heavily on JNDI and the ENC context for information: first for obtaining the Sequence bean's home interface, and second for obtaining the constant for the key name of the OFFICES table. While both of these could be obtained in more "normal" ways, such as looking up the JNDI name of the home interface, and using a Java constant for the key name, using the environment context adds options for the deployer. For example, changing the name of the OFFICES table would not affect the bean; the

---

* If this is confusing, note that the CreateException that the home interface declares is thrown by the remote stub when problems occur with network communication, RMI, and other client-side components. Therefore, for the server-side component to throw the same Exception, the throws clause must be added to the bean method declaration.

deployer could change the CMP mapping and the JNDI constant for the table name, but no recompilation would be needed. The same thing applies to the Sequence bean; it can be deployed into a different container, bound to a different JNDI name, or changed in a variety of other fashions, all without bothering the code. Deploying the beans with a different XML deployment descriptor is all that is needed to modify the bean that is returned from the ENC context. And finally, several different Exceptions that can occur are caught and re-thrown as CreateExceptions. Once the bean and key name are obtained through JNDI, it's a piece of cake to use the getNextValue( ) method coded earlier to obtain the next available primary key value.

With these code changes in place, all that's left is to handle binding these objects into the ENC context. The simplest change is adding an environment entry for the OFFICES table key name; adding a reference to the Sequence bean for use by the Office bean is only slightly more complex. The first task is accomplished through the env-entry (environment entry) element. The second is done with the ejb-local-ref (EJB reference) element. Note that the local version of this is used to accommodate the local interfaces used in the Sequence bean. Also ensure that the value of the ejb-link element in your ejb-local-ref matches the ejb-name of the bean you are referencing; this means using the value SequenceBean in both cases. Make the following changes to the deployment descriptor:

```
<entity>
  <description>
    This Office bean represents a Forethought office,
       including its location.
  </description>
  <display-name>OfficeBean</display-name>
  <ejb-name>OfficeBean</ejb-name>
  <home>com.forethought.ejb.office.OfficeHome</home>
  <remote>com.forethought.ejb.office.Office</remote>
  <local-home>com.forethought.ejb.office.OfficeLocalHome</local-home>
  <local>com.forethought.ejb.office.OfficeLocal</local>
  <ejb-class>com.forethought.ejb.office.OfficeBean</ejb-class>
  <persistence-type>Container</persistence-type>
  <prim-key-class>java.lang.Integer</prim-key-class>
  <reentrant>False</reentrant>

  <abstract-schema-name>OFFICES</abstract-schema-name>
  <cmp-field><field-name>id</field-name></cmp-field>
  <cmp-field><field-name>city</field-name></cmp-field>
  <cmp-field><field-name>state</field-name></cmp-field>
  <primkey-field>id</primkey-field>

  <env-entry>
    <env-entry-name>constants/OfficeKey</env-entry-name>
    <env-entry-type>java.lang.String</env-entry-type>
    <env-entry-value>OFFICES</env-entry-value>
  </env-entry>
  <ejb-local-ref>
    <ejb-ref-name>ejb/SequenceLocalHome</ejb-ref-name>
```

```
      <ejb-ref-type>Session</ejb-ref-type>
      <local-home>com.forethought.ejb.sequence.SequenceLocalHome</local-home>
      <local>com.forethought.ejb.sequence.SequenceLocal</local>
      <ejb-link>SequenceBean</ejb-link>
    </ejb-local-ref>
  </entity>
```

Compiling and repackaging the session and entity beans with these changes is a piece of cake. Simply compile the *SessionAdapter.java*, *SequenceException.java*, *SequenceLocal.java*, *SequenceBean.java*, and *SequenceLocalHome.java* classes, and recompile the *Office.java*, *OfficeHome.java*, and *OfficeBean.java* source files. JAR these and the previously compiled EntityAdapter classes into *forethoughtEntities.jar* along with the modified *ejb-jar.xml* deployment descriptor. You might wonder at the name "forethoughtEntities". But there's a session bean in there, right? Absolutely! The JAR file doesn't represent entity *beans*, it represents *business* entities. In this case, it takes a session bean to represent these entities. If there were ten session beans, two entity beans, and three standalone Java classes that represented the entities, they would be in the JAR file. In other words, the naming in the application is functional, not typological. Staying with this pattern will help you keep your application well documented, rather than technically documented; this difference can save other developers and deployers time and effort in understanding the application's organization. So just like that (well, it was a little harder than that!), you have handled the problem of primary keys and sequence values for entity beans.

Details, Details, Details

Continuing on with a look at common problems in EJB, it's time to move to one area that *is* fairly well understood: the overhead of RMI traffic. More often than not, more time is spent waiting for networks to respond than on actual processing when dealing with EJB. So far, I have spent a lot of time talking about creating a new entity, such as the Forethought office. In that case, very little "back-and-forth" traffic occurs:

```
Object ref = context.lookup("java:comp/env/ejb/OfficeHome");
OfficeHome home = (OfficeHome)
    PortableRemoteObject.narrow(ref, OfficeHome.class);
Office office = home.create("Dallas", "TX");
```

In this case, once the home interface of the bean is located, a single call creates the new office. However, when obtaining information about an office, more calls are needed:

```
String city = office.getCity();
String state = office.getState();
```

While these two calls look pretty harmless, each requires a round-trip RMI call. The remote stub has its method invoked, initiates a remote method invocation, waits for a response, and returns that response. All this depends on network latency and all the other costly issues that surround any network transmission. While even this doesn't seem too bad, take a look at a slightly more complex object:

```
String sku = product.getSKU( );
String name = product.getName( );
String description = product.getDescription( );
float price = product.getPrice( );
// etc...
```

Here, multiple trips over the network are required for these simple method calls, and the application quickly becomes bogged down waiting on even the fastest networks. This is a common peril in using EJB. Happily, though, it can easily be remedied.

Instead of returning field-level values through these calls, you can set your beans up to return *object maps*. In this case, an object map is a normal Java object that corresponds to the entity returning it. This object is then used to find out information about the entity. In this way, a single remote call occurs, and a local object map is returned. This map has all the information a client might need to query about the entity, and therefore this information can be obtained through local calls, instead of expensive remote calls. Let's look at doing this with the Office bean and see exactly how this problem can be handled.

The OfficeInfo Class

All you need to do to utilize object maps is create a class, very similar to the actual OfficeBean class, but without all of the EJB semantics. The class then needs to provide simple accessor and mutator methods for these fields (with just an accessor for the id field). Since these methods will be calls on a local object, rather than a remote stub, they give a performance gain. The only other requirement for the class is that it implements java.io.Serializable; this requirement must be fulfilled by any object that can be returned via RMI. The code for this class is shown in Example 5-10.

Example 5-10. The OfficeInfo Details Class

```
package com.forethought.ejb.office;

import java.io.Serializable;

public class OfficeInfo implements Serializable {

    /** The ID of this office */
    private int id;

    /** The city this office is in */
    private String city;

    /** The state this office is in */
    private String state;

    OfficeInfo(int id, String city, String state) {
        this.id = id;
        this.city = city;
        this.state = state;
```

Example 5-10. The OfficeInfo Details Class (continued)

```java
    }

    public int getId( ) {
        return id;
    }

    public String getCity( ) {
        return city;
    }

    public void setCity(String city) {
        this.city = city;
    }

    public String getState( ) {
        return state;
    }

    public void setState(String state) {
        this.state = state;
    }
}
```

This code is very similar to the Office remote interface. That should make perfect sense: you want the functionality of the entity bean's remote interface, without the penalties for use that RMI imposes. As this class is essentially a part of the bean, you should include it in the same package, com.forethought.ejb.office. Additionally, any bean client that uses the Office bean will already have to import the OfficeHome and Office classes, both in the same package; adding another import for this new class in the same package is no big deal.

 There is one difference in the details object as compared to the remote interface: the type of the primary key. Note that the method getId( ) in the details object returns an int, not an Integer. Again, this is by design rather than accident. First, because the details object is immutable, there is not as much need to differentiate the data type by using an object instead of a primitive. More importantly, the details object is simply snapshot data, often thrown away after a single use, and is intended to be convenient. This would move you towards providing the easier data type (int) for use, rather than the more complex data type (Integer). This may seem a little odd at first, but I've found it to be perfectly intuitive in an actual application.

Also notice that the constructor for the class is package-protected, which means that a client application will not be able to perform the following operation:

```java
// Create a new office in an ILLEGAL WAY!!
OfficeInfo officeInfo = new OfficeInfo(2459, "Portland", "Oregon");
```

This innocent-looking code fragment is a real problem; it gives the client the impression of creating a new office, but has no effect on a data store anywhere else in the application. Only the Office bean can create a new details object, and the client is then only allowed to set values on an existing object:

```
// Create a new office, the RIGHT WAY!
Office office = officeHome.create("Portland", "OR");

// Get the detail object for a bean
OfficeInfo officeInfo = office.getInfo();

// Change the details of the office
officeInfo.setCity("Boston");
officeInfo.setState("MA");

// Set these changes back to the database
office.setInfo(officeInfo);
```

This provides easy access to data for the user without lots of RMI, but also protects that user from making mistakes in office creation.

The final note is the name of the class used. I've called this class OfficeInfo. The methodology or design pattern outlined in this section is often called the *details pattern*, or the *value pattern*. Following that name, the class in this case would be called OfficeDetails, or OfficeValue. However (and maybe this is just me), the term "details" seems to imply that there is a view of the entity somewhere else that is *not* detailed. Of course, this isn't the case. And the term "value" implies a single value for a single field, rather than a set of values that compose a complex object. For these reasons, the term "information" seems more applicable; the class provides information about an entity. And as I'm a programmer, I've naturally shortened "information" to "info." The end result is that I use OfficeInfo for the class name, and it clearly represents the purpose of the class.

Modifying the Entity Bean

So now you have a class that provides a map of the office entity. However, you'll need to make some modifications to your bean classes to put it into use. First, you should add a means of obtaining the map of an entity, as well as a means of retrieving it. Of course, this is the key; once this object is retrieved via RMI, the information on the entity can be obtained through local method calls. Example 5-11 shows the modified Office class, the bean's remote interface.

Example 5-11. The Modified Office Remote Interface

```
package com.forethought.ejb.office;

import java.rmi.RemoteException;
import javax.ejb.EJBObject;
```

Example 5-11. The Modified Office Remote Interface (continued)

```
public interface Office extends EJBObject {

    public OfficeInfo getInfo( ) throws RemoteException;
    public void setInfo(OfficeInfo officeInfo) throws RemoteException;

    // Other accessor and mutator methods not included for brevity
}
```

One change you do *not* want to make is to add a new create( ) method for the home interface of the bean. While it might make sense, at least at first thought, to add a means of creating an office through supplying a details object, this breaks down on closer inspection. It would require the client to create an OfficeInfo instance and pass in an ID value; of course, this practice goes against everything I've been talking about with regard to sequences, and isn't such a good idea. In fact, the only object that should *create* details objects is the bean implementation, which needs to return the map of its data. Clients should never create instances of OfficeInfo; instead, they should obtain them from the getInfo( ) method of the Office remote interface. In this sense, it works a lot like obtaining a remote interface through a home interface: the client uses the home interface as a factory. In the same way, the client uses the remote interface as a provider for the details object.

Finally, you need to add the implementation of the remote interface methods. The accessor and mutator methods that deal with the OfficeInfo class are very simple, and the required changes to the OfficeBean class are shown here:

```
public OfficeInfo getInfo( ) {
    return new OfficeInfo(getId( ).intValue( ), getCity( ), getState( ));
}

public void setInfo(OfficeInfo officeInfo) {
    setId(new Integer(officeInfo.getId( )));
    setCity(officeInfo.getCity( ));
    setState(officeInfo.getState( ));
}
```

Remember that the get/setId( ), get/setCity( ), and get/setState( ) methods are all local in the bean class, so no RMI traffic is occurring in these methods.

Compile all these classes (including the new *OfficeInfo.java* source file), add them to the *forethoughtEntities.jar* archive, and ensure that you can still deploy the Forethought entities. Once that is in place, you're ready to go on. However, there are still a few items related to the details pattern worth mentioning (just so you remain the expert among your friends!).

Leaving Out Details

You should realize that there are times when details objects are *not* useful. In the Office bean, the details object was supplied for use by clients through the bean's remote interface. However, you should not duplicate these accessor methods on the Office bean's local interface. Because local interfaces allow for (essentially) in-JVM calls, the reasons for using details objects become null and void. It's simpler to just directly access the variables needed through normal local interface methods.

So in this case, a details object is not warranted. By the time values are copied into the details object and that object is serialized, the single call needed to operate with a local object (as is the case when using local interfaces) would have been just as efficient. For that reason, simple objects like the Forethought "type" objects do not use details objects. In your own applications, you will need to make these sorts of decisions all the time; rarely is any advice absolute.

As another example of when details objects should be left out, consider the UserType and AccountType beans (I haven't discussed these other than by reference in the data design, but they are in Appendix E). Both of these beans provide only local interfaces, as they are used internally by other beans but never directly by a client. Because of this restriction, and because the beans will always interact locally, the advantages of using details objects become inconsequential, just as in the Office bean. This is even more the case because both of these objects represent only two database fields: an ID and a type. Again, it is better to leave out use of the details objects (as is done in the code in Appendix E).

Data Modeling

A final couple of words on entity beans are merited before moving on. The Office bean has remained very simple so far, allowing you to overlook a few problems related to dealing with entity beans in a large application. This simplicity exists for two reasons: first, the bean stands on its own, and second, it is a frequently changed object. These two facts are discussed in the following sections.

Independent and Dependent Data Objects

The fact that an office is a complete entity means that it is an independent data object. In other words, a Forethought office does not depend on any other data to be complete. Additionally, an office has meaning on its own. A states table, for example, might not have this quality; for our purposes, a state's name and abbreviation are not really useful on their own, and the state has purpose only within the context of another entity that references the states table. In this case, you would want the client to deal with the overall office entity, perhaps setting its name, and the bean would then use the states bean to work with that entity. In that way, the states entity becomes a *dependent object*. On the other hand, the office entity is an *independent object*.

It is also important to understand that just because an entity is used by another entity, it is not necessarily dependent. The office entity is again a perfect example: it is referenced by the users entity, specifying the office the user works in. But the office entity is *not* dependent, because it has business meaning on its own. There are many cases where the office may need to be used alone, such as locating the nearest Forethought office. Because of these uses, you don't want to prevent access to the office entity; however, you would prevent similar access for states.

EJB 2.0 provides for relationships between beans, and it is here that dependent objects begin to play an important role in the application. The new CMP 2.0 in the EJB specification allows for much easier handling of this information, as you'll see in examples in the appendixes and throughout the rest of the book. Because that's a fairly routine EJB practice, though, I'll leave further details about bean relationships to basic EJB books, and not address it here. Other than a few additional abstract methods and a few entries in a deployment descriptor, the container takes care of all the relationship work, so there's no special work required on your part.

When Entity Beans Don't Make Sense

The second characteristic of offices in the Forethought application is that they are often changed, updated, added, and deleted. This makes them good candidates for entity beans, as such actions can occur in transactions. However, there are times when an entity bean is overkill. A good example in our application is the USER_TYPES table, which, at least in the Forethought application, acts more like a constants pool than an entity. It will most likely be populated with some initial data that is never changed; the table's only purpose is to read these values ("Employee" or "Client") and nothing else. The expensive RMI calls that are involved with EJBs and transactions are essentially wasted on this table, as they aren't ever taken advantage of, yet they are still paid for. The same principles apply to the ACCOUNT_TYPES table, which acts as a constants pool for accounts.

However, the decision of how to handle the table is still difficult. Reading the previous paragraph, it may seem that you should just use JDBC and not worry about it. It's not that easy, however. On the one hand, when almost all of the entities in the database are represented by entity beans (as in the Forethought application), you have already committed a lot of resources to EJB. In that respect, changing two classes to JDBC units of work, while leaving ten or more as EJB, counteracts most of the advantages of using JDBC on its own. Additionally, you have the extremely useful ENC context available in your beans, which is not as easily accessible in straight JDBC classes. On the other hand, as the number of classes that directly use JDBC grows, the balance begins to shift. A good rule of thumb is that when you have half as many JDBC candidates as you do full-blown entity beans, go ahead and use straight JDBC for those classes, and entity beans for the rest. You will see quite a performance improvement. However, this isn't the case in this application, so I don't suggest changing any classes to straight JDBC; the performance gain would be negligible.

The bottom line here, though, is that it isn't always an automatic choice to use entity beans for every case of data access. In fact, in many applications where transactions aren't crucial and financial information isn't being transferred, you may not want to use EJB at all. Of course, the Forethought application both needs transactions and sends financial computations across the wire, so you should use EJB.

Filling in the Blanks

Well, I've spent quite a while discussing how to handle Forethought offices in this chapter. Of course, there is a lot more than just an office to be dealt with in the application; there are also data entities for users, funds, accounts, and the other data structures created in the database. Trying to detail beans for the numerous tables in even this sample application would take another fifty pages or so. Of course, doing so would cloud the point of this chapter, which is EJB design and related patterns.

Appendix E is full of supplemental code that was used in this book but didn't fit into a chapter, and it's where the entity bean code for the rest of the Forethought entities lies. You can also download the code for the entire book from *http://www. newInstance.com*. You should take the time now to enter in all this code, or download it, compile it, and add it to the *forethoughtEntities.jar* archive. Deploy this into your EJB container to ensure it is ready for use, and then continue. The rest of the book assumes that you have available not only the Office bean, but all of the Forethought entity beans detailed in Appendix E, and you will have problems if they are not. You can also see some of the additional concepts discussed in this and the previous chapter in action in these supplemental code listings. For example, handling dependent objects, like the user's type in the User bean, is a perfect example, and you'll see how that works.

What's Next?

I've covered a lot of EJB concepts in this chapter, rarely taking a break. Hopefully you've been able to get everything working with the help of the appendixes, and now have the complete set of Forethought entities available for use. Even more importantly, you should have an understanding of the advanced concepts in EJB, and of how to use them in your own applications.

In the next chapter, you'll complement your work on entity beans, the base of the Forethought application, with access to a directory server, which completes the application foundation. We'll look at JNDI again and see how it can help in accessing LDAP providers, as well as beans and Java objects bound to the registry. By the end of the next chapter, you'll have a complete data layer, and can move on to the business layer of the application. So buckle up, fire up your directory server, and let's get to it.

CHAPTER 6

Managers

Now that you have your database accessible through entity beans, you're ready to move on to providing access to the Forethought directory server. Like the entity beans, classes that provide LDAP access are at a lower level of the application than that which clients will access. The classes from the last chapter, and in this one, will never be touched directly by application clients, or even by the first tier of the application. The application's business layer will utilize these tools to access raw data and assemble that data into meaningful computations and groupings.

In this chapter, then, I'll start by comparing entities with a new type of component, *managers*. You'll see why using a manager for directory server access makes more sense than using a set of entities. You'll then construct a basic class to allow access to a directory server. From there, I'll move on to adding some performance tweaks to your existing code, ensuring that the application doesn't spend unnecessary amounts of time waiting for a connection to the directory server to be established. I'll also explain the process of managing connections to multiple servers, and touch on caching and persistence at the connection layer. This will finish up the manager class, and you'll finally have a complete data layer.

Managers and Entities

So far, I have talked exclusively about entity components. Each instance of an entity component represents a corresponding data object, and can also store related data objects, such as the User entity bean (from Appendix E). That bean provides a means to get an Office entity directly from the User entity. In other words, a single object instance in Java maps directly to a data entity from the data store. Entities work extremely well when you have data objects that you need to work with as a whole; for example, you'll almost always have to work with more than just the user's first name; you'll also need the last name, distinguished name (DN), and other information about that user. However, this will not always be the case when dealing with data.

Remember that in the directory server, all that is being stored is the username, password, and information about groups that a user is in. This data is accessed through a username, generally asking only for a password match in return. In other words, data is supplied to the server, and if the data matches, a confirmation occurs; otherwise, a denial occurs:

```
// Obtain the username and password from the request
String username = request.getUsername();
String password = request.getPassword();

// Get LDAP connection object
LDAPManager manager =
    new LDAPManager("ldap://galadriel.middleearth.com", 389);

// Validate user
if (manager.authenticate(username, password)) {
    // Allow access to application
} else {
    // Deny access
}
```

In this code fragment, there is clearly no need to obtain a Java representation of the user's data object from the directory server. Instead, it is just as simple to connect to the directory server and authenticate the user. The user's credentials are either accepted or denied, and the application flow can continue. Since no other information about the user is stored in the directory server, there isn't a need to operate upon a data object.

This is a perfect example of when you should use the *manager* component. In a sense, a manager is like a wrapper for dealing with specific entities. It is best used when an actual entity does not need to be accessed directly, but instead operations need to be performed upon specific parts of it. A manager can be used as part of the façade pattern that I mentioned in Chapter 4, or in lieu of coding entities at all. In either case, though, keep in mind that a manager does not perform business logic; it merely allows simple queries and updates to underlying data. For example, the following is a typical method for a manager to provide:

```
public class LDAPManager {

    public void addUser(String username, String password) {
        // Method implementation
    }
}
```

This code simply operates upon data without doing anything business-specific. However, the following method would not be a valid method for a manager component to provide, as it performs business logic and data manipulation rather than simple data access:

```
public class LDAPManager {

    /**
     * <p>
     *  This will remove all users that are of the user type "client".
     * </p>
     */
    public void removeClients() {
        // Method implementation
    }
}
```

Think about it this way: the first method, addUser( ), is applicable to any application, since all directory servers in all applications have users (otherwise, a directory server wouldn't be used). The second method, removeClients( ), is not useful in any case, though. It depends, first, on there being different types of users in the directory server. Further, it requires that one of those types be "client". Finally, it might even require that database access be performed to link users with their types, if types are stored in the database. This is clearly a method that belongs in the business layer rather than in the data layer.

This type of component can be presented as either a session bean that accesses entity beans, or as a standalone Java class that does not use entity beans at all. I'll look at both and explain which is most appropriate for handling access to directory servers.

Managers as Session Beans

The most common type of manager component you will come across is the session bean manager. Almost all of these types of managers occur in beans used for data administration. Remember that you don't want to allow any direct access to your entity beans, as it would expose too much information about the underlying data structure. Direct access also requires validation at the entity bean level, and it makes managing beans extremely complex, as both session and entity beans would have to be made available to the application layer. What is needed is an abstraction layer, sandwiched between application and business logic and raw data.

Session beans provide that abstraction. So far, I have mainly discussed session beans in the context of performing business logic and computations. In a similar way, session bean managers normally use multiple entity beans, piecing data from various tables and sources together to generate meaningful business results. However, they perform data logic, providing access to database rows or directory server stores rather than doing business-related computations. With that in mind, you can apply these concepts to the Forethought application.

You already know that the application will need to manage investments, funds, users, and more. Many times, even a simple investment consists of data in many places; the Fund bean, the Investment bean, the User bean, the Account bean, and more are all involved in this rather basic operation. However, these all depend on even more basic data in the database. As an example, take a fund from the application. While Forethought clients don't need to manipulate this data, the brokers need to be able to add and delete funds, or update information about the funds. There is no business logic involved here, just straight data manipulation. In this case, a manager comes into play. A session bean can provide a proxy-like access to the Fund entity bean, but the methods on the session bean, which I'll refer to as FundManager, are simple: add( ), remove( ), update( ), and others. In fact, you'll find that almost all manager beans have these same method names, which provides a simple means of using any manager.

Now that you've seen the case for session bean managers, you should already be guessing that almost all of the Forethought entity beans will have complementary managers in the business layer. There will be a UserManager to administrate new users in the database (which will be used in tandem with the LDAPManager to manage users, as they are stored in both the database and the directory server), the FundManager that I just discussed, an OfficeManager, and so on. I'll look at the code for each of these later. Figure 6-1 shows the flow of data into a manager component and how it interacts with entity beans and the underlying database. You can compare this to the flow I'll look at next, when a Java class (that is not a session bean) is used as a manager.

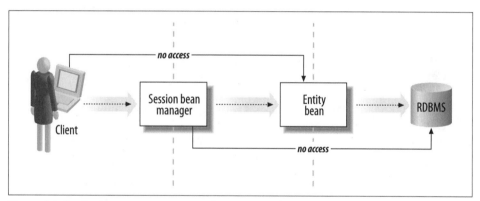

Figure 6-1. Session bean acting as a manager to an entity bean

Managers as Java Classes

The case of using a normal Java class, where "normal" simply means the class isn't a bean or other specific format, is a bit different from the session bean case. Often, the primary difference is not as much in the manager class itself, but in what is actually being managed. This means that bean manager components generally use entity beans for data access, making the manager's code pretty simple. The data access actually occurs in the entity bean. However, managers that are not session beans generally access a data store directly, which means that their implementation is often more complex to code.

The advantage of this type of manager component is that it can dramatically improve performance, at least in certain areas. I've already talked about the dangers of over-using RMI in Enterprise JavaBeans, and shown how local interfaces can often help improve performance. Add to that the EJB container transaction and security processes, and you have quite a bit of overhead. If you are working with a database, where entity beans provide significant advantages to counterbalance these penalties, beans make perfect sense. However, other types of data stores do not fit into that model. Directory servers are one of those types of stores; there is simply no advantage to using beans in this case. Transactions become essentially meaningless, and even when beans are used, they must be bean-managed and coded completely by hand.

It would be unfair not to point out that some application servers provide hooks into directory servers, often requiring little to no coding. However, these servers are not J2EE-required or even standard APIs or methods, which means that your code is not at all portable. Additionally, you lose an element of control; remember that there were lots of modifications made to the default directory server schema. Even if your application server provides these sorts of hooks, it may not support the custom object classes used in the Forethought application or those that you may need in your own applications. So what is the moral of this story? Learn JNDI and the `javax.naming.directory` package that I cover in this chapter, and code directory server access on your own (or use the code provided in this chapter).

When dealing with a directory server, it simply makes more sense to create a standard Java class, use JNDI directly, and not pay the performance penalties associated with EJB. Additionally, you gain some other advantages. Using a manager component results in the developer having complete control over the connection to the directory server. It also allows you to stretch the rules of object-oriented (OO) programming a bit, resulting in even better performance. Let me explain this in more detail.

Consider the case of operating upon a user in the directory server. In a strict object-oriented environment, a user would be added through the manager. The result of this method would probably be the new user object itself (making the manager act much like a constructor and the Java new keyword):

```
User user = LDAPManager.createUser("bmclaugh", "Brett", "McLaughlin");
```

Then additional operations, such as modifying the user's attributes, would be performed upon that user object, rather than through the manager itself:

```
user.joinGroup("administrators");

out.println(user.getFirstName() + " " + user.getLastName());
user.setUID("bmclaughlin");
```

While this approach is very object-oriented, it turns out to be a bad idea, and here's why: the user object now has to manage the directory server connection itself.

Remember that when you get an entity bean's remote interface, connections to the database are taking place behind the scenes; as previously mentioned, it's better to allow the manager to handle those connections. If the manager creates objects, though, each object must also be able to handle connecting to the directory.

The only other option is for created objects to reference the manager that created them; that approach has its own set of problems, though. While it is possible to have the LDAP user object maintain a reference to its manager, you then have to start worrying about distributing the components; what happens if the LDAP user object is serialized and sent across the network, for example? The reference to its manager would become meaningless. The related code would need permission and group objects as well, so now you have four objects (the manager, user, group, and permission objects) that have to deal with JNDI calls and directory service interaction. This strategy becomes even more complex if you want to try and employ any connection pooling or caching at all. In other words, this object-oriented approach, where operations on an object are accomplished through methods on that object, breaks down. It makes sense to take a slightly different tack.

So instead of using this OO approach, you can bend the rules a bit. (It's OK to do this as long as you know what rules you are bending and why they should be bent.) Here you need to have all calls upon any objects in the directory go through the manager component. In a strictly OO environment, you would have code similar to this:

```
// Connect to LDAP directory server
LDAPManager manager = new LDAPManager("galadriel.middleearth.com");

// Create new user
LDAPUser user = manager.getUser("shirlbg");
user.setPassword(userPassword);

// Add the user to a group
LDAPGroup clients = manager.getGroup("clients");
clients.addMember(user);
```

To illustrate how this approach increases in complexity the more that clients access the manager and obtain objects, Figure 6-2 shows how the flow moves from client to directory server. Note how each object returned from the manager results in another component that must access the directory server.

However, it's possible to change that approach, and instead have all the LDAP-related methods invoked on the manager component. So you will have code that looks more like this:

```
// Connect to LDAP directory server
LDAPManager manager = new LDAPManager("galadriel.middleearth.com");

// Create new user
manager.updateUser("shirlbg", "Shirley", "Greathouse", userPassword);

// Add the user to a group
manager.assignUser("shirlbg", "clients");
```

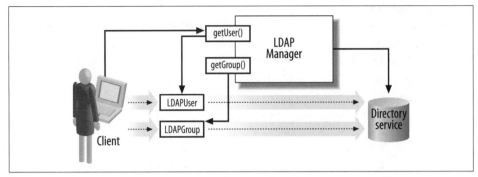

Figure 6-2. Manager object returning LDAP objects to client (strict OO approach)

You can see that the program control here has been inverted; instead of using the manager to get individual objects, and then operating upon those objects, the manager actually maintains control and manipulates any objects needed internally, behind the scenes.* This makes the client's job much simpler; although there are more methods on the manager component, the client only has to deal with that single component.

The other major advantage, besides simplicity, is that the manager component is the only object that needs to deal with connections. This brings back the possibility of using connection pooling, caching, and other performance-driven enhancements that were overly complex in the more OO environment. This approach is clearly superior, and the small change in mentality involved with always operating upon the manager object is well worth the advantages gained in performance and usability. Figure 6-3 shows this new program flow, which is quite a bit different (and notably simpler) than what it was in Figure 6-2. This flow is exactly the flow desired, and it is how the LDAPManager class will be modeled.

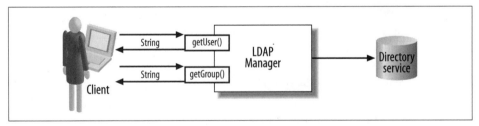

Figure 6-3. Manager object handling all interaction with a directory server (less OO approach)

---

* It is actually possible to not create *any* objects internally, or at the least to use only the Sun-provided JNDI objects, rather than user-friendly objects like the LDAPUser and LDAPGroup classes shown in the first code sample. This is exactly the approach taken with the LDAPManager class, reducing garbage collection and overhead from excessive object creation.

The LDAPManager Class

With the basic principles of manager classes under your belt, you're ready to look at the LDAPManager class. This chapter involves a rapid run through some LDAP and JNDI concepts that you should already be familiar with; if you get lost in the details of the code samples, pick up *Java Enterprise in a Nutshell*, which spends a lot of time on JNDI. Once you've got a handle on the basics, the code itself should illustrate any tricky issues.

The LDAPManager class belongs in a package structure that mirrors the com.forethought.ejb package: com.forethought.ldap. There are a few constants that can be defined right off the bat. First, the default port for LDAP, 389, is stored, which allows clients to specify only a hostname, and possibly authentication credentials, when connecting, rather than also having to specify the default port when appropriate. Additionally, some basic member variables are defined: one for the hostname to connect to, and one for the port. These variables are used when the manager needs to connect and reconnect to the directory server, or authenticate users when a connection is already in place. Finally, the manager needs to store a connection object itself, a javax.naming.directory.DirContext instance.

Skeletons and Outlines

Using JNDI for directory server access will require a bit of a change in thinking. Everything in JNDI revolves around the idea of a Context; this should seem familiar, as I discussed getting an InitialContext object in Chapter 5. While this was taken for granted in that chapter, I need to talk a little more about it here. First, it's possible to outline this new manager class and see how the Context object fits into the bigger picture. Example 6-1 shows the bare-bones skeleton of the LDAPManager class. It provides several constructors, all deferring to an overloaded constructor, which uses the provided information to obtain a DirContext instance. Fire up your editor and type in the code listing; you'll be adding to this class throughout the rest of the chapter.*

Example 6-1. The LDAPManager Skeleton

```
package com.forethought.ldap;

import java.util.Properties;
import java.util.LinkedList;
import java.util.List;
import javax.naming.Context;
import javax.naming.NameNotFoundException;
```

---

* I'm cheating a bit in this code listing; you will add quite a few methods to the LDAPManager class throughout this chapter, and adding each needed import statement as we go would be fairly confusing. Instead, all the needed import statements for the class are included in Example 6-1. Be sure to include all of them, as they are required for later methods.

Example 6-1. The LDAPManager Skeleton (continued)

```java
import javax.naming.NamingEnumeration;
import javax.naming.NamingException;
import javax.naming.directory.Attribute;
import javax.naming.directory.AttributeInUseException;
import javax.naming.directory.Attributes;
import javax.naming.directory.BasicAttribute;
import javax.naming.directory.BasicAttributes;
import javax.naming.directory.DirContext;
import javax.naming.directory.InitialDirContext;
import javax.naming.directory.ModificationItem;
import javax.naming.directory.NoSuchAttributeException;
import javax.naming.directory.SearchControls;
import javax.naming.directory.SearchResult;

public class LDAPManager {

    /** The default LDAP port */
    private static final int DEFAULT_PORT = 389;

    /** The connection, through a <code>DirContext</code>, to LDAP */
    private DirContext context;

    /** The hostname connected to */
    private String hostname;

    /** The port connected to */
    private int port;

    public LDAPManager(String hostname, int port,
                       String username, String password)
        throws NamingException {

        context = getInitialContext(hostname, port, username, password);

        // Only save data if we got connected
        this.hostname = hostname;
        this.port = port;
    }

    public LDAPManager(String hostname, int port)
        throws NamingException {

        this(hostname, port, null, null);
    }

    public LDAPManager(String hostname) throws NamingException {
        this(hostname, DEFAULT_PORT);
    }
}
```

Nothing really surprising here; it's apparent that the interesting action is in the
getInitialContext( ) method. In the last chapter, the entity beans needed only a

basic `InitialContext` object. This object provided the beans access to the application server's default JNDI provider, which was either specified in a *jndi.properties* file or through a specific programmatic means. In both cases, the naming system was controlled by the application server. In other words, the bean code only requested a connection to the application server's naming provider, and was not concerned with how the server dealt with naming. However, this manager needs to take some of that control back.

 Lest you get confused, the code in Example 6-1 will not yet compile, because there is no implementation of the `getInitialContext()` method. I'll detail this method in the next section, so things will work out then; however, expect compilation errors at this point.

Naming in Detail

A *naming service* is simply a means of binding objects to arbitrary names and allowing clients to look up objects by those names. This is used instead of (for example) a memory address, which is how references in Java usually work. The details of handling these object-to-name mappings are fairly flexible; anything from a filesystem to a directory server to an RMI registry is allowed. This means that the client doesn't have to worry about *how* the objects are bound, but instead just needs to access those objects. As if that didn't make it easy enough for programmer types, the bulk of JNDI complexity is left to the service provider, usually the application server vendor. Sun makes life even easier by supplying providers for many naming services. So while the service provider gets to spend lots of time implementing the `javax.naming. spi` interfaces, the client merely needs to provide a URL for the provider and the context factory class, and then use the naming service. For a lot more on JNDI, as well as related topics, you can pick up *Java Enterprise in a Nutshell*.

This means that most times, a naming service is used for the functionality it provides, and the actual details of how objects are bound become irrelevant. This is the case in application servers, and it also held true in the last chapter; you don't care how the server stores entity bean mappings, as long as you can look them up by their JNDI names. In fact, many servers provide multiple naming service providers, and allow the server deployer (usually a system administrator) to select an RMI registry, filesystem, or even directory server to store those mappings. As it doesn't affect the code that the objects are looked up in, these details don't usually bother us geeks in the cubes.

However, in the case of using the Forethought directory server, you will need to focus on these often-irrelevant details about a service provider; you will need to use a specific type of naming service, and functionality is secondary. Here, you aren't looking for a means to map objects to names, but rather to interface with objects in a specific medium. For that reason, you should not use the generic means of obtaining an

`InitialContext` that I have talked about so far, but instead specifically define the context factory to use. That provider is Sun's LDAP (v3) context factory, which is specifically designed for use with a directory server; the relevant class is `com.sun.jndi.ldap.LdapCtxFactory`. The result is that with this class and a provider URL, your code can connect to a directory server. As a side effect, you end up using JNDI. This isn't a bad thing, either. Instead of choosing to use JNDI, which happens to use a directory server for mappings, you are using a directory server, and accessing that server in a vendor-neutral way that just happens to involve using JNDI. Sorry to drag you through all these details, but hopefully it helps you see exactly why you need to not only use JNDI, but also to supply a specific context factory class instead of relying on an application server to handle that detail. In addition to that specificity, you also need to use a `javax.naming.directory.DirContext`, specifically designed for LDAP access, instead of the more generic `javax.naming.Context` object used in the last chapter.

The end result? Well, it's only about fifteen lines of code, but it establishes a connection to a directory server and returns that connection in the form of a `DirContext` object instance. This method replaces the context factory variable with Sun's LDAP provider instead of one of the vendor-specific classes you might see in your server's example code. It takes in the hostname and port number to connect to, as well as a username and password. The username and password can be `null` (the overloaded constructors pass in the `null` value when no username or password is provided), but if they are non-null, authentication to the directory server also occurs in this method. This authentication turns out to be vital; the user supplied will be the user under which actions like adding users, assigning permissions, and deleting groups are performed. If that user doesn't have sufficient permissions to perform these actions, the actions will fail. You'll see that when using the manager, the directory manager user is usually preferred for this initial connection. Add the following method, which puts all of these details into action, to the LDAPManager class:

```
private DirContext getInitialContext(String hostname, int port,
                                     String username, String password)
    throws NamingException {

    String providerURL =
        new StringBuffer("ldap://")
            .append(hostname)
            .append(":")
            .append(port)
            .toString();

    Properties props = new Properties();
    props.put(Context.INITIAL_CONTEXT_FACTORY,
            "com.sun.jndi.ldap.LdapCtxFactory");
    props.put(Context.PROVIDER_URL, providerURL);

    if ((username != null) && (!username.equals(""))) {
        props.put(Context.SECURITY_AUTHENTICATION, "simple");
        props.put(Context.SECURITY_PRINCIPAL, username);
        props.put(Context.SECURITY_CREDENTIALS,
            ((password == null) ? "" : password));
    }

    return new InitialDirContext(props);
}
```

Once a constructor invokes this method, the manager component has a DirContext to operate upon. But how does this relate to the directory server's structure? JNDI does not use semantics like "connection" or "organizational unit." So just as it is important to understand how service providers work, it is vital to grasp how the JNDI structures—the Context objects—relate to the directory server structure.

When the getInitialContext( ) method returns a DirContext instance, that instance is mapped to the very top level of the directory server's structure. In the Forethought case, this is the "root" of the tree where the organization is "forethought.com" (*o=forethought.com*). Objects bound to the naming service are then referred to in JNDI as *subcontexts*. Each subcontext is bound to a name, the object's DN. So for the user whose username is "shirlbg" and whose DN is *uid=shirlbg,ou=People, o=forethought.com*, the object is bound to the subcontext *uid=shirlbg,ou=People, o=forethought.com* under the top-level context. The DN of an object identifies not only the path to that object in the directory, but also the mapping of that object under the top-level directory context. Figure 6-4 shows how the JNDI contexts relate to the directory server hierarchy (you will remember this structure from Figure 3-11).

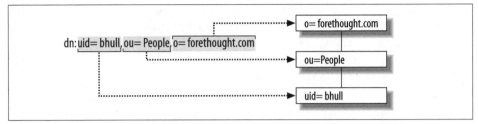

Figure 6-4. Mapping JNDI contexts to the Forethought directory server

The only other item you will have to deal with in detail is the javax.naming. directory.Attribute class. Each instance of this class represents a specific attribute for an object class. Thus, the common name, or cn, attribute of the *inetOrgPerson* object class can be retrieved, modified, and deleted using the Attribute class. Figure 6-5 takes a specific entry from the Forethought directory server, the sample user Shirley Greathouse* that I have been using in the examples in this chapter, and shows how its attributes relate to the JNDI Attribute class.

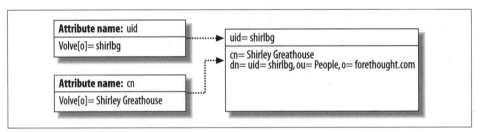

Figure 6-5. Attributes and directory server entries

Users

Now that you have a skeleton to build on, you simply need to add support for the object types used in the Forethought application: users, groups, and permissions. I'll start with users, as they are basic to any application. There are three main tasks when dealing with users. First, you need to convert from the user's username, which the application works with, to the user's distinguished name, which JNDI works with. Next, you will learn to add and delete users. Finally, you'll code a method that allows you to authenticate a user, which is part of the login process used later on in the application. I'll detail these tasks one at a time.

Getting the distinguished name

As mentioned in previous JNDI discussions, the contexts within JNDI related to the directory server are all identified by a distinguished name (DN). This means that

---

* If your directory server doesn't have this entry yet, don't worry. I'm just using this as a sample, and you will populate your server and database in the next chapter.

while all user-related methods should take and return usernames (or group names, or permission names), they must pass DNs to the JNDI methods. Therefore, your first task is to create two methods: one that converts a username to a user's DN, and one that converts from a DN to a username. Both of these depend on knowing where within the directory hierarchy users are stored, so that a constant can be defined (USERS_OU) that specifies the organizational unit that users are bound under.

With that constant in place, it's trivial to code a getUserDN( ) method, which takes in a user's username and returns the DN. Since a username becomes the uid attribute, the DN of the username "gqg10012" can easily be constructed as *uid=gqg1001, ou=People,o=forethought.com*, where *ou=People,o=forethought.com* is the organizational unit represented by the USERS_OU constant. It becomes a simple matter of String concatenation.[*] Converting from a DN to a username with the getUserUID( ) method simply involves reversing the process and splitting the username from its surroundings (the string "uid=" before it and a comma directly after it). There is also some minor error checking; in the case of a relative DN, such as *uid=shirlbg* (you'll see this in searches detailed a little later on), if no trailing comma is found, the end variable is simply set to the length of the userDN string. In either case, you will get the desired result. So add the constant and two methods shown here to your LDAPManager source; they will be used in all of the other user methods:

```
/** The OU (organizational unit) to add users to */
private static final String USERS_OU =
    "ou=People,o=forethought.com";

private String getUserDN(String username) {
    return new StringBuffer( )
            .append("uid=")
            .append(username)
            .append(",")
            .append(USERS_OU)
            .toString( );
}

private String getUserUID(String userDN) {
    int start = userDN.indexOf("=");
    int end = userDN.indexOf(",");

    if (end == -1) {
        end = userDN.length( );
    }

    return userDN.substring(start+1, end);
}
```

---

[*] In the actual method, a StringBuffer is used; this is Java 101, in essence. You should never, ever concatenate Java Strings directly with the + operator. Instead, use a buffer to perform any needed concatenation, and then convert that buffer with the toString( ) method. Not following this advice will result in a horribly large String pool, drastically reducing application performance.

Adding and deleting

With conversion in place, you can now move to the next task, adding and deleting users. Both of these operations are keyed upon the target user's username, which becomes a DN by virtue of the getUserDN( ) method just coded. When adding a user, you will need to require a password, as well as a first name and last name. The first and last names of the user are not used functionally, as these values are stored in the database and are available through the User entity bean. However, the cn (common name) and sn (surname) attributes are required for the *inetOrgPerson* object class that users are stored within. While you could fill these attributes with meaningless values or even the username, using accurate first and last names helps describe the users a little better. Also remember that adding a user will involve both the database and directory server, so your code will have the first and last name values available when users are added, and that code can take care of supplying these values easily.

The key operation in adding a user is invoking the createSubcontext( ) method on the manager's DirContext. This binds the set of user attributes the code creates to the user's DN. An instance of the javax.naming.directory.Attribute class discussed earlier represents each of the user's attributes. You also will use the javax.naming. directory.Attributes class* to hold the various attributes. In other words, an Attributes instance holds Attribute instances, which as a group are supplied when creating a new entry in the directory server. To create these, you will need to instantiate implementations of the two interfaces; the BasicAttributes and BasicAttribute classes (also in the javax.naming.directory package) fit the bill perfectly.

So you will need to create a new BasicAttribute for all of the attributes used in the new object class. This includes the cn, sn, givenName, userPassword, and uid attributes. The other attribute you will need to worry about is the objectClass attribute. It specifies the object class hierarchy that the new object will have; we discussed directory hierarchies and object class hierarchies in Chapter 3. Creating this attribute and adding the object classes to the hierarchy also reveals something important about the Attribute class: it can have multiple values. This will also be important when looking at adding users to groups, which involves assigning multiple values (user DNs) to a group's uniqueMember attribute. Once all of the individual Attribute objects are created, they must be assigned to the Attributes object. Finally, this container is passed on to the createSubcontext( ) method, and the result is a new entry in the LDAP tree. You should also note that the addUser( ) method, as well as almost all of the methods in the LDAPManager class, throws a NamingException. This exception can occur when connections have failed, and also when an object already exists with the supplied DN. Later, you'll code business objects that create users, and handle these errors and report problems back to the user in a more meaningful format. For

---

* Actually, both the Attribute and Attributes classes are interfaces, but you will see that this is not a problem, as the manager code will use implementations of these as needed.

now, just throw the error back to the client component. Add this method to the LDAPManager source file, and the manager will be equipped to add new users to the directory:

```
public void addUser(String username, String firstName,
                    String lastName, String password)
    throws NamingException {

    // Create a container set of attributes
    Attributes container = new BasicAttributes( );

    // Create the objectclass to add
    Attribute objClasses = new BasicAttribute("objectClass");
    objClasses.add("top");
    objClasses.add("person");
    objClasses.add("organizationalPerson");
    objClasses.add("inetOrgPerson");

    // Assign the username, first name, and last name
    String cnValue = new StringBuffer(firstName)
        .append(" ")
        .append(lastName)
        .toString( );
    Attribute cn = new BasicAttribute("cn", cnValue);
    Attribute givenName = new BasicAttribute("givenName", firstName);
    Attribute sn = new BasicAttribute("sn", lastName);
    Attribute uid = new BasicAttribute("uid", username);

    // Add password
    Attribute userPassword =
        new BasicAttribute("userpassword", password);

    // Add these to the container
    container.put(objClasses);
    container.put(cn);
    container.put(sn);
    container.put(givenName);
    container.put(uid);
    container.put(userPassword);

    // Create the entry
    context.createSubcontext(getUserDN(username), container);
}
```

Deleting users, or any type of subcontext, is a much simpler task. All you need to do is identify the name that the subcontext is bound to (in this case, the user's DN), and invoke the destroySubcontext( ) method on the manager's DirContext object. Additionally, while the method still throws a NamingException, it should trap one specific problem, the NameNotFoundException. This exception is thrown when the requested subcontext does not exist within the directory; however, because ensuring that the DN for the user specified *doesn't* exist is the point of the deleteUser( ) method, this problem is ignored. Whether the specified user is deleted, or did not exist prior to the method call, is irrelevant to the client. Add the deleteUser( ) method shown here to your source code:

```
public void deleteUser(String username) throws NamingException {
    try {
        context.destroySubcontext(getUserDN(username));
    } catch (NameNotFoundException e) {
        // If the user is not found, ignore the error
    }
}
```

Any other exceptions that might result, such as connection failures, are still reported through the NamingException that can be thrown in the method.

With these two methods in place, all user manipulation can be handled. You will notice, though, that I haven't discussed any methods to allow user modification. It would seem that without these methods, a user's password could not be changed, and their first or last name could not be updated. However, this is not the case. Instead of providing a method to allow those operations, it is easier to require components using the manager to delete the user and then re-create that user with the updated information. While this might seem a bit of a pain, keep in mind that you will have a component that handles all user actions and abstracts both this manager and the entity beans from the application layer. In other words, ease of use is not the primary concern in the manager. The advantage in not providing update methods is that it keeps the manager clear and simple; additionally, for the sake of only four attributes (if you count the username, which should not change anyway), update methods are simply not worth the trouble.

Authenticating the user

The last task the manager needs to perform that directly involves users (and only users; I'll look at working with users and other objects together a little later) is authentication. When a user first accesses the Forethought application, he or she will eventually try to access protected resources. At that point, authentication needs to occur; permissions and groups can be looked up, but first the user must provide a username and password. These, of course, must be pushed back to the directory server, and the manager should let the client component know if the username and password combination is valid.

The code for this is a piece of cake; in fact, you've already written it! Remember that the getInitialContext( ) method took a username and password in addition to a hostname and port number. You can use this same method with the username and password supplied to the new authentication method, isValidUser( ). The method then simply catches any exceptions that may occur. If there are no errors, a successful context was obtained and the user is valid; if errors occur, then problems resulted from authentication, and the user is rejected.

Any exception results in the isValidUser( ) method returning false, indicating that a login has failed. In a strict sense, this can return some false negatives; if the connection to a directory server has dropped, for example, the method returns false. This is somewhat deceptive, and in an industrial-strength application, a reconnection might be attempted in this case. However, in even medium-sized applications, a downed directory server will cripple an application anyway, so denying a user access is still the right thing to do. In other words, while the false result may not indicate a failed authentication, it does indicate that the user should not be allowed to continue.

You also need to be sure that you don't overwrite the existing DirContext instance, the member variable called context in the LDAPManager class, with any returned DirContext instance obtained in this method. If that happened, the credentials used in this method would determine what actions could be performed by the other methods. Few, if any, users other than the Directory Manager would be able to add, delete, and modify objects in the directory. You could end up with a very subtle bug that causes all operations on the directory to suddenly begin to fail. To avoid this, your code should create a local DirContext object (local to the method) called context,* and use that for obtaining a new context. This object is then automatically thrown away when the method exits. Enter in this method, as shown here:

```
public boolean isValidUser(String username, String password) {
    try {
        DirContext context =
            getInitialContext(hostname, port, getUserDN(username),
                              password);
        return true;
    } catch (NamingException e) {
        // Any error indicates couldn't log user in
        return false;
    }
}
```

Realize that in this example, assuming that your directory server is running on an unencrypted port, the user's password will be sent across the network as clear text. There is still a lot of protection in place, though, as the clients for this manager component will be within the application itself (in the servlet/login layer, which will be covered in detail in Volume II). However, you can increase security even further by installing your directory server on the SSL-enabled port, which by default is 636. This will allow encryption of all communication to the server, adding additional layers of protection for your users' passwords.

---

* Although this object shares the same name as the LDAPManager class's member variable, Java's rules of scoping take care of keeping the two distinct; one stays around in memory (the member variable) and one exists only for the duration of the isValidUser( ) method.

Groups

The next task involving directory servers is dealing with groups. The manager needs to allow clients to supply simple group names as opposed to group DNs, just as with users. Next, the manager needs to provide analogs to the addUser( ) and deleteUser( ) methods for adding and removing groups. You don't have to worry about group authentication. Later in this chapter, when we look at operations that involve more than one object (groups and users, permissions and groups, etc.), I'll look at some more group operations; for now, though, the conversion of group names and adding and deleting groups is all that is required.

Getting the distinguished name

As when dealing with users, you must first create a means to convert between a group's name (which is also the value of its cn attribute) and its distinguished name. First, define the GROUPS_OU constant, referring to the organizational unit under which groups are stored. Then, the manager can build the same sort of formula with String concatenation that was used to get the user DN. For a group called "clients", the DN becomes *cn=clients,ou=Groups,o=forethought.com*. Add the new constant and methods to your source file, as shown here:

```
/** The OU (organizational unit) to add groups to */
private static final String GROUPS_OU =
    "ou=Groups,o=forethought.com";

private String getGroupDN(String name) {
    return new StringBuffer( )
            .append("cn=")
            .append(name)
            .append(",")
            .append(GROUPS_OU)
            .toString( );
}

private String getGroupCN(String groupDN) {
    int start = groupDN.indexOf("=");
    int end = groupDN.indexOf(",");

    if (end == -1) {
        end = groupDN.length( );
    }

    return groupDN.substring(start+1, end);
}
```

Adding and deleting

Next, the manager needs to add and delete groups, just as it offers the ability to add and delete users. The only differences here are the object class hierarchy and the required attributes. The class hierarchy runs from the top-level object, appropriately named *top*, to *groupOfUniqueNames*, the default group object class, to *groupOfForethoughtNames*, the custom object class created in Chapter 3. The required attributes for a group are only its objectClass and cn (the group name). Add the method shown here:

```
public void addGroup(String name, String description)
    throws NamingException {

    // Create a container set of attributes
    Attributes container = new BasicAttributes();

    // Create the objectclass to add
    Attribute objClasses = new BasicAttribute("objectClass");
    objClasses.add("top");
    objClasses.add("groupOfUniqueNames");
    objClasses.add("groupOfForethoughtNames");

    // Assign the name and description to the group
    Attribute cn = new BasicAttribute("cn", name);
    Attribute desc = new BasicAttribute("description", description);

    // Add these to the container
    container.put(objClasses);
    container.put(cn);
    container.put(desc);

    // Create the entry
    context.createSubcontext(getGroupDN(name), container);
}
```

Just like deleting a user, deleting a group is a piece of cake. All we need to do is convert the group's name to the appropriate DN, and then destroy that subcontext:

```
public void deleteGroup(String name) throws NamingException {
    try {
        context.destroySubcontext(getGroupDN(name));
    } catch (NameNotFoundException e) {
        // If the group is not found, ignore the error
    }
}
```

And, as simple as that, you are finished with basic group interactions.

Permissions

This is starting to sound like something from the department of redundancy department, but you now need to duplicate the functionality for working with groups and users to allow the manager to add and remove permissions. This should be a piece of cake at this point.

Getting the distinguished name

By now, you should know the formula by heart. Find out the organizational unit under which permissions should exist, and create a PERMISSIONS_OU constant. Determine what attribute the permission's name is stored as (in this case, cn); look at the permission's name and DN (for the name "addUser", the DN is *cn=addUser, ou=Permissions,o=forethought.com*), and code the appropriate conversion methods. The code to add to your source is shown here:

```
/** The OU (organizational unit) to add permissions to */
private static final String PERMISSIONS_OU =
    "ou=Permissions,o=forethought.com";

private String getPermissionDN(String name) {
    return new StringBuffer( )
            .append("cn=")
            .append(name)
            .append(",")
            .append(PERMISSIONS_OU)
            .toString( );
}

private String getPermissionCN(String permissionDN) {
    int start = permissionDN.indexOf("=");
    int end = permissionDN.indexOf(",");

    if (end == -1) {
        end = permissionDN.length( );
    }

    return permissionDN.substring(start+1, end);
}
```

Adding and deleting

There is not much surprising here either. The class hierarchy is the simplest yet, starting at the *top* object class and moving on to the custom class *forethoughtPermission*. The required attributes are the objectClass and cn of the permission, and you can throw in a description value for good measure. Add in the following method:

```
public void addPermission(String name, String description)
        throws NamingException {

    // Create a container set of attributes
    Attributes container = new BasicAttributes( );

    // Create the objectclass to add
    Attribute objClasses = new BasicAttribute("objectClass");
    objClasses.add("top");
    objClasses.add("forethoughtPermission");
```

```
    // Assign the name and description to the group
    Attribute cn = new BasicAttribute("cn", name);
    Attribute desc = new BasicAttribute("description", description);

    // Add these to the container
    container.put(objClasses);
    container.put(cn);
    container.put(desc);

    // Create the entry
    context.createSubcontext(getPermissionDN(name), container);
}
```

Same song, third verse. Converting a permission's name to its DN and destroying that subcontext takes care of the deletePermission( ) method. Add this in now:

```
public void deletePermission(String name) throws NamingException {
    try {
        context.destroySubcontext(getPermissionDN(name));
    } catch (NameNotFoundException e) {
        // If the permission is not found, ignore the error
    }
}
```

With manipulation of these three basic object types complete, it's time to move on to adding some glue between the types. We'll now look at adding users to groups and permissions to groups, joining these objects in the directory in a usable way.

Tying It Together

It's time to build some more useful features into the manager. Assignment operations will be used far more often than simple addition and deletion methods, so in this section, I discuss establishing links between users and groups and between groups and permissions.

It's important at this point to get an idea of how the Forethought application will use groups and permissions. First, it is possible to establish that users will never have individual permissions assigned to them; I talked about this in some detail in Chapter 3. In fact, the *inetOrgPerson* object class has no attribute for assigning permissions at all. Instead, permissions will be assigned to groups, and then groups will have users assigned to them. This ends up as a rather standard-looking schema, where the groups in the directory act as a join table. Figure 6-6 illustrates this relationship.

In the Forethought application, both groups and permissions are required. A group provides a coarse-grained security mechanism. Group membership implies a general area of operation; for example, a user may be assigned to the *Employee*, *Broker*, and *Manager* groups. This doesn't necessarily say that the user can create a new fund; that level of access would be associated with a specific permission. However, many components, such as a company directory component, would allow anyone in the

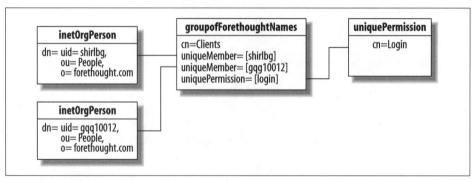

Figure 6-6. Relating permissions to users

Employee group some level of access; this is an example of a coarse-grained access control. Permissions, in contrast, are intended to be much more granular. While a group may provide access to a specific component, a permission might determine the data returned from that component. For example, all members of the *Employee* group can access the company directory, but only users with the *updateUsers* permission are given access to an "Update" link in the directory form. This isn't to say that groups cannot be used for this sort of access, just that it is more common to ask for a specific permission, as that permission might be assigned to multiple groups. With that in mind, you're ready to create relationships between users, groups, and permissions.

Addition and removal of users

As you can see from Figure 6-6, one half of the bridge between users and permissions is the assignment of a user to a group. I will look at this part of the bridge here; in the next section, we'll build the other half.

First, the manager needs to handle the addition of a user to a group; this merely requires the client to supply the username and group name. Like the other manager methods, conversions from a username to a user DN and from a group name to a group DN are handled by the utility methods getUserDN( ) and getGroupDN( ).

The membership of a user in a group is stored within the group's uniqueMember attribute. Adding a user to a group entails simply locating the group and adding the user's DN to that group's uniqueMember attribute. You'll remember that attributes in an object class can have multiple values, which is the case here. You should create a new BasicAttribute, assign it the attribute name "uniqueMember", and then give it the value of the supplied user's distinguished name. This method also introduces a new JNDI class: the javax.naming.directory.ModificationItem class. When a context has attributes modified in a directory server, JNDI clients need to use the modifyAttributes( ) method of the DirContext class. This method takes as an argument the name of the context to modify (the group's DN), and an array of ModificationItem objects. Conveniently, this allows modification of multiple attributes in one method call; in this case, though, the manager is making only a single change.

The constructor of a ModificationItem takes as arguments the type of modification and the attribute being modified (an instance of the Attribute class, or rather one of its implementations). The DirContext class provides constants for the types of modifications allowed; these constants are summarized in Table 6-1.

Table 6-1. The DirContext constants for modification types

Constant	Purpose	Example
ADD_ATTRIBUTE	Adds a new value to the attribute supplied.	Adds a member to a group.
REMOVE_ATTRIBUTE	Removes a value from the attribute supplied.	Removes a member from a group.
REPLACE_ATTRIBUTE	Replaces an existing value with the supplied value.	Replaces the last name of a user with a (different) married name.

In the case of adding a user, you should use the ADD_ATTRIBUTE constant; for deleting, use REMOVE_ATTRIBUTE. You can create an array of requested modifications (an array of one, in both adding and deleting), create the attribute class and value to be added, drop that attribute into the array of modifications, and then invoke the modifyAttributes( ) method with the group's DN and modification. The only other note is that when adding a user, you should ignore the AttributeInUseException; this indicates that the attribute, in the case of ADD_ATTRIBUTE, is already added. In other words, the user is already a member of the supplied group. This is fine, so no error needs to be reported back to the client. In the case of deletion, the same process occurs; however, in that case the code should ignore the NoSuchAttribute exception, which indicates that the user requested for removal wasn't in the requested group to begin with. This is all you need to know to implement the assignUser( ) and removeUser( ) methods, which are shown here:

```java
public void assignUser(String username, String groupName)
    throws NamingException {

    try {
        ModificationItem[] mods = new ModificationItem[1];

        Attribute mod =
            new BasicAttribute("uniqueMember",
                            getUserDN(username));
        mods[0] =
            new ModificationItem(DirContext.ADD_ATTRIBUTE, mod);
        context.modifyAttributes(getGroupDN(groupName), mods);
    } catch (AttributeInUseException e) {
        // If user is already added, ignore exception
    }
}
```

```
public void removeUser(String username, String groupName)
    throws NamingException {

    try {
        ModificationItem[] mods = new ModificationItem[1];

        Attribute mod =
            new BasicAttribute("uniqueMember",
                                getUserDN(username));
        mods[0] =
            new ModificationItem(DirContext.REMOVE_ATTRIBUTE, mod);
        context.modifyAttributes(getGroupDN(groupName), mods);
    } catch (NoSuchAttributeException e) {
        // If user is not assigned, ignore the error
    }
}
```

Verification of group memberships

Once groups and users are tied together, the next logical step is to be able to verify, programmatically, what these ties are for a certain user. Assigning user "shirlbg" to the "clients" group doesn't do much good if clients can't later determine whether she is in that group. Therefore, the manager needs a userInGroup( ) method. This method will take a username and group name as arguments, and return true if the specified user is in the supplied group, false if not. It also makes sense to provide a means of obtaining *all* users within a group, the getMembers( ) method. This ability is useful in two cases: first, as an administration utility, and second, as a means of not having to constantly access the directory server with userInGroup( ) method invocations.

In both of these cases, the manager code will use the getAttributes( ) method that the DirContext class provides. This method takes a subcontext identifier (in this case, the DN of the group being checked), and optionally an array of Strings, each with the name of an attribute to search for. If no array is provided, all attributes on the specified subcontext are returned. Providing this array is a good idea, though, as it reduces the attributes that must be searched within the directory. In both of these methods, only values for the uniqueMember attribute are needed. These values are provided as an array to the getAttributes( ) method; the array is a list of one, the single value "uniqueMember". This method returns an Attributes object with all the requested values. Here, though, this is a list of one, containing just the single Attribute class correlating to the uniqueMember attribute.

The work isn't quite complete yet; remember that a single LDAP attribute can have multiple values. Because of this, you can't get a single value from the Attribute instance; instead you need to iterate through all of the values for that attribute. The NamingEnumeration class aids in moving through these values. At this point, the two methods slightly diverge: the userInGroup( ) method returns true as soon as it finds an entry that matches the user's DN; the getMembers( ) method adds all returned members to a List and returns that List to the invoking component.

If you check the JNDI documentation, you will notice that the Attribute class provides a method called get() that takes a Java Object and returns a boolean indicating whether the Attribute has that object value. You might be tempted to use that method in the userInGroup() method instead of running through a NamingEnumeration and performing comparisons. However, the get() method provides no means of performing a case-insensitive comparison, and instead would perform case-sensitive String comparison; since the DNs in a directory are case-insensitive, this would cause problems. Use the code as-is, or be prepared for some nasty surprises!

You can add these two new methods, shown here, to your LDAPManager source file:

```
public boolean userInGroup(String username, String groupName)
    throws NamingException {

    // Set up attributes to search for
    String[] searchAttributes = new String[1];
    searchAttributes[0] = "uniqueMember";

    Attributes attributes =
        context.getAttributes(getGroupDN(groupName),
                              searchAttributes);
    if (attributes != null) {
        Attribute memberAtts = attributes.get("uniqueMember");
        if (memberAtts != null) {
            for (NamingEnumeration vals = memberAtts.getAll();
                vals.hasMoreElements();
                ) {
                if (username.equalsIgnoreCase(
                    getUserUID((String)vals.nextElement()))) {
                    return true;
                }
            }
        }
    }

    return false;
}

public List getMembers(String groupName) throws NamingException {
    List members = new LinkedList();

    // Set up attributes to search for
    String[] searchAttributes = new String[1];
    searchAttributes[0] = "uniqueMember";

    Attributes attributes =
        context.getAttributes(getGroupDN(groupName),
                              searchAttributes);
    if (attributes != null) {
        Attribute memberAtts = attributes.get("uniqueMember");
        if (memberAtts != null) {
```

```
        for (NamingEnumeration vals = memberAtts.getAll( );
            vals.hasMoreElements( );
            members.add(
                getUserUID((String)vals.nextElement( )))) ;
    }
}

    return members;
}
```

While this handles any lookups from the group side, it still leaves one task undone from the user angle: clients need to be able to find all the groups that a user is in. This task is little trickier than it appears; remember that the group object has knowledge about the users belonging to it, but users have no easy means of tracing the relationship the other way. (Refer back to Figure 6-6 if you need to.) As a result, it is not possible to locate a user and look up the user's groups through an attribute, as you could to find the members of a group. To address this issue, I'll now introduce the search( ) method on the DirContext object. This method is for cases just like this, where the developer needs to "take control" and directly specify search criteria that go beyond the simple relationships discussed so far. The search( ) method takes three parameters: the context to start searching at, a search filter, and a SearchControls object, which specifies constraints on how searching is performed.

The context allows you to narrow the portion of the directory searched; obviously, broader searches, which start at the root or high up in the tree, take more time to perform. In this case, you are looking specifically for groups, and know that all groups are located under the organizational unit *Groups*. In fact, there is already a constant for that subcontext, GROUPS_OU. So the context is taken care of.

The next piece of information, the search filter, becomes the key in most searches. The first step in building this filter is identifying the criteria (not necessarily in code format, but with simple words), which in this case is fairly simple. First, you want to locate all groups, as you are interested only in group objects. It is possible to isolate these objects by their objectClass attribute, which you know will always be groupOfForethoughtNames. The filter format for this is simply (objectClass= groupOfForethoughtNames). All search criteria must be enclosed in parentheses; this allows combination of expressions, which you'll want in just a moment. Within those parentheses simply provide the attribute name, the equals sign, and the value you are searching for. Wildcards are also acceptable, so a criterion of (cn=s*) would return all users whose cn attribute starts with the letter "s". This would include "Shirley Greathouse" as well as "Sergei Zubov". Adding to this filter, you need to request that for all the groups found, return only those whose uniqueMember attribute contains the DN of the user supplied. This portion of the search criteria, then, becomes (uniqueMember=userDN), where userDN is the supplied user's distinguished name. Finally, you need to tie the two search criteria together through reverse polish notation,* where the format of an expression is (operator operand operand). The operands are the two expressions, and the operator is the ampersand (&), which indicates a logical AND. The result of this rather strange discussion is the expression (&(objectClass=groupOfForethoughtNames)(uniqueMember= userDN)). So now you have the second item in the search criteria.

Directory Names and Directory Names

So far, I have used Java Strings for specifying the names of subcontexts in the various JNDI methods, including the getAttributes( ) method and the search( ) method. However, this is only one way to deal with directory subcontext names; the javax.naming.Name class provides another. This class allows for a greater degree of manipulation of JNDI names, as it has methods to allow composition of a name. In other words, you can take multiple Name objects and compose them into a single (new) Name, perhaps adding an organizational unit (*ou=People*) to a directory server's root (*o=forethought.com*). This is especially usefully when working with programs that browse directories, needing to add a new context name to an existing context name. All of the methods you have seen that take a simple String for a context's name also will accept a JNDI Name object. In the application so far, though, you have always known the exact name of the desired subcontext, and so have not needed this additional functionality. You can certainly use both forms of naming in your own JNDI-based applications.

All that's left is the SearchControls object, which allows for constraining the search to only part of a tree in order to limit the number of results and the time spent in searching. I will touch on it here only briefly, so consult the JNDI documentation for more information about this useful class. In this case, you'll use it to limit the scope of the search. Recall that all groups are directly under the *Groups* organizational unit, which was specified as the context to start searching at. This enables the code to specify that it wants only one level of the LDAP tree to be searched, as opposed to the entire tree, which is the default option. Figure 6-7 shows the difference, and it is obvious that you will get performance gains from this constraint.

On the left side of Figure 6-7, you see the result of searching all of a tree below the starting point, specified by the constant SearchControls.SUBTREE_SCOPE. Compare this to searching only one level deep, using the SearchControls.ONELEVEL_SCOPE, which is shown on the right. This is the only option to set on the search constraints; then, the manager is finally ready to search the directory. The result of the search is a

---

* If you've ever used a graphical or higher-end mathematical calculator, you've probably dealt with this; reverse polish calculators were very popular in the early 90's. I have no idea if they are still popular today, as I left high school and college well behind me!

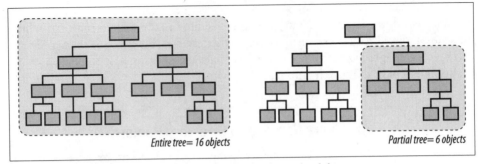

Entire tree= 16 objects   *Partial tree= 6 objects*

Figure 6-7. Searching an entire tree versus searching only one level deep

NamingEnumeration instance, which the manager can iterate through, converting each returned group DN into a simple name and adding the name to the groups list. This completed list is then returned to the invoker of the method.

 It is important to note that the values returned, all of type javax.naming. directory.SearchResult, have names that are DNs. What is actually interesting is the DN itself, in that it is relative to the starting context of the search. In other words, the name of the group "Administrators" is not reported as *cn=Administrators,ou=Groups,o=forethought.com*, because the starting context was *ou=Groups,o=forethought.com*. Relative to that context, the group's name becomes simply *cn=Administrators*. When this is sent to our getGroupCN( ) method, the check to set the end variable to the length of the input String, when there is no trailing comma in the group's DN, comes into play. Failing to do that check would result in the returned String either being gibberish, or creating an error before it was even sent back to the caller.

Enter this method as shown here:

```
public List getGroups(String username) throws NamingException {
    List groups = new LinkedList( );

    // Set up criteria to search on
    String filter = new StringBuffer( )
        .append("(&")
        .append("(objectClass=groupOfForethoughtNames)")
        .append("(uniqueMember=")
        .append(getUserDN(username))
        .append(")")
        .append(")")
        .toString( );

    // Set up search constraints
    SearchControls cons = new SearchControls( );
    cons.setSearchScope(SearchControls.ONELEVEL_SCOPE);

    NamingEnumeration results =
        context.search(GROUPS_OU, filter, cons);
```

```
    while (results.hasMore()) {
        SearchResult result = (SearchResult)results.next();
        groups.add(getGroupCN(result.getName()));
    }

    return groups;
}
```

With this method in place, you have all the tools needed to determine whether a user is in a group, as well as to find the members of a group and the groups of a user. You can now move on to permissions.

Assignment and revocation of permissions

The other half of the bridge between users and permissions is the link from groups to permissions. As with assigning a user to a group, the manager needs to allow assignment of a permission to a group and revocation of a permission from a group. In fact, other than some semantics ("assign" instead of "add", and "revoke" instead of "remove"), the methods to assign and revoke permissions to and from groups are nearly identical to the addition and removal of users to and from groups. The only other significant change is the attribute being modified: uniquePermission as compared to uniqueMember. I won't bore you with explanation of concepts already covered, and instead I'll just show you the code that needs to be added to the LDAPManager class:

```
public void assignPermission(String groupName, String permissionName)
    throws NamingException {

    try {
        ModificationItem[] mods = new ModificationItem[1];

        Attribute mod =
            new BasicAttribute("uniquePermission",
                            getPermissionDN(permissionName));
        mods[0] =
            new ModificationItem(DirContext.ADD_ATTRIBUTE, mod);
        context.modifyAttributes(getGroupDN(groupName), mods);
    } catch (AttributeInUseException e) {
        // Ignore the attribute if it is already assigned
    }
}

public void revokePermission(String groupName, String permissionName)
    throws NamingException {

    try {
        ModificationItem[] mods = new ModificationItem[1];

        Attribute mod =
            new BasicAttribute("uniquePermission",
                            getPermissionDN(permissionName));
```

```
        mods[0] =
            new ModificationItem(DirContext.REMOVE_ATTRIBUTE, mod);
        context.modifyAttributes(getGroupDN(groupName), mods);
    } catch (NoSuchAttributeException e) {
        // Ignore errors if the attribute doesn't exist
    }
}
```

Verification of permissions

In addition to finding out if a certain group has a particular member, you also need to be able to determine if a group has a particular permission assigned to it. In the same vein, the manager needs to be able to obtain all of the permissions assigned to a particular group. Fortunately, the two methods needed, hasPermission( ) and getPermissions( ), are simple cut-and-paste operations from the userInGroup( ) and isMember( ) methods. Just change the attribute searched on from uniqueMember to uniquePermission, and you're home free. Enter in the methods as shown here:

```
public boolean hasPermission(String groupName, String permissionName)
    throws NamingException {

    // Set up attributes to search for
    String[] searchAttributes = new String[1];
    searchAttributes[0] = "uniquePermission";

    Attributes attributes =
        context.getAttributes(getGroupDN(groupName),
                              searchAttributes);
    if (attributes != null) {
        Attribute permAtts = attributes.get("uniquePermission");
        if (permAtts != null) {
            for (NamingEnumeration vals = permAtts.getAll( );
                 vals.hasMoreElements( );
                 ) {
                if (permissionName.equalsIgnoreCase(
                    getPermissionCN((String)vals.nextElement( )))) {
                    return true;
                }
            }
        }
    }

    return false;
}

public List getPermissions(String groupName) throws NamingException {
    List permissions = new LinkedList( );

    // Set up attributes to search for
    String[] searchAttributes = new String[1];
    searchAttributes[0] = "uniquePermission";
```

```
Attributes attributes =
    context.getAttributes(getGroupDN(groupName),
                          searchAttributes);
if (attributes != null) {
    Attribute permAtts = attributes.get("uniquePermission");
    if (permAtts != null) {
        for (NamingEnumeration vals = permAtts.getAll();
             vals.hasMoreElements();
             permissions.add(
                 getPermissionCN((String)vals.nextElement()))) ;
    }
}

return permissions;
}
```

You've now added the needed functionality to interact with the Forethought directory server (or any other directory server, with very small changes). There are some higher-level interactions you'll need, such as finding out if a specific user has a specific permission, but I'll leave these computations to session beans and other components layered on top of the LDAPManager component.

What's Next?

You're almost finished with the Forethought data layer, which is a major milestone in any application development. In the next chapter, I'll spend some time looking at a few odds and ends. These little details will make the application perform a little better and be easier to use, and will help you in your other programming tasks. From there, you will populate the database and directory server. In addition to seeding the application with data, this will show you how clients interact with the programming constructs already developed.

## CHAPTER 7

Completing the Data Layer

You've made it through the first section of the application, the data structure. Of course, this is simply the raw information used in the application. While it's almost time to begin coding the next tier of the application, the business layer, it's worth taking a moment to make sure things are working correctly, and perform a few optimizations and clean-up tasks.

In this chapter, I'll first look at several items that can help improve the efficiency, performance, and cleanliness of the application code discussed so far. As in the creation of any application, a lot of ground has been covered very quickly. It is worth taking a short break from adding features in order to really wrap up the data layer; those who inherit your code some day will be glad you did. From there, I'll move on to showing you how to realistically test your application, and write a client for the various beans and the LDAP manager that are in place. This also gives you a chance to populate your data stores, so the examples in the rest of the book will be using the same data as in my version of the application. More importantly, if you're not familiar with using RMI, JNDI, and contexts with your beans, you'll see this sort of client in action. At the end of the chapter, you can say you've got a complete, functional, polished data layer, which is quite an accomplishment.

Odds and Ends

So far, you have concentrated completely on data layer functionality; while this results in a working application, it doesn't necessarily produce a *good* application. To start with, look again at the LDAPManager class. The biggest problem in this manager component is that, at best, it does a mediocre job of managing connections to the directory server. When dealing with entity beans, this was a minor issue; the EJB container was handling all database connections, and was presumably using some connection pools and object caching to improve performance. However, with the LDAP manager, there is no container to take care of these details. This means that when users complain of latency when accessing your directory server, the blame falls squarely on your shoulders (and mine).

Currently, each client of the directory server interacts with the manager by invoking the LDAPManager constructor and using the new keyword. However, each invocation of the constructor results in a new connection being created to the directory server. Not only does this add overhead to the clients, but it also could easily result in ten, fifteen, or even more connections to the same directory server being open at any point in time. So clients pay for a new connection, but then accessing the server is slowed because multiple connections are vying for the same server and data. This is not scalable in any reasonable way. In this section, I'll detail some minor changes to the manager component that will enable connection sharing and reuse. These simple changes will take the LDAPManager component from simply functional to scalable in a high-volume, distributed application.

Connection Sharing

The simplest change to make to the manager component is to move the connection from an instance level to a class level. In this way, the manager can create a single connection for *all* instances, instead of a connection for *each* instance. There are actually two ways to handle this. The first involves moving the DirContext instance in the class from a normal member variable to a static variable of the class. The second is to actually turn the manager into a singleton, and share a single LDAPManager instance (not just the DirContext object) for all requests. Figure 7-1 illustrates the difference between these two approaches.

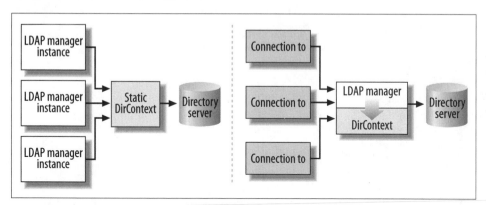

Figure 7-1. Sharing the DirContext instance versus sharing the LDAPManager instance

At first glance, these might seem identical; however, the difference is in the information that becomes shared. In the approach on the left in Figure 7-1, sharing just the DirContext, no other instance variables are shared. The problem here is that it is possible to end up with a connection (the DirContext object) that is shared, but local variables (like the port and hostname variables) that are different for various clients. This is certainly not a desired result, and can become quite confusing to a client. In contrast, the approach on the right, sharing a single LDAPManager instance, allows clients to share instance information as well. This ensures that the hostname, port, and other instance variables are kept in sync across all clients, reducing confusion. This approach is obviously preferable to simply sharing a connection, as the instance variables are used in methods like isValidUser( ) and need to be managed across all clients.

To effect this change, then, you should create a static variable in the LDAPManager class that will be the single, shared instance. Add this variable to the source file:

```
/** The LDAPManager instance object */
private static LDAPManager instance = null;

/** The connection, through a <code>DirContext</code>, to LDAP */
private DirContext context;

/** The hostname connected to */
private String hostname;

/** The port connected to */
private int port;
```

Once this variable is in place, you also need to ensure that clients cannot create instances on their own; otherwise, this shared connection becomes useless, as some clients will use it and others will create their own manager instances. The simplest means of preventing this problem is to make the constructor for the class inaccessible. You can change the accessor from public to protected to effect this change. You can then also discard all of the overloaded constructors, as the overloading will be on the method that returns the shared instance. Make the changes shown here:

```
protected LDAPManager(String hostname, int port,
                       String username, String password)
    throws NamingException {

    context = getInitialContext(hostname, port, username, password);

    // Only save data if we got connected
    this.hostname = hostname;
    this.port = port;
}

// All other constructors are removed
```

Now, you can create the analog of these constructors, a set of methods that returns this shared instance. Call this method getInstance( ); this is the standard practice when using the singleton pattern. This method has the same arguments supplied to it as your old constructors, and it's simple to overload these, providing three versions of getInstance( ), as well. This method should also be made static so that clients can access it, as shown here:

```
// Get the shared instance
LDAPManager manager =
    LDAPManager.getInstance("galadriel.middleearth.com",
                            389);
```

```
manager.addUser("shirlbg", "Shirley", "Greathouse", "nellbell");
// other manager operations
```

All that's left, then, is the implementation. Since the instance variable was assigned an initial value of null, getInstance() can check against this value to see if a new instance needs to be created, or if an existing one can be returned. If an instance does need to be created, some synchronization is called for. You should synchronize here to ensure that two simultaneous requests don't *both* create new instances, as that would result in dual instances being supplied to clients. Once the code is in a synchronized block, it again compares the instance variable to null. Why? For the exact same reason discussed previously. If two requests come in and both find the instance variable equal to null, one will obtain the object lock and create a new LDAPManager instance; the second, once it obtains the lock, should not create a new instance. Thus, a second comparison within the synchronized block ensures that only one instance is created. Finally, the ready-for-use instance is returned, as it was either ready to use in the first place or was newly created. It is this set of operations that results in the class being a singleton. A single instance is being made available to all clients, rather than direct object instantiation occurring. Enter these changes as they are shown here:

```
public static LDAPManager getInstance(String hostname,
                                      int port,
                                      String username,
                                      String password)
    throws NamingException {

    if (instance == null) {
        synchronized (LDAPManager.class) {
            if (instance == null) {
                instance =
                    new LDAPManager(hostname, port,
                                    username, password);
            }
        }
    }
    return instance;
}

public static LDAPManager getInstance(String hostname, int port)
    throws NamingException {

    return getInstance(hostname, port, null, null);
}

public static LDAPManager getInstance(String hostname)
    throws NamingException {

    return getInstance(hostname, DEFAULT_PORT, null, null);
}
```

The result of this is that only one connection to a directory server is used for all clients. Therefore, clients requesting an instance of the manager get faster responses, as they are not waiting for a new connection to be made. Response time for all methods is also reduced, as multiple connections are not competing for the same resources.

 To clarify, the instance of the LDAPManager class will be shared across all clients in the same Java virtual machine (JVM). If you have multiple JVMs on the same machine, or if your application is spread across multiple servers (both common occurrences in enterprise applications), multiple instances of the manager component will occur. However, the result is still a drastic improvement in performance. This situation also doesn't require a change in your code, other than perhaps raising some synchronization issues, which I address now.

Synchronization

All of you Java threading experts out there are probably just dying to throw some synchronized keywords into the rest of the manager code now. However, hold off on that; the manager doesn't need them. Let me explain a little further. Now that there is only a single shared instance, it is possible that multiple clients will request the same method with the same data. Imagine that the user with username "gqg10012", first name "Gary", last name "Greathouse", and password "hunting" is requested for addition by two different clients, at the same time.

While you could synchronize all of the manager's methods, particularly the addXXX( ) and assignXXX( ) methods, this really isn't such a good idea. It adds a lot of overhead, as only one thread can invoke the method at a time. More pointedly, is it really that common for the same exact user or group to be added to an application at the same time? In fact, is it common for *any* object to be added very often to the directory? The truth of the matter is that it is not. Generally, a single client adds users in batches, or rarely; in these cases, synchronization is not an issue.

Since you will rarely encounter threading problems, synchronizing all of the manager's methods is certain to slow down all clients for the sake of a very small percentage of them. In the very odd occasion that you do run into this problem, a NamingException will be thrown, and clients can easily handle that case. But clearly, an occasional error is well worth it for the sake of greatly speeding up the rest of your application. Leave the methods as-is; your users will thank you for it.

Multiple Directory Servers

There is one more issue to address before leaving the LDAP manager component, and that is the very subtle problem left in the manager code. It is illustrated in Figure 7-2, and should worry you quite a bit.

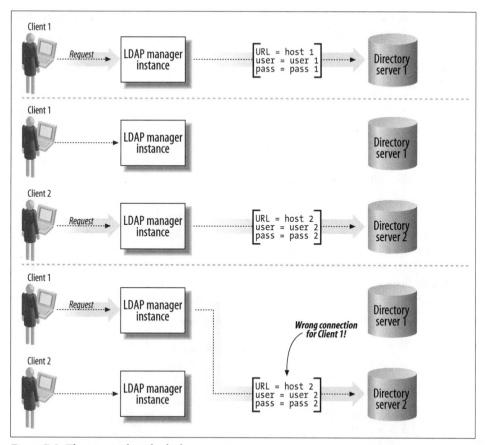

Figure 7-2. The issue with multiple directory servers

What happens here is that client 1 requests an instance of LDAPManager, with the hostname and port of directory server 1. An instance is created, and returned to client 1. Now, because this is a particularly robust application, directory server 2 is used as well. Perhaps a different user class is stored here, or entirely different information altogether; in either case, two servers are used for performance and scalability. So client 2 requests a connection, through the LDAPManager component, to directory server 2. The LDAPManager class receives the hostname and port for this server, and as its instance variable is already created (and therefore non-null), it happily returns the instance connected to directory server 1. And then…well, things get pretty ugly.

To prevent this situation, you should make a final modification to the way shared instances are handled. Instead of maintaining a single instance, the manager needs to maintain a single instance *per* hostname, port number, and credentials combination. This is not particularly hard to do; the manager can store instances in a Java Map structure, using a unique key for each combination of connection information. First, add the needed import statements:

```
import java.util.Properties;
import java.util.HashMap;
import java.util.LinkedList;
import java.util.List;
import java.util.Map;
// Other import statements...
```

Additionally, you need to change the single instance variable to the Map structure:

```
/** The LDAPManager instance object */
private static Map instances = new HashMap();
```

Finally, change the getInstance() method, the version that is called by all of the others. The change requires that a key value first be constructed for the map, which will be unique for each combination of server details and authentication credentials. The method should also ensure that no NullPointerExceptions occur by checking the values of the username and password variables before using them. It then checks to see whether an instance exists for that key, and returns that instance if it does; if not, the method creates one and returns that. Make the changes shown here:

```
public static LDAPManager getInstance(String hostname,
                                      int port,
                                      String username,
                                      String password)
    throws NamingException {

    // Construct the key for the supplied information
    String key = new StringBuffer()
        .append(hostname)
        .append(":")
        .append(port)
        .append("|")
        .append((username == null ? "" : username))
        .append("|")
        .append((password == null ? "" : password))
        .toString();

    if (!instances.containsKey(key)) {
        synchronized (LDAPManager.class) {
            if (!instances.containsKey(key)) {
                LDAPManager instance =
                    new LDAPManager(hostname, port,
                                    username, password);
                instances.put(key, instance);
                return instance;
            }
        }
    }

    return (LDAPManager)instances.get(key);
}
```

Error Reporting

Last, but not least, there are some details left unfinished with regard to error reporting. So far, I haven't covered error conditions in the manager, other than the basic NamingException that can occur. For example, consider the isValidUser() method, whose signature is shown here:

```
public boolean isValidUser(String username, String password);
```

This method simply returns true or false, depending on whether the credentials supplied result in a successful authentication. However, is it accurate to have only two possible results from this set of credentials? Table 7-1 lists the possibilities that can occur, and indicates a third result that the isValid() method currently masks.

Table 7-1. Results from user credentials check

Username	Password	Current result	Desired result
Valid	Invalid	False	False
Valid	Valid	True	True
Invalid	Invalid	False	???

As you can see, a client cannot distinguish between an invalid user, who should be denied access, and a valid user with an incorrect password, who might be given a chance to request their password by email, for example. You therefore need a means of reporting the condition where the username supplied is not found. Because this is an *exceptional* case, using an Exception class makes perfect sense:

```
public boolean isValidUser(String username, String password)
    throws UserNotFoundException;
```

You can extend the basic ForethoughtException class discussed in Chapter 5 to report this problem; you simply need to store some information specific to the error being reported. In this case, holding the username that was specified can make the error message much more informative. Additionally, a first name and last name are stored, in the event that this exception is later used by methods that search by a user's complete name rather than username. Example 7-1 shows this new exception class, which inherits from ForethoughtException.

Example 7-1. The UserNotFound Exception Class

```
package com.forethought.ldap;

import com.forethought.ForethoughtException;

public class UserNotFoundException extends ForethoughtException {

    /** The username searched for */
    private String username;
```

Example 7-1. The UserNotFound Exception Class (continued)

```
    /** The user's first name searched for */
    private String firstName;

    /** The user's last name searched for */
    private String lastName;

    public UserNotFoundException(String username) {
        super("A user with the username " + username +
            " could not be found.");
        this.username = username;
    }

    public UserNotFoundException(String firstName, String lastName) {
        super("A user with the name " + firstName +
            " " + lastName + " could not be found.");
        this.username = username;
    }

    public String getUsername( ) {
        return username;
    }

    public String getFirstName( ) {
        return firstName;
    }

    public String getLastName( ) {
        return lastName;
    }
}
```

With these two exceptions ready for use, you can go back and update the isValidUser( ) method to use the new exception system:

```
    public boolean isValidUser(String username, String password)
        throws UserNotFoundException {
        try {
            DirContext context =
                getInitialContext(hostname, port, getUserDN(username),
                                  password);
            return true;
        } catch (javax.naming.NameNotFoundException) {
            throw new UserNotFoundException(username);
        } catch (NamingException e) {
            // Any other error indicates couldn't log user in
            return false;
        }
    }
```

Finally, it's time to compile and close up shop on the LDAPManager class, and populate your application's data store.

Checkpoint

You are now ready to prepare a client to access your beans and manager, and populate the data stores. Before coding this test client, ensure that you have all your Java classes set up and ready for use. As this is a book about enterprise applications, usually distributed across multiple machines, this is not as simple as in a traditional, standalone application. Often certain classes are on one server, while others are on another server; there are backups, load-balanced servers, fail-over servers, and so on. The Forethought application has a fairly simplistic setup: all classes are located on a single server. This represents the logical unit, which in your own applications may be a single physical server, or may be multiple servers. For example, you might have entity beans on one server, session beans on another, your web server on a third, and then have multiple machines for backup on top of those.

Additionally, you will have clients that are presumably separate from the server. I *will* assume that any clients are physically separate from the server and its code, as that is the typical case in enterprise applications. The trick, then, is getting the right classes on the server for the server to operate, and then the right classes on the client to allow access to the server. Server classes are simple: for the most part, you'll just throw everything on the server. With EJB, for example, the remote and home interface, the primary key class, a value class (if there is one), and the implementation class should all be on the server. The task of setting the client up, though, is not as simple.

In the case of a web client, nothing is needed on the client, as a simple web browser is used and all program execution occurs on the server. However, you aren't quite to that point yet; you need a client that can operate upon your EJB entity beans directly. Therefore, the client must be able to access the remote interface of the EJBs locally. But to get to the remote interface, you need to also make the home interface available for looking up beans. Additionally, if finders are used, the primary key class is often required on the client. And finally, the value objects that are used by the client to cut down on all that RMI traffic need to be present. So for EJB work, all but the implementation classes are needed on both server and client, and the implementation classes are also needed on the server. Any beans not directly accessed by clients, like our Sequence bean, are also kept only on the server. And for directory server access, our LDAPManager class needs to reside on the client. While that class is not technically needed on the server yet, you should go ahead and put it there as well: you'll have session beans that use it later.

So you now need to check and ensure that all of your classes are in the right place. Figure 7-3 shows the structure you should have in place on your server.

Once you have the server setup, you can create a similar organization for your client's classes. This is shown in Figure 7-4.

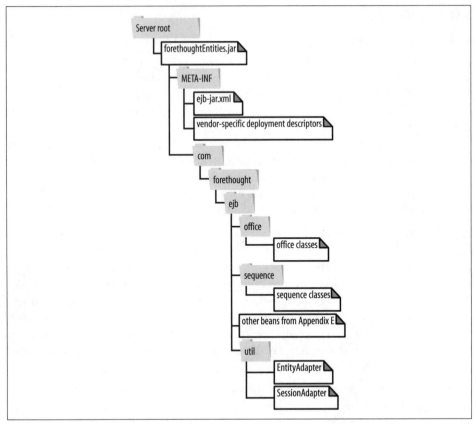

Figure 7-3. Server class hierarchy

 If you have only a single physical machine at your disposal, you can use the CLASSPATH environment variable on your system to mimic this client/server setup. For example, if you have a directory called *serverclasses/* and one called *clientclasses/*, you could put your server classes in the former and client classes in the latter. Then open up two (different) console windows or DOS prompts. In the server window, set the CLASSPATH variable to include only the *serverclasses/* classes, and in the client window, make only the *clientclasses/* classes available to the JVM. This effectively mimics the setup of two different machines, and will allow you to test your configuration as if you had two servers.

Populating the Data Stores

Once everything is in place, you are ready to get to data population. Example 7-2 shows a client class, called EntityCreator, that connects to the application server, creates a lot of sample data, and then does the same for the directory server. While the class is fairly long, it does almost nothing very exciting. Your work through the

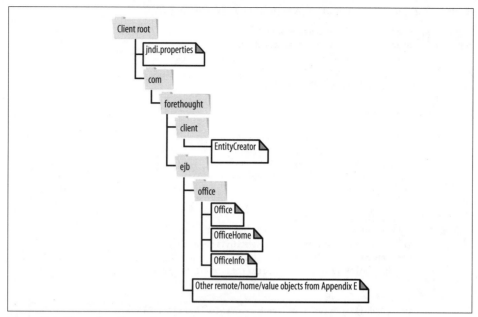

Figure 7-4. Client class hierarchy

first chapters should make this all fairly simple stuff by now. Enter in the source code and compile it, and get ready to test the application data stores.

Example 7-2. The EntityCreator Data Population Class

```
package com.forethought.client;

import java.rmi.RemoteException;
import java.util.Properties;
import javax.ejb.CreateException;
import javax.naming.Context;
import javax.naming.InitialContext;
import javax.naming.NamingException;
import javax.rmi.PortableRemoteObject;

// Office bean
import com.forethought.ejb.office.Office;
import com.forethought.ejb.office.OfficeHome;

// User bean
import com.forethought.ejb.user.User;
import com.forethought.ejb.user.UserHome;

// Fund bean
import com.forethought.ejb.fund.Fund;
import com.forethought.ejb.fund.FundHome;

// Account bean
```

Example 7-2. The EntityCreator Data Population Class (continued)

```java
import com.forethought.ejb.account.Account;
import com.forethought.ejb.account.AccountHome;

// LDAP Manager
import com.forethought.ldap.LDAPManager;

public class EntityCreator {

    public static void main(String[] args) {
        try {
            // Get an InitialContext
            Context context = new InitialContext( );
            Object ref = null;

            // Look up the Office bean
            System.out.println("Looking up the Office bean.");
            ref = context.lookup("forethought.OfficeHome");
            OfficeHome officeHome = (OfficeHome)
                PortableRemoteObject.narrow(ref, OfficeHome.class);

            // Create offices
            Office dallasOffice = officeHome.create("Dallas", "TX");
            Office chicagoOffice = officeHome.create("Chicago", "IL");
            Office bostonOffice = officeHome.create("Boston", "MA");
            Office denverOffice = officeHome.create("Denver", "CO");
            Office newYorkOffice = officeHome.create("New York", "NY");
            Office sanFranciscoOffice = OfficeHome.create("San Francisco", "CA");
            Office sanJoseOffice = officeHome.create("San Jose", "CA");
            System.out.println("Created Forethought Offices.\n");

            // Look up the Funds bean
            System.out.println("Looking up the Fund bean.");
            ref = context.lookup("forethought.FundHome");
            FundHome fundHome = (FundHome)
                javax.rmi.PortableRemoteObject.narrow(ref,
                    FundHome.class);

            // Create funds
            fundHome.create("Industrial Select",
                "This fund is based on industrial stocks such as oil, " +
                "gas, and other utilities.");
            fundHome.create("Money Market Fund",
                "This fund is based on money market accounts, and is " +
                "intended to provide a steady rate of return over time.");
            fundHome.create("Stable Economic",
                "This fund is focused on commodoties that are stable " +
                "and have predictable (albeit smaller) yields.");
            fundHome.create("Technology Saver",
                "This fund is concentrated on technology stocks, but " +
                "larger and proven ones (Fortune 1000 companies).");
            fundHome.create("Technology Select",
                "This fund is concentrated on technology stocks and " +
                "high yield investments.");
```

Example 7-2. The EntityCreator Data Population Class (continued)

```
fundHome.create("Universal",
    "This fund is spread through proven stocks across the " +
    "board, basing selection on yield rather than industry.");
System.out.println("Created Forethought Funds.\n");

// Get LDAPManager to add users and groups/permissions
System.out.println("Looking up the LDAP Manager.");
LDAPManager manager =
    LDAPManager.getInstance("localhost", 389,
                            "cn=Directory Manager",
                            "forethought");

// Create permissions in LDAP
manager.addPermission("Add User",
                        "Add a new Forethought user");
manager.addPermission("Edit User",
                        "Edit a Forethought user");
manager.addPermission("Delete User",
                        "Delete a Forethought user");
manager.addPermission("Login",
                        "Login to the Forethought application.");
manager.addPermission("Update Profile",
                        "Update a user's own profile.");
manager.addPermission("Change Password",
                        "Change a user's own password.");
manager.addPermission("Manage Funds",
                        "Add a new Forethought fund.");
manager.addPermission("View Funds",
                        "View Forethought funds.");
manager.addPermission("View Brokers",
                        "View Forethought brokers");
manager.addPermission("View Internal News",
                        "View Forethought internal news.");
System.out.println("Added Forethought Permissions.\n");

// Create groups in LDAP
manager.addGroup("Application Users",
                    "Users of the Forethought application");
manager.addGroup("Clients", "Forethought clients");
manager.addGroup("Employees", "Forethought employees");
manager.addGroup("Managers", "Forethought managers");
manager.addGroup("Brokers", "Forethought brokers");
manager.addGroup("Administrators",
                    "Forethought application administrators");
System.out.println("Added Forethought Groups.\n");

// Create groups-permission links
manager.assignPermission("Application Users", "Login");
manager.assignPermission("Application Users",
                        "Update Profile");
manager.assignPermission("Application Users",
                        "Change Password");
```

Example 7-2. The EntityCreator Data Population Class (continued)

```
                manager.assignPermission("Clients", "View Funds");
                manager.assignPermission("Clients", "View Brokers");

                manager.assignPermission("Employees", "View Internal News");

                manager.assignPermission("Managers", "Edit User");

                manager.assignPermission("Brokers", "Manage Funds");

                manager.assignPermission("Administrators", "Login");
                manager.assignPermission("Administrators", "Add User");
                manager.assignPermission("Administrators", "Edit User");
                manager.assignPermission("Administrators", "Delete User");

                System.out.println("Assigned Forethought Permissions.\n");

                // Add users
                manager.addUser("shirlbg", "Shirley", "Greathouse", "nellie");
                manager.addUser("gqg10012", "Gary", "Greathouse", "chunk");
                manager.addUser("bsturm", "Bob", "Sturm", "shaft");
                manager.addUser("danm", "Dan", "McDowell", "tablespoon");
                manager.addUser("rhyner", "Mike", "Rhyner", "wolf");
                manager.addUser("greggo", "Greg", "Williams", "motorcycle");
                manager.addUser("norm", "Norm", "Hitzges", "chophouse");
                System.out.println("Added Forethought Users to LDAP.\n");

                // Assign users to groups
                manager.assignUser("shirlbg", "Application Users");
                manager.assignUser("shirlbg", "Clients");

                manager.assignUser("gqg10012", "Application Users");
                manager.assignUser("gqg10012", "Clients");

                manager.assignUser("bsturm", "Employees");
                manager.assignUser("bsturm", "Brokers");

                manager.assignUser("danm", "Employees");
                manager.assignUser("danm", "Brokers");

                manager.assignUser("rhyner", "Employees");
                manager.assignUser("rhyner", "Managers");

                manager.assignUser("greggo", "Employees");
                manager.assignUser("greggo", "Managers");

                manager.assignUser("norm", "Administrators");

                System.out.println("Assigned Forethought Users to Groups.\n");

                // Look up the User bean
                System.out.println("Looking up the User bean.");
                ref = context.lookup("forethought.UserHome");
```

Example 7-2. The EntityCreator Data Population Class (continued)

```
            UserHome userHome = (UserHome)
                javax.rmi.PortableRemoteObject.narrow(ref,
                    UserHome.class);

            // Create users (without offices)
            System.out.println("Creating Forethought clients.");
            User shirley = userHome.create("uid=\"shirlbg\",ou=\"People\"," +
                            "o=\"forethought.com\"",
                            "Client", "Shirley", "Greathouse", null);
            User gary = userHome.create("uid=\"gqg10012\",ou=\"People\"," +
                        "o=\"forethought.com\"",
                        "Client", "Gary", "Greathouse", null);

            // Create users (with offices)
            System.out.println("Creating Forethought employees.");
            userHome.create("uid=\"bsturm\",ou=\"People\"," +
                        "o=\"forethought.com\"",
                        "Employee", "Bob", "Sturm", bostonOffice);
            userHome.create("uid=\"danm\",ou=\"People\"," +
                        "o=\"forethought.com\"",
                        "Employee", "Dan", "McDowell", denverOffice);
            userHome.create("uid=\"rhyner\",ou=\"People\"," +
                        "o=\"forethought.com\"",
                        "Employee", "Mike", "Rhyner", chicagoOffice);
            userHome.create("uid=\"greggo\",ou=\"People\"," +
                        "o=\"forethought.com\"",
                        "Employee", "Greg", "Williams", sanJoseOffice);
            userHome.create("uid=\"norm\",ou=\"People\"," +
                        "o=\"forethought.com\"",
                        "Employee", "Norm", "Hitzges", dallasOffice);
            System.out.println("Created Forethought Users.\n");

            // Look up the Account bean
            System.out.println("Looking up the Account bean.");
            ref = context.lookup("forethought.AccountHome");
            AccountHome accountHome = (AccountHome)
                javax.rmi.PortableRemoteObject.narrow(ref,
                    AccountHome.class);

            // Create accounts
            accountHome.create("Everyday", 900, shirley);
            accountHome.create("Money Market", 2500, shirley);
            accountHome.create("Savings", 5000, shirley);

            accountHome.create("Investment Plus", 10000, gary);
            accountHome.create("Money Market", 5000, gary);
            System.out.println("Created Forethought Accounts.\n");
        } catch (Exception e) {
            e.printStackTrace( );
        }
    }
}
```

Compile this class (ensuring that you have your environment set up with the EJB and LDAP classes, or by using the `compileClients` target in the Ant build file), and run it. You can use the `createEntities` target of the supplied Ant build file to accomplish this, as shown here:

```
C:\dev\javaentI>ant createEntities
Buildfile: build.xml

init:

prepare:

compileUtilityClasses:
    [echo] Compiling the Forethought utility classes.

compileSequenceBean:
    [echo] Compiling the Forethought Sequence Bean classes.

compileTypeBeans:
    [echo] Compiling the Forethought Typed Bean classes.

compileOfficeBean:
    [echo] Compiling the Forethought Office Bean classes.

compileUserBean:
    [echo] Compiling the Forethought User Bean classes.

compileFundBean:
    [echo] Compiling the Forethought Fund Bean classes.

compileAccountBean:
    [echo] Compiling the Forethought Account Bean classes.

compileTransactionBean:
    [echo] Compiling the Forethought Transaction Bean classes.

compileLDAPClasses:
    [echo] Compiling the Forethought LDAP classes.

compile:

compileClients:
    [echo] Compiling Forethought application clients.

createClientJar:
    [echo] Creating the Forethought client jar.
     [jar] Updating jar: C:\dev\javaentI\output\forethoughtClient.jar

createEntities:
    [echo] Creating the Forethought entities...
    [java] Looking up the Office bean.
    [java] Created Forethought Offices.
    [java]
```

```
[java] Looking up the Fund bean.
[java] Created Forethought Funds.
[java]
[java] Looking up the LDAP Manager.
[java] Added Forethought Permissions.
[java]
[java] Added Forethought Groups.
[java]
[java] Assigned Forethought Permissions.
[java]
[java] Added Forethought Users to LDAP.
[java]
[java] Assigned Forethought Users to Groups.
[java]
[java] Looking up the User bean.
[java] Creating Forethought clients.
[java] Creating Forethought employees.
[java] Created Forethought Users.
[java]
[java] Looking up the Account bean.
[java] Created Forethought Accounts.
[java]

BUILD SUCCESSFUL

Total time: 15 seconds
```

And, as simple as that, you have a structure with data in place, ready for use. I'd encourage you to use a database query tool to verify that the data has been inserted into your database, and any tools that your directory server provides to do the same for your data store. Of course, you could take a moment to write some simple Java classes to perform these tasks; certainly the work done here should make that job fairly easy. You can also write a client to use the LDAPManager class to view various users, groups, and permissions in the directory. Once you are confident that your data stores are populated, it's time to move on to the next section of the application.

What's Next?

You are finally ready to move on to the business tier of the application, where business logic is handled. The business tier is made up largely of session beans, and you'll use it to build out the infrastructure of the Forethought application. This tier will of course rest upon the structure already in place, and will use this foundation for access to the database and directory server. Expect to deal with lots of logic for handling user administration, investments, transactions, account queries, and more in the next section of the book; we'll also look at the Java Messaging Service (JMS) to handle communication of time-sensitive data. Make sure your entity beans and LDAPManager classes are ready to go, and dive into the next chapters.

CHAPTER 8

Business Logic

You have now completed the data layer of your application, and are ready to dive into the business layer. If you recall from Chapter 2, the business layer incorporates your application's *business logic*. Specifically, you will need to provide access to your entity beans, business calculations, and a scheduling facility. In this chapter, I'll detail the access to entity beans already in place, and discuss how to handle more complex business tasks. Chapter 9 then details the scheduling process.

First, I'll discuss the *façade pattern*, in which you use session beans to access entity beans. This access method is used instead of allowing direct access to entity beans, and is key to a sound strategy in building enterprise applications. I'll also outline the problems and penalties associated with this approach, giving you the information you need to make good decisions in your own applications. This pattern goes hand in hand with the manager component discussed in Chapter 6 when working with directory servers. I'll illustrate the pattern with a simple example, an OfficeManager session bean.

From there, I'll move on to slightly more complex session beans. You'll see how a single session bean can perform operations on multiple beans and on other Java components. You'll build a UserManager component, which will administer users, and will operate upon the User entity bean as well as the LDAPManager directory server component. This should give you an idea of how to handle these more complex tasks.

Finally, I'll spend some time detailing the difference between stateless and stateful beans, and demonstrate how stateful beans can generally be converted into simpler, more efficient stateless session beans. You'll also see how helper classes can make stateless beans appear as stateful ones, allowing your clients to get simple interfaces while your beans remain fast and lightweight. I'll explore these concepts in developing an AccountManager component for working with user accounts.

The Façade Pattern

I've already mentioned the façade pattern in several earlier chapters, but never truly delved into the pattern's details. It's appropriate to do that now, and see why an extra layer of abstraction is necessary. In practice, most developers instinctively know that they should use a layer of session beans that prevent direct entity bean access, but then convince themselves to abandon this approach because they cannot justify it. I'll try and provide you some justification for that decision here.

Data Schema Exposure

The most obvious rationale for using session beans to abstract entity beans is that the approach also abstracts the structure of your data stores. To understand this better, you may want to take a second look at the actual structure of the Forethought database schema, and the SQL used to create it. Figure 8-1 shows the Forethought OFFICES table to serve as an example.

Figure 8-1. The Forethought OFFICES table

The presumption is that you do not want to expose the inner workings of your application's data store, or even the specifics of how that data is stored. In other words, letting users (also known as potential hackers) know your database schema is a bad idea. Problems in this area arise when allowing direct access to the entity bean layer. The methods in entity beans typically map directly to underlying fields in the data schema, as shown in Figure 8-2.

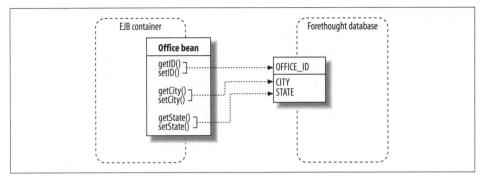

Figure 8-2. Mapping the Office entity bean to the OFFICES table

As you can see, for each column in the OFFICES table, a corresponding method exists in the Office entity bean. The same, of course, occurs for the rest of the database schema.

It is trivial to examine entity beans and then extrapolate the data schema from them, which is precisely the situation you are trying to avoid in application design. This problem is simplified by the introduction of session beans that abstract these details. For example, consider an OfficeManager bean that provides methods to add, update, and delete Forethought offices. The remote interface for this bean is shown in Example 8-1.

Example 8-1. The OfficeManager Remote Interface

```
package com.forethought.ejb.office;

import java.rmi.RemoteException;
import javax.ejb.EJBObject;

public interface OfficeManager extends EJBObject {

    public OfficeInfo get(String city, String state) throws RemoteException;

    public OfficeInfo add(String city, String state) throws RemoteException;

    public void update(OfficeInfo officeInfo) throws RemoteException;

    public boolean delete(String city, String state) throws RemoteException;
    public boolean delete(OfficeInfo officeInfo) throws RemoteException;
}
```

This interface manages to hide some of the details of database schema implementation. While it might seem obvious to you that the OFFICES table contains a CITY and STATE text column, you are seeing through the eyes of someone who already knows the database schema. Figure 8-3 shows how this exact session bean might map to several different database implementations; therefore, it does hide the database schema by providing *logical* methods on entities, instead of *physical* methods.

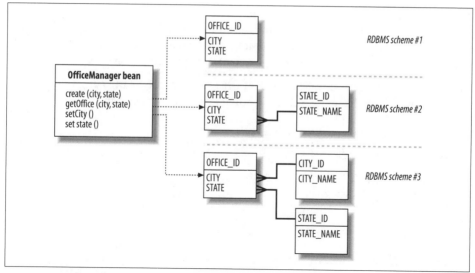

Figure 8-3. Mapping the OfficeManager to different database schemas

You can see that it's no longer obvious exactly how the database is laid out. Using session beans and the façade design pattern will aid in security by providing this layer of obfuscation* over the data schema.

Finally, for those of you still unsure why this is worth going on about, let me explain why this obfuscation is so critical. Many of you are probably wondering why it is important to abstract your database schema from your presentation layer; wouldn't the developers and designers of one layer work with, or even be the same people as, the developers and designers of the other? That would seem to be the case, at least in many situations. In fact, you will code the Forethought application from front to back, so it might seem silly to go to this trouble.

However, as the era of service-based computing takes off, this process becomes vital. Instead of providing complete applications, the J2EE specification (as well as Microsoft's .NET platform, UDDI, SOAP, and other developments) indicates that organizations are focusing more on components than on complete applications. Interchanging data components from one application and company with presentation components from another application and company is becoming common and even standard. As a result, it is unsafe to assume that only you or your company's developers will be accessing your business layer and EJBs. You should assume that your EJB layer will be exposed to many others, some of whom you want to provide access but not application information to. For all of these reasons, a sound design of

---

* *Obfuscation* means "to make so confused or opaque as to be difficult to perceive or understand." It's often used to describe the process of scrambling bytecode so that it cannot be decompiled, and is used here to represent the same concept with respect to the database schema in use.

the business layer can save you some trouble, even make you a hero, when your pointy-haired boss insists that now the beans you worked on must be accessible by a new partner, but that the partner doesn't get database schema information. Suddenly, the work done on your session beans really begins to pay off!

I'll run briefly through the rest of the OfficeManager classes, as the actual implementation is fairly trivial. Example 8-2 is the home interface for the bean.

Example 8-2. The OfficeManager Home Interface

```
package com.forethought.ejb.office;

import java.rmi.RemoteException;
import javax.ejb.CreateException;
import javax.ejb.EJBHome;

public interface OfficeManagerHome extends EJBHome {

    public OfficeManager create( ) throws CreateException, RemoteException;
}
```

As you can see, this is a stateless session bean, which is the most efficient session bean. I'll discuss this more later. You can see from the implementation class in Example 8-3 that no state is required for the bean to function, and therefore using a stateless bean makes sense in this case.

Example 8-3. The OfficeManager Implementation Class

```
package com.forethought.ejb.office;

import java.rmi.RemoteException;
import javax.ejb.CreateException;
import javax.ejb.EJBHome;
import javax.naming.Context;
import javax.naming.InitialContext;

import com.forethought.ejb.util.SessionAdapter;

public class OfficeManagerBean extends SessionAdapter {

    public void ejbCreate( ) throws CreateException {
        // No action required for stateless session beans
    }

    public OfficeInfo get(String city, String state) throws RemoteException {
        Office office = getOffice(city, state);
        if (office != null) {
            return office.getInfo( );
        } else {
            return null;
        }
    }
}
```

Example 8-3. The OfficeManager Implementation Class (continued)

```java
    public OfficeInfo add(String city, String state) {
        try {
            // Get an InitialContext
            Context context = new InitialContext();

            // Look up the Office bean
            OfficeHome officeHome = (OfficeHome)
                context.lookup("java:comp/env/ejb/OfficeHome");
            Office office = officeHome.create(city, state);

            return office.getInfo();
        } catch (Exception e) {
            // Any problems - just return null
            return null;
        }
    }

    public void update(OfficeInfo officeInfo) throws RemoteException {
        Office office = getOffice(officeInfo.getId());
        office.setInfo(officeInfo);
    }

    public boolean delete(String city, String state) {
        Office office = getOffice(city, state);
        return delete(office);
    }

    public boolean delete(OfficeInfo officeInfo) {
        Office office = getOffice(officeInfo.getId());
        return delete(office);
    }

    private Office getOffice(int id) {
        try {
            // Get an InitialContext
            Context context = new InitialContext();

            // Look up the Office bean
            OfficeHome officeHome = (OfficeHome)
                context.lookup("java:comp/env/ejb/OfficeHome");
            Office office = officeHome.findByPrimaryKey(new Integer(id));

            return office;
        } catch (Exception e) {
            // Any problems - just return null
            return null;
        }
    }

    private boolean delete(Office office) {
        if (office == null) {
            return true;
```

Example 8-3. The OfficeManager Implementation Class (continued)

```
        }

        try {
            office.remove();
            return true;
        } catch (Exception e) {
            // any problems - return false
            return false;
        }
    }

    private Office getOffice(String city, String state) {
        try {
            // Get an InitialContext
            Context context = new InitialContext();

            // Look up the Office bean
            OfficeHome officeHome = (OfficeHome)
                context.lookup("java:comp/env/ejb/OfficeHome");
            Office office = officeHome.findByLocation(city, state);

            return office;
        } catch (Exception e) {
            // Any problems - just return null
            return null;
        }
    }
}
```

You'll notice that this bean uses a new finder method on the Office entity bean, findByLocation( ). You can add this method to your OfficeHome class:

```
public Office findByLocation(String city, String state)
    throws FinderException, RemoteException;
```

Here's the relevant addition for the *ejb-jar.xml* file:

```
<query>
  <query-method>
    <method-name>findByLocation</method-name>
    <method-params>
      <method-param>java.lang.String</method-param>
      <method-param>java.lang.String</method-param>
    </method-params>
  </query-method>
  <ejb-ql>
    <![CDATA[WHERE city = ?1 AND state = ?2]]>
  </ejb-ql>
</query>
```

Before leaving the façade pattern behind, there are a few other details related to this first business-related bean worth detailing. First, notice that the manager beans are placed within the same package as the related entity bean. This provides logical groupings of managers and the related entities, and also makes access from manager component to entity bean simple (notice that there weren't a lot of `import` statements required in the source code).

Additionally, the method names have been changed a bit; instead of `create( )`, `setCity( )`, and `getState( )`, the more conventional method names `add( )`, `update( )`, and `delete( )` are used. This is more in line with an administrative component, and moves away from the strict conventions required in CMP entity beans. It also provides an easier-to-use interface for client code.

Performance Penalties

In the interests of full disclosure, you should be aware that the façade pattern, with all of its positives, does have some negatives. The significant problem with using this pattern is that it can introduce some performance penalties into your applications. Using an extra bean for communication (the session manager component) means that additional RMI calls must be made. This, of course, causes increases in network traffic, serialization of arguments, and all of the costs that any RMI call has. If both entity beans and session beans reside in the same EJB container on a single server, these costs shrink to almost nothing;[*] however, this is often not the case. It's more common to have session beans in one EJB container and entity beans in another, often on completely different physical machines.

However, even this problem can be overcome. Instead of packaging all entity beans and deploying them on one server, and packaging all session beans and deploying them on another, you can use more logical (and sensible) groupings to improve performance. Remember that you packaged a session bean, the `SequenceBean`, with the Forethought entities already. In this same fashion, manager components that implement the façade design pattern can be packaged with entity beans, ensuring that RMI communication is as fast as possible; this also provides logical divisions between entities and their accessor classes (the manager components) and business-driven components (the rest of the session beans). Figure 8-4 shows this configuration in action. Here, the manager components are packaged in the *forethoughtEntities.jar* archive, and in that way, become simple entities.

Additionally, almost all manager components turn out to be stateless; in other words, each method of the component operates on its own without any saved information. Using stateless components also helps to offset penalties incurred through using the façade pattern. As mentioned several times, stateless session beans outperform all other types of entity beans substantially. Interestingly enough, entity beans consume the most resources of any bean, as often one single instance is shared for

---

[*] In fact, most advanced EJB containers have optimizations for these "in-VM" calls, and will essentially drop the calls off the RMI stack and make the calls locally, removing any RMI penalties at all.

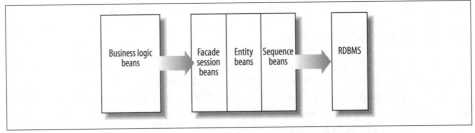

Figure 8-4. Logical separation of beans

containers (although there are as many variations on this theme as there are container vendors). So it is safe to make your manager session beans stateless.

These changes address the major downside of using the façade pattern; there are really no other penalties (other than some extra coding) to this approach. Clearly it makes sense, then, to implement it in the Forethought application as well as in your own.

The UserManager

Once offices are set up, the next logical step is to deal with Forethought users. Users are crucial to any application, which makes the UserManager component a critical part of the Forethought application. This particular manager component will also illustrate some of the important reasons for using managers at all. Chief among those reasons are data source transparency and data format transparency. Both offer advantages to the manager clients and provide many of the security and ease-of-use benefits discussed earlier with regard to the OfficeManager.

Data Source Transparency

In the case of Forethought offices, all information related to an office is stored in a single table, in a single data source: the Forethought RDBMS OFFICES table, which we set up in Chapter 3. While extremely convenient, this is most often *not* the case. It's a lot more common to find that a single logical entity (like a user) has its information stored in multiple tables (like the USERS and USER_TYPES tables), and even in multiple data sources (like the Forethought database and the Forethought directory server). As a result, working with one *logical* piece of data often requires operating upon multiple *physical* pieces of data. This can become quite a pain for application clients: they must use JDBC to connect to a database, SQL to select from and join together tables, and then JNDI to operate upon a directory server; finally, the resultant information has to be spliced together in some meaningful form. As a good developer, you should seek to avoid this complexity.

The User entity bean and the LDAPManager component have already alleviated some of these problems; these two components abstract all the details of connection and specific SQL and LDAP statements from the client. However, a client (or piece of code) would still have to know that the core information about a user is in the database, and therefore an entity bean is needed, while the authentication information is in a directory server, so the manager is employed. Add to that the need to not only utilize the User entity bean, but the UserType and possibly Office entity beans as well, and things are only marginally better than they were without beans and managers at all. What is obviously needed here is another level of abstraction. As the saying goes, "Everything in programming can be solved with another layer of abstraction." It is here that UserManager-type components come in. By providing a single component for working with users, the data sources involved with that component are hidden from the client. For example, consider the process of adding a new user. Figure 8-5 shows that while the client makes one single method invocation (to add( )), the UserManager bean actually operates upon the directory server as well as multiple entity beans. This transparency of data source not only results in the client having a much easier means of adding a user, but also removes any exposure of the underlying data schema.

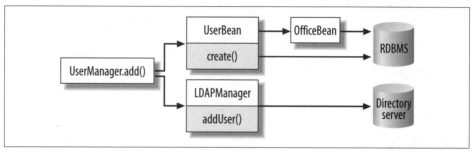

Figure 8-5. The UserManager's add( ) method in action

Data Format Transparency

In addition to data *source* transparency, designers of complex systems often need to worry about data *format* transparency. Data format transparency basically means that a client does not have to make distinctions in data that characterize best practices in data storage. In other words, a client does not have to worry about how data is actually stored. The back-end can be designed according to the best practices in data storage; the client doesn't know or care about the details. In other words, a client can act *logically* without having to think *physically*. Of course, I've been addressing this logical-versus-physical concern for this entire chapter, so there should be no surprises here. Consider that a client will be dealing with a user most often by that user's username (such as "gqg10012"). However, the directory server and database deal with the user's distinguished name (such as *uid=gqg10012,ou=People, o=forethought.com*). Forcing the client to worry about that lengthier and less meaningful format is clearly not desired. Your manager components can hide these format details.

As an example, the UserManager component allows users to be specified by their usernames, and then internally handles conversion to distinguished names. Of course, you already have a method to do just this in the LDAPManager component. To accommodate new needs here, it makes sense to make that method public. Additionally, there is no compelling need to require an instance of LDAPManager to be available for using the method; as a result, the method can be modified to be static, as well:

```
public static String getUserDN(String username) {
    return new StringBuffer()
            .append("uid=")
            .append(username)
            .append(",")
            .append(USERS_OU)
            .toString();
}
```

You'll want to make this change in your own manager component (including the getGroupDN() and getPermissionDN() methods). With that done, the UserManager component, as well as any other session bean dealing with users, can have interactions with users based simply on a supplied username. As a result, clients don't need to deal with, or even be aware of, the format in which usernames are stored in the data sources. In this way, your managers provide data format transparency. Of course, this same principle could be applied to allowing complete names to be specified ("Mike Rhyner" would become "Mike" and "Rhyner" as first and last names), state conversions ("Texas" would become "TX"), and so forth. In these ways, manager components can allow you to simplify the job of a client.

Getting to It

You're now ready to look at the code that composes the UserManager component, and everything will become crystal clear. As always, I start with the remote interface. This is very similar to the OfficeManager interface in the standard methods that it provides for working with Forethought users. However, as users are a bit different than other Forethought entities, you will notice a few extra methods, as shown in the code listing in Example 8-4. In addition to providing two flavors of user creation (one with an office, and one without), there are methods to authenticate a user and to change a user's password. Both of these deal specifically with the authentication credentials of a user, and are common tasks in any application in which security is used. Of course, these are fairly trivial "pass-through" style methods, in which calls are made to the LDAPManager component to achieve the requested result.

Example 8-4. The UserManager Remote Interface

```
package com.forethought.ejb.user;

import java.rmi.RemoteException;
import javax.ejb.EJBObject;
```

Example 8-4. The UserManager Remote Interface (continued)

```
// Office bean
import com.forethought.ejb.office.OfficeInfo;

// UserType bean
import com.forethought.ejb.userType.UnknownUserTypeException;

// LDAPManager component
import com.forethought.ldap.UserNotFoundException;

public interface UserManager extends EJBObject {

    public UserInfo get(String username) throws RemoteException;

    public UserInfo add(String username, String password,
                        String firstName, String lastName,
                        String userType)
        throws RemoteException, UnknownUserTypeException;

    public UserInfo add(String username, String password,
                        String firstName, String lastName,
                        String userType, OfficeInfo officeInfo)
        throws RemoteException, UnknownUserTypeException;

    public void update(UserInfo userInfo)
        throws RemoteException, UnknownUserTypeException;

    public boolean setPassword(String username, String oldPassword,
                               String newPassword)
        throws RemoteException, UserNotFoundException;


    public boolean authenticate(String username, String password)
        throws RemoteException, UserNotFoundException;

    public boolean delete(String username) throws RemoteException;
    public boolean delete(UserInfo userInfo) throws RemoteException;
}
```

Example 8-5 shows the home interface for the UserManager component.

Example 8-5. The UserManager Home Interface

```
package com.forethought.ejb.user;

import java.rmi.RemoteException;
import javax.ejb.CreateException;
import javax.ejb.EJBHome;

public interface UserManagerHome extends EJBHome {

    public UserManager create( ) throws CreateException, RemoteException;
}
```

Note that several of these methods throw a UserNotFoundException; I mentioned this class and its use in Chapter 7. However, I left the details of putting the class into use in the LDAPManager component to you, as an exercise. Here's my modified version of the isValidUser( ) method of LDAPManager, which issues this exception if authentication is attempted with a nonexistent username:

```
public boolean isValidUser(String username, String password)
    throws UserNotFoundException {

    try {
        DirContext context =
            getInitialContext(hostname, port, getUserDN(username),
                              password);
        return true;
    } catch (NamingException e) {
        // See if this was a missing user
        if (e instanceof javax.naming.AuthenticationException) {
            javax.naming.AuthenticationException ae =
                (javax.naming.AuthenticationException)e;
            if (ae.getResolvedObj( ) == null) {
                throw new UserNotFoundException(username);
            }
        }
        // Any error indicates couldn't log user in
        return false;
    }
}
```

There are certainly other ways to handle this problem that return the same result, but this was the simplest I found. Since users with invalid passwords will have related resolved objects, a test against null determines whether the authentication problem was in the supplied password or the supplied username. You should make an equivalent change in your own LDAPManager component before coding the UserManager's implementation class.

Additionally, you'll notice that this new manager has a method to update a user's password, setPassword( ). This makes perfect sense; however, no such method exists on the LDAPManager component. You'll need to add this method into that class, as shown here:

```
public boolean updatePassword(String username, String oldPassword,
                              String newPassword)
    throws UserNotFoundException {

    // Ensure this is a valid user, with a valid (old) password
    boolean isValidUser = isValidUser(username, oldPassword);
    if (!isValidUser) {
        return false;
    }

    try {
        // Get the user
```

```
        DirContext userContext =
            (DirContext)context.lookup(getUserDN(username));

        ModificationItem[] mods = new ModificationItem[1];

        // Create new password attribute
        mods[0] = new ModificationItem(DirContext.REPLACE_ATTRIBUTE,
            new BasicAttribute("userPassword", newPassword));

        // Replace old with new
        userContext.modifyAttributes("", mods);

        return true;
    } catch (NamingException e) {
        e.printStackTrace();
        return false;
    }
  }
}
```

Why All the Back and Forth?

If you are following along with the code in this book, you may be wondering why I am doing a lot of "back and forth" with adding methods, changing home interfaces, updating existing methods, and so on. I certainly could have made any later changes to my own code appear in earlier chapters (through the magic of editing and book production). However, this book is about enterprise application programming, and the constant refining of code is very much a part of that process. In other words, I'm trying to give you at least a semi-realistic view of how real-life programming works. Of course, you can download completed code for all classes online at *http://www.newInstance. com* if you don't want to deal with these issues.

All that's left at this point is the session bean's implementation class. There is very little explanation needed for this class; if you followed along in Chapters 6 and 7, you can quickly pick up the code shown in Example 8-6. In a nutshell, the component acts as a client to various entity beans and LDAP components, piecing together disparate functions into one logical method. You should examine the groupings used for each method, and see how the underlying data sources and data formats are harnessed into easy-to-use methods for manager clients.

Example 8-6. The UserManager Implementation Class

```
package com.forethought.ejb.user;

import java.rmi.RemoteException;
import javax.ejb.CreateException;
import javax.ejb.EJBHome;
import javax.naming.Context;
```

Example 8-6. The UserManager Implementation Class (continued)

```java
import javax.naming.InitialContext;
import javax.naming.NamingException;

import com.forethought.ejb.util.SessionAdapter;

// Office bean
import com.forethought.ejb.office.OfficeInfo;

// UserType bean
import com.forethought.ejb.userType.UnknownUserTypeException;

// LDAPManager component
import com.forethought.ldap.LDAPManager;
import com.forethought.ldap.UserNotFoundException;

public class UserManagerBean extends SessionAdapter {

    /** <p> Required method for allowing bean lookups. </p> */
    public void ejbCreate( ) throws CreateException {
        // No action required for stateless session beans
    }

    public UserInfo get(String username) throws RemoteException {
        User user = getUser(username);
        if (user != null) {
            return user.getInfo( );
        } else {
            return null;
        }
    }

    public UserInfo add(String username, String password,
                        String firstName, String lastName,
                        String userType)
        throws RemoteException, UnknownUserTypeException {

        // Simply delegate, without an office
        return add(username, password, firstName, lastName, userType, null);
    }

    public UserInfo add(String username, String password,
                        String firstName, String lastName,
                        String userType, OfficeInfo officeInfo)
        throws RemoteException, UnknownUserTypeException {

        boolean addedToDirectory = false;
        LDAPManager manager = null;
        try {
            // Add user to directory server
            manager = getLDAPManager( );
            manager.addUser(username, firstName, lastName, password);
            addedToDirectory = true;
```

Example 8-6. The UserManager Implementation Class (continued)

```
                // Get an InitialContext
                Context context = new InitialContext( );

                // Add user to database
                UserHome userHome = (UserHome)
                    context.lookup("java:comp/env/ejb/UserHome");
                User user = userHome.create(LDAPManager.getUserDN(username),
                                            userType, firstName, lastName,
                                            officeInfo);

                return user.getInfo( );
        } catch (NamingException e) {
            /*
             * If added to directory, but not to database, remove back from
             * directory server
             */
            if (addedToDirectory) {
                try {
                    manager.deleteUser(username);
                } catch (Exception ignored) {
                    // If this dies, we're done
                }
            }
        } catch (CreateException e) {
            if (addedToDirectory) {
                try {
                    manager.deleteUser(username);
                } catch (Exception ignored) {
                    // If this dies, we're done
                }
            }
        }

        // If we got here, things failed
        return null;
    }

    public void update(UserInfo userInfo)
        throws RemoteException, UnknownUserTypeException {

        // This only involves database fields, so no LDAP access needed
        User user = getUser(userInfo.getId( ));
        user.setInfo(userInfo);
    }

    public boolean setPassword(String username, String oldPassword,
                               String newPassword)
        throws UserNotFoundException {

        try {
            LDAPManager manager = getLDAPManager( );
            return manager.updatePassword(username, oldPassword, newPassword);
```

Example 8-6. The UserManager Implementation Class (continued)

```
        } catch (NamingException e) {
            return false;
        }
    }

    public boolean authenticate(String username, String password)
        throws UserNotFoundException {

        try {
            return getLDAPManager( ).isValidUser(username, password);
        } catch (NamingException e) {
            return false;
        }
    }

    public boolean delete(String username){
        User user = getUser(username);
        return delete(user);
    }

    public boolean delete(UserInfo userInfo) {
        User user = getUser(userInfo.getId( ));
        return delete(user);
    }

    private User getUser(int id) {
        try {
            // Get an InitialContext
            Context context = new InitialContext( );

            // Look up the User bean
            UserHome userHome = (UserHome)
                context.lookup("java:comp/env/ejb/UserHome");
            User user = userHome.findByPrimaryKey(new Integer(id));

            return user;
        } catch (Exception e) {
            // Any problems - just return null
            return null;
        }
    }

    private User getUser(String username) {
        try {
            // Get an InitialContext
            Context context = new InitialContext( );

            // Look up the User bean
            UserHome userHome = (UserHome)
                context.lookup("java:comp/env/ejb/UserHome");
            User user = userHome.findByUserDn(LDAPManager.getUserDN(username));
```

Example 8-6. The UserManager Implementation Class (continued)

```
            return user;
        } catch (Exception e) {
            // Any problems - just return null
            return null;
        }
    }

    private boolean delete(User user) {
        if (user == null) {
            return true;
        }
        try {
            user.remove( );
            return true;
        } catch (Exception e) {
            // Any problems - return false
            return false;
        }
    }

    private LDAPManager getLDAPManager( ) throws NamingException {
        /**
         * This could be set up to read from a properties file, but I have
         * kept it simple for example purposes.
         */
        LDAPManager manager =
            LDAPManager.getInstance("localhost", 389,
                                    "cn=Directory Manager",
                                    "forethought");
        return manager;
    }
}
```

Almost all of the code shown is fairly straightforward: simple JNDI lookups for entity beans and operations upon those beans make up most of the class. Use of the LDAPManager component makes up almost all of the rest of the code. As you can see, the process of using two (or more) data sources, formats, or types is all abstracted nicely in the UserManager bean, and allows the client to happily add, delete, and update users without worrying about physical data storage details.

State Design

Continuing on with the Forethought business logic, I want to spend some time on the issue of stateful versus stateless beans. I refer to it as an issue because it almost always manages to come up when working with session beans, and can have a drastic effect on your application's performance. Specifically, stateless session beans are much more efficient than stateful session beans.

For a more detailed discussion on the issue, you can check out Richard Monson-Haefel's *Enterprise JavaBeans*, which spends a great deal of print on how a container handles these two kinds of beans. I'll briefly sum up the relevant portions here. A stateless session bean is a very lightweight bean, since it needs to carry around only EJB-mandated variables, not programmer-defined ones. As a result, most containers have pools of stateless beans. Because no single client needs to have access to a specific stateless bean instance (no state is being kept, remember), a single instance can serve two, three, ten, or even a hundred clients. This allows the bean pool to be kept small, and negates a frequent need to grow or shrink the pool, which would take valuable processor cycles.

A stateful bean is just the opposite: an instance is tied to the client that invoked its create( ) method. This means that an instance must exist for every client accessing the stateful bean. Therefore, the bean pools must be larger, or must frequently be grown as more requests come in. The end result is longer process times, more beans, and fewer clients being served. The moral of this technology tale is that if at all possible, you should use stateless session beans.

The following sections demonstrate these principles, and specifically how a bean that appears to be a better stateful bean can easily be converted into a stateless one. This should provide you with some good ideas about state design and some handy tips on how to convert your own stateful beans into stateless ones.

Starting Stateful

Take the case of an AccountManager bean that will handle a single user's accounts. For this exercise, I'll keep the methods required for the bean simple. Example 8-7 shows the remote interface for this bean.

Example 8-7. The AccountManager Remote Interface

```
package com.forethought.ejb.account;

import java.rmi.RemoteException;
import java.util.List;
import javax.ejb.EJBObject;

// Account bean
import com.forethought.ejb.account.AccountInfo;

// AccountType bean
import com.forethought.ejb.accountType.UnknownAccountTypeException;

public interface AccountManager extends EJBObject {

    public AccountInfo add(String type, float balance)
        throws RemoteException, UnknownAccountTypeException;

    public AccountInfo get(int accountId) throws RemoteException;
```

Example 8-7. The AccountManager Remote Interface (continued)

```
    public List getAll( ) throws RemoteException;

    public AccountInfo deposit(AccountInfo accountInfo, float amount)
        throws RemoteException;

    public AccountInfo withdraw(AccountInfo accountInfo, float amount)
        throws RemoteException;

    public float getBalance(int accountId) throws RemoteException;

    public boolean delete(int accountId) throws RemoteException;
}
```

As you can see, the manager operates upon a single account for a single user. This design allows a client to simply pass in the user's username one time (using the create( ) method), and worry about details of the account independently of keeping up with a username. Example 8-8 shows this method in the manager's home interface.

Example 8-8. The AccountManager Home Interface

```
package com.forethought.ejb.account;

import java.rmi.RemoteException;
import javax.ejb.CreateException;
import javax.ejb.EJBHome;

public interface AccountManagerHome extends EJBHome {

    public AccountManager create(String username)
        throws CreateException, RemoteException;
}
```

This interface provides a means to create a new account or to find all existing accounts for a given username. Because the bean is keeping up with the account's user and the account's ID, both required for entity bean interaction, the bean *must* be stateful. That is, since each individual method uses the data, this information must be kept in the bean instance between requests. For a better understanding of these details, review the bean's implementation code in Example 8-9.

Example 8-9. The AccountManager Implementation Class

```
package com.forethought.ejb.account;

import java.rmi.RemoteException;
import java.util.Collection;
import java.util.Iterator;
import java.util.LinkedList;
import java.util.List;
import javax.ejb.CreateException;
```

Example 8-9. The AccountManager Implementation Class (continued)

```
import javax.ejb.FinderException;
import javax.ejb.EJBHome;
import javax.naming.Context;
import javax.naming.InitialContext;
import javax.naming.NamingException;

import com.forethought.ejb.util.SessionAdapter;

// Account bean
import com.forethought.ejb.account.Account;
import com.forethought.ejb.account.AccountHome;
import com.forethought.ejb.account.AccountInfo;

// AccountType bean
import com.forethought.ejb.accountType.UnknownAccountTypeException;

// User bean
import com.forethought.ejb.user.User;
import com.forethought.ejb.user.UserHome;

// LDAPManager (for utility method)
import com.forethought.ldap.LDAPManager;

public class AccountManagerBean extends SessionAdapter {

    /** Username related to this account */
    private String username;

    /** User bean for this account's user */
    private User user;

    /** <p> Required method for allowing bean lookups. </p> */
    public void ejbCreate(String username)
        throws CreateException, RemoteException {

        this.username = username;

        try {
            // Get an InitialContext
            Context context = new InitialContext( );

            // Look up the Account bean
            UserHome userHome = (UserHome)
                context.lookup("java:comp/env/ejb/UserHome");
            this.user = userHome.findByUserDn(LDAPManager.getUserDN(username));
        } catch (NamingException e) {
            throw new CreateException("Could not load underlying User bean.");
        } catch (FinderException e) {
            throw new CreateException("Could not locate specified user.");
        }
    }
```

Example 8-9. The AccountManager Implementation Class (continued)

```
    public AccountInfo add(String type, float balance)
        throws UnknownAccountTypeException {

        try {
            // Get an InitialContext
            Context context = new InitialContext( );

            // Look up the Account bean
            AccountHome accountHome = (AccountHome)
                context.lookup("java:comp/env/ejb/AccountHome");
            Account account = accountHome.create(type, balance, user);
            return account.getInfo( );
        } catch (RemoteException e) {
            return null;
        } catch (CreateException e) {
            return null;
        } catch (NamingException e) {
            return null;
        }
    }

    public AccountInfo get(int accountId) throws RemoteException {
        return getAccount(accountId).getInfo( );
    }

    public List getAll( ) {
        List accounts = new LinkedList( );

        try {
            Integer userId = user.getId( );

            // Get an InitialContext
            Context context = new InitialContext( );

            // Look up the Account bean
            AccountHome accountHome = (AccountHome)
                context.lookup("java:comp/env/ejb/AccountHome");
            Collection userAccounts = accountHome.findByUserId(userId);
            for (Iterator i = userAccounts.iterator( ); i.hasNext( ); ) {
                Account account = (Account)i.next( );
                accounts.add(account.getInfo( ));
            }
        } catch (Exception e) {
            // Let fall through to the return statement
        }
        return accounts;
    }

    public AccountInfo deposit(AccountInfo accountInfo, float amount)
        throws RemoteException {

        // Look up bean, to ensure most current view of data
```

Example 8-9. The AccountManager Implementation Class (continued)

```
        Account account = getAccount(accountInfo.getId());
        AccountInfo info = account.getInfo();

        // Update balance
        info.setBalance(info.getBalance() + amount);
        try {
            account.setInfo(info);
        } catch (UnknownAccountTypeException neverHappens) { }
        return info;
    }

    public AccountInfo withdraw(AccountInfo accountInfo, float amount)
        throws RemoteException {

        // Look up bean, to ensure most current view of data
        Account account = getAccount(accountInfo.getId());
        AccountInfo info = account.getInfo();

        // Update balance
        info.setBalance(info.getBalance() - amount);
        try {
            account.setInfo(info);
        } catch (UnknownAccountTypeException neverHappens) { }
        return info;
    }

    public boolean delete(int accountId) {
        try {
            Account account = getAccount(accountId);
            account.remove();
            return true;
        } catch (Exception e) {
            return false;
        }
    }

    public float getBalance(int accountId) throws RemoteException {
        return getAccount(accountId).getBalance();
    }

    private Account getAccount(int id) {
        try {
            // Get an InitialContext
            Context context = new InitialContext();

            // Look up the Account bean
            AccountHome accountHome = (AccountHome)
                context.lookup("java:comp/env/ejb/AccountHome");
            Account account = accountHome.findByPrimaryKey(new Integer(id));

            return account;
        } catch (Exception e) {
```

Example 8-9. The AccountManager Implementation Class (continued)

```
        // Any problems - just return null
        return null;
    }
  }
}
```

This is all basic EJB material, and shouldn't cause you any problems. You'll notice that this class also uses a new finder method on the Account bean:

```
public Collection findByUserId(Integer userId)
    throws FinderException, RemoteException;
```

The accompanying query element in the Account bean's entry in the *ejb-jar.xml* descriptor would look like this:

```
<query>
  <query-method>
    <method-name>findByUserId</method-name>
    <method-params>
      <method-param>java.lang.Integer</method-param>
    </method-params>
  </query-method>
  <ejb-ql>
    <![CDATA[WHERE userLocal.id = ?1]]>
  </ejb-ql>
</query>
```

To deploy the AccountManager bean, you would use this (additional) XML entry in your *ejb-jar.xml* deployment descriptor:

```
<session>
  <description>
    This AccountManager bean allows administration of Forethought accounts.
  </description>
  <ejb-name>AccountManagerBean</ejb-name>
  <home>com.forethought.ejb.account.AccountManagerHome</home>
  <remote>com.forethought.ejb.account.AccountManager</remote>
  <ejb-class>com.forethought.ejb.account.AccountManagerBean</ejb-class>
  <session-type>Stateful</session-type>
  <transaction-type>Container</transaction-type>
  <ejb-ref>
    <ejb-ref-name>ejb/AccountHome</ejb-ref-name>
    <ejb-ref-type>Entity</ejb-ref-type>
    <home>com.forethought.ejb.account.AccountHome</home>
    <remote>com.forethought.ejb.account.Account</remote>
    <ejb-link>AccountBean</ejb-link>
  </ejb-ref>
</session>
```

Additions to your application server's vendor-specific descriptors should be equally simple. With this bean in stateful form ready for use, it's time to see how it can be turned into a better-performing stateless session bean.

Going Stateless

To move this bean into stateless territory, you first need to change the home interface's create( ) signature. Since stateless beans can't maintain any information
between method calls, passing in a username (or any other data) to the create( )
method is useless. Make the following change:

```
public AccountManager create( )
    throws CreateException, RemoteException;
```

Once this change has been made, you need to determine which methods advertised
by the bean require a username for operation. In other words, browse through your
bean's implementation class and note any method that uses the username or user
method variable. Once you've determined the methods in this category, you will
need to change the signature for those methods in the remote interface:

```
public interface AccountManager extends EJBObject {

    public AccountInfo add(String username, String type, float balance)
        throws RemoteException, UnknownAccountTypeException;

    public AccountInfo get(int accountId) throws RemoteException;

    public List getAll(String username) throws RemoteException;

    public AccountInfo deposit(AccountInfo accountInfo, float amount)
        throws RemoteException;

    public AccountInfo withdraw(AccountInfo accountInfo, float amount)
        throws RemoteException;

    public float getBalance(int accountId) throws RemoteException;

    public boolean delete(int accountId) throws RemoteException;
}
```

In this case, only two methods require this information, so it's not terribly inconve-
nient. However, in many cases conversion from stateful to stateless requires a param-
eter to be added to ten, twenty, or more methods. Even though this example is
somewhat trivial, I want to continue the discussion assuming that it is a major issue
to have to keep the username around for these multiple method calls. Before getting
to the solution, though, you'll need to update your bean implementation class to
operate without maintaining state. First, add a utility method to the end of the class:

```
private User getUser(String username) throws RemoteException {
    try {
        // Get an InitialContext
        Context context = new InitialContext( );

        // Look up the Account bean
        UserHome userHome = (UserHome)
            context.lookup("java:comp/env/ejb/UserHome");
```

```
        User user = userHome.findByUserDn(LDAPManager.getUserDN(username));
        return user;
    } catch (NamingException e) {
        throw new RemoteException("Could not load underlying User bean.");
    } catch (FinderException e) {
        throw new RemoteException("Could not locate specified user.");
    }
}
```

Then remove the username and user member variables, and modify three methods
(those affected by the change to stateless):

```
public void ejbCreate() throws CreateException {
    // Nothing to be done for stateless beans
}

public AccountInfo add(String username, String type, float balance)
    throws UnknownAccountTypeException {

    try {
        // Get an InitialContext
        Context context = new InitialContext();

        // Get the correct user
        User user = getUser(username);

        // Look up the Account bean
        AccountHome accountHome = (AccountHome)
            context.lookup("java:comp/env/ejb/AccountHome");
        Account account = accountHome.create(type, balance, user);
        return account.getInfo();
    } catch (RemoteException e) {
        return null;
    } catch (CreateException e) {
        return null;
    } catch (NamingException e) {
        return null;
    }
}

public List getAll(String username) {
    List accounts = new LinkedList();

    try {
        User user = getUser(username);
        Integer userId = user.getId();

        // Get an InitialContext
        Context context = new InitialContext();

        // Look up the Account bean
        AccountHome accountHome = (AccountHome)
            context.lookup("java:comp/env/ejb/AccountHome");
        Collection userAccounts = accountHome.findByUserId(userId);
```

```
            for (Iterator i = userAccounts.iterator(); i.hasNext(); ) {
                Account account = (Account)i.next();
                accounts.add(account.getInfo());
            }
        } catch (Exception e) {
            // Let fall through to the return statement
        }
        return accounts;
    }
```

Finally, don't forget to change your deployment descriptor:

```
<session>
    <description>
        This AccountManager bean allows administration of Forethought accounts.
    </description>
    <ejb-name>AccountManagerBean</ejb-name>
    <home>com.forethought.ejb.account.AccountManagerHome</home>
    <remote>com.forethought.ejb.account.AccountManager</remote>
    <ejb-class>com.forethought.ejb.account.AccountManagerBean</ejb-class>
    <session-type>Stateless</session-type>
    <transaction-type>Container</transaction-type>·
    <ejb-ref>
        <ejb-ref-name>ejb/AccountHome</ejb-ref-name>
        <ejb-ref-type>Entity</ejb-ref-type>
        <home>com.forethought.ejb.account.AccountHome</home>
        <remote>com.forethought.ejb.account.Account</remote>
        <ejb-link>AccountBean</ejb-link>
    </ejb-ref>
    <ejb-ref>
        <ejb-ref-name>ejb/UserHome</ejb-ref-name>
        <ejb-ref-type>Entity</ejb-ref-type>
        <home>com.forethought.ejb.user.UserHome</home>
        <remote>com.forethought.ejb.user.User</remote>
        <ejb-link>UserBean</ejb-link>
    </ejb-ref>
</session>
```

All things considered, these changes are relatively simple to make, and have the net effect of making your bean faster, more efficient, and only marginally harder to use.

However, as I mentioned, there are times when the changes to the bean's remote interface are more difficult. Passing in a username or any other piece of data ten, twenty, or more times to a bean's methods can result in pain for the developer, and less-clear code. In these cases, a simple helper class on the client can make a stateless session bean behave just as a stateful one did. Example 8-10 shows this principle in action, detailing the AccountManagerHelper utility class.

Example 8-10. An AccountManager Helper Class

```
package com.forethought.client;

import java.rmi.RemoteException;
import java.util.List;
```

Example 8-10. An AccountManager Helper Class (continued)

```java
import javax.ejb.CreateException;
import javax.naming.Context;
import javax.naming.InitialContext;
import javax.naming.NamingException;
import javax.rmi.PortableRemoteObject;

// Account bean
import com.forethought.ejb.account.AccountInfo;
import com.forethought.ejb.account.AccountManager;
import com.forethought.ejb.account.AccountManagerHome;

// AccountType bean
import com.forethought.ejb.accountType.UnknownAccountTypeException;

public class AccountManagerHelper {

    /** The username for this account's user */
    private String username;

    /** The <code>AccountManager</code> bean instance */
    private AccountManager manager;

    public AccountManagerHelper(String username)
        throws CreateException, NamingException, RemoteException {

        this.username = username;

        Context context = new InitialContext();

        // Get the stateless bean instance
        Object ref = context.lookup("forethought.AccountManagerHome");
        AccountManagerHome accountManagerHome = (AccountManagerHome)
            PortableRemoteObject.narrow(ref, AccountManagerHome.class);
        this.manager = accountManagerHome.create();
    }

    public AccountInfo add(String type, float balance)
        throws RemoteException, UnknownAccountTypeException {

        return manager.add(username, type, balance);
    }

    public AccountInfo get(int accountId) throws RemoteException {
        return manager.get(accountId);
    }

    public List getAll() throws RemoteException {
        return manager.getAll(username);
    }

    public AccountInfo deposit(AccountInfo accountInfo, float amount)
        throws RemoteException {
```

Example 8-10. An AccountManager Helper Class (continued)

```
        return manager.deposit(accountInfo, amount);
    }

    public AccountInfo withdraw(AccountInfo accountInfo, float amount)
        throws RemoteException {

        return manager.withdraw(accountInfo, amount);
    }

    public boolean delete(int accountId) throws RemoteException {
        return manager.delete(accountId);
    }

    public float getBalance(int accountId) throws RemoteException {
        return manager.getBalance(accountId);
    }
}
```

Looking at the methods available on this helper class, you should realize pretty quickly that it mirrors the remote interface of the AccountManager session bean; however, it looks like the stateful bean version, rather than the new stateless version. The constructor for the class then takes the place of the old stateful bean's create( ) method from the home interface. This class then maintains a bean instance, the user-name for the manager, and delegates to the session bean. All of the same exceptions are passed through to the client, so the interface is very similar; the only difference is that context lookups are handled within the helper class. This makes the client code even simpler, as this code fragment shows:

```
// Look up the AccountManager bean
System.out.println("Looking up the AccountManager bean.");
AccountManagerHelper accountHelper =
    new AccountManagerHelper("gqg10012");

// Create an account
AccountInfo everydayAccount = accountHelper.add("Everyday", 5000);
if (everydayAccount == null) {
    System.out.println("Failed to add account.\n");
    return;
}
System.out.println("Added account.\n");

// Get all accounts
List accounts = accountHelper.getAll();
for (Iterator  i = accounts.iterator(); i.hasNext(); ) {
    AccountInfo accountInfo = (AccountInfo)i.next();
    System.out.println("Account ID: " + accountInfo.getId());
    System.out.println("Account Type: " + accountInfo.getType());
    System.out.println("Account Balance: " +
        accountInfo.getBalance() + "\n");
}
```

```
// Deposit
accountHelper.deposit(everydayAccount, 2700);
System.out.println("New balance in everyday account: " +
    accountHelper.getBalance(everydayAccount.getId( )) + "\n");

// Withdraw
accountHelper.withdraw(everydayAccount, 500);
System.out.println("New balance in everyday account: " +
    accountHelper.getBalance(everydayAccount.getId( )) + "\n");

// Delete account
accountHelper.delete(everydayAccount.getId( ));
System.out.println("Deleted everyday account.");
```

You may find that helper classes like this can simplify your own client code, even if you don't need to provide stateful session bean *masquerading*, where a stateless bean is made to look like a stateful one. In any case, this approach provides the best of both session bean types: the performance of a stateless bean with the interface of a stateful one. This technique will allow you to convert all of your application's stateful session beans into stateless ones, which will yield some dramatic performance improvements.

What's Next?

You now have the tools to build the back-end of almost any enterprise application you may come across, and apply your knowledge to most of the problems you will encounter in the enterprise Java space. In the next chapter, though, I want to move beyond the basics into the less-used realm of the Java Message Service (and specifically, message-driven beans). Although it is still somewhat unusual to see these kinds of beans in action, you will find that JMS offers several attractive features. I'll detail these and how they can help in asynchronous tasks in the next chapter, which focuses specifically on messaging in enterprise applications.

CHAPTER 9

Messaging and Packaging

Up until now, everything detailed in the Forethought application has been based on *synchronous processing*. This simply means that an event is triggered by some client, then responded to by an application component, and finally an answer is returned to that client. For example, when a Java class requests that a new user be created, the UserManager accesses the User bean, that bean interacts with the database, and an acknowledgment is triggered back up the calling stack. The extensive coverage of this type of interaction is justified, as you will be dealing with synchronous processing far more often than not.

However, there are times when you want more of a listener paradigm. In this case, an application component waits for certain types of events and responds only when those events occur. That component is called a *listener*, because it listens for application events. When it is activated, it takes some sort of action, often interacting with various other components in the application. It typically does not send any acknowledgment when its actions are done, making it asynchronous in operation. I'll detail this sort of behavior in this chapter, focusing on the scheduling component of the Forethought application. Meetings will be added to the Forethought queue and reported to a scheduling client, which simply spits these meetings back out to waiting recipients.

Additionally, this chapter will wrap up some loose ends by detailing the final packaging of the enterprise beans detailed in this and previous chapters. This will fill in the blanks on assembly descriptors, method permissions, and other deployment descriptor options previously left uncovered. At the end of this chapter, you'll have a complete, working application foundation, ready for use.

Messaging on the Server

To begin the discussion on messaging, I want to focus on the scheduling component of the Forethought application. Specifically, I want to look at messaging components on the server. By "the server," I simply mean the back-end of the application, as distinguished from any set of application clients. This may or may not be a separate physical machine, but in either case, it is distinct from application clients such as desktop programs or other application interface tools. Once you understand how this messaging operates within the application, you will be ready for the next section, where clients are discussed and built.

Premise

First, let's revisit the scheduler facility for the Forethought application. The application should be able to store events that are important to the company. As you recall from Chapter 3, the EVENTS table is set up for just such a purpose. Then, users in the Forethought application are associated with these events and become attendees (not surprisingly, stored in the ATTENDEES table). This is all fairly basic material.

Scheduling comes into play when you realize that individual employees will probably run some type of calendar or scheduling software on their computers. For the sake of this discussion, assume that this software is customizable, and that you can add features to it. That is important, as it allows the messaging and scheduling components in the application to be hooked into their desktop software. Given that assumption, the task becomes clear.

Each time a new event is added to the data store, a message should be fired off. This message should indicate that a new event has been created, and also include the attendees for that event. Since you should already have an Event entity bean (from Appendix E), it is fairly easy to extrapolate the need for a session bean to handle the addition of data to that bean, as discussed in the last chapter. I'll call this session bean Scheduler. While it could have been called EventManager, I've used a different name to indicate that it is not a simple administrative component, as the other manager beans were. This component will handle creation of events, and then send off a Java Message Service (JMS) message indicating this creation.

The purpose of this message is simple: it allows any application client subscribed to the same JMS topic to which these messages are sent to consume the new message. The client can examine the new event, and if the event has a certain individual as an attendee, it can sound an alarm, send email, or otherwise notify the relevant attendee. I'll delve into specific examples of these actions in the section "Messaging on the Client." However, understand that once your component makes these messages available through JMS, the possibilities for client interaction become nearly limitless.

The EventManager Bean

Actually putting these principles into practice is not nearly as complex as you might expect. First, you should already have the Event bean coded from Appendix E. You'll then need to code up a manager session bean to allow access to this entity. I've kept this bean extremely simple, as it's not the focus of this discussion. Example 9-1 shows the remote interface for this new manager.

Example 9-1. The EventManager Remote Interface

```java
package com.forethought.ejb.event;

import java.rmi.RemoteException;
import java.util.Collection;
import java.util.Date;
import javax.ejb.EJBObject;

public interface EventManager extends EJBObject {

    public EventInfo addEvent(String description, Date dateTime,
                                    Collection attendees)
        throws RemoteException;

    public boolean removeEvent(EventInfo eventInfo) throws RemoteException;
}
```

Example 9-2 is the home interface for the new manager.

Example 9-2. The EventManager Home Interface

```java
package com.forethought.ejb.event;

import java.rmi.RemoteException;
import javax.ejb.CreateException;
import javax.ejb.EJBHome;

public interface EventManagerHome extends EJBHome {

    public EventManager create()
        throws CreateException, RemoteException;
}
```

Example 9-3 is the implementation class for this bean, and introduces some basic JMS concepts.

Example 9-3. The EventManager Bean

```java
package com.forethought.ejb.event;

import java.rmi.RemoteException;
import java.util.Collection;
import java.util.Date;
import javax.ejb.CreateException;
import javax.ejb.EJBHome;
import javax.jms.JMSException;
import javax.jms.ObjectMessage;
import javax.jms.Topic;
import javax.jms.TopicConnection;
import javax.jms.TopicConnectionFactory;
```

Example 9-3. The EventManager Bean (continued)

```
import javax.jms.TopicPublisher;
import javax.jms.TopicSession;
import javax.naming.Context;
import javax.naming.InitialContext;
import javax.naming.NamingException;

import com.forethought.ejb.util.SessionAdapter;

public class EventManagerBean extends SessionAdapter {

    /** <p> Required method for allowing bean lookups. </p> */
    public void ejbCreate( ) throws CreateException {
        // No action required for stateless session beans
    }

    public EventInfo addEvent(String description, Date dateTime,
                              Collection attendees)
        throws RemoteException {

        try {
            // Get an InitialContext
            Context context = new InitialContext( );

            // Add event to database
            EventHome eventHome = (EventHome)
                context.lookup("java:comp/env/ejb/EventHome");
            Event event = eventHome.create(description, dateTime, attendees);
            EventInfo eventInfo = event.getInfo( );

            // Get topic factory
            TopicConnectionFactory factory =
                (TopicConnectionFactory)context.lookup(
                    "java:comp/env/jms/TopicFactory");
            Topic topic =
                (Topic)context.lookup("java:comp/env/jms/SchedulerTopic");

            // Connect to topic
            TopicConnection connection = factory.createTopicConnection( );

            // Send off notification of this event creation
            TopicSession session =
                connection.createTopicSession(false,
                    javax.jms.Session.AUTO_ACKNOWLEDGE);
            TopicPublisher publisher = session.createPublisher(topic);

            // Send message
            ObjectMessage message = session.createObjectMessage( );
            message.setStringProperty("Action", "create");
            message.setObject(eventInfo);
            publisher.publish(message);
            connection.close( );
```

Example 9-3. The EventManager Bean (continued)

```
            return eventInfo;
        } catch (NamingException e) {
            throw new RemoteException(e.getMessage());
        } catch (CreateException e) {
            throw new RemoteException(e.getMessage());
        } catch (JMSException e) {
            throw new RemoteException(e.getMessage());
        }
    }

    public boolean removeEvent(EventInfo eventInfo) throws RemoteException {
        Event event = getEvent(eventInfo.getId());

        boolean deleted = delete(event);
        if (deleted) {
            try {
                // Get an InitialContext
                Context context = new InitialContext();

                // Get topic factory
                TopicConnectionFactory factory =
                    (TopicConnectionFactory)context.lookup(
                        "java:comp/env/jms/TopicFactory");
                Topic topic =
                    (Topic)context.lookup("java:comp/env/jms/SchedulerTopic");

                // Connect to topic
                TopicConnection connection = factory.createTopicConnection();

                // Send off notification of this event
                TopicSession session =
                    connection.createTopicSession(false,
                        javax.jms.Session.AUTO_ACKNOWLEDGE);
                TopicPublisher publisher = session.createPublisher(topic);

                // Send message
                ObjectMessage message = session.createObjectMessage();
                message.setStringProperty("Action", "delete");
                message.setObject(eventInfo);
                publisher.publish(message);
                connection.close();
            } catch (JMSException e) {
                throw new RemoteException(e.getMessage());
            } catch (NamingException e) {
                throw new RemoteException(e.getMessage());
            }
        }

        return deleted;
    }

    private Event getEvent(int id) {
```

Example 9-3. The EventManager Bean (continued)

```
        try {
            // Get an InitialContext
            Context context = new InitialContext();

            // Look up the User bean
            EventHome eventHome = (EventHome)
                context.lookup("java:comp/env/ejb/EventHome");
            Event event = eventHome.findByPrimaryKey(new Integer(id));

            return event;
        } catch (Exception e) {
            // Any problems - just return null
            return null;
        }
    }

    private boolean delete(Event event) {
        if (event == null) {
            return true;
        }
        try {
            event.remove();
            return true;
        } catch (Exception e) {
            // any problems - return false
            return false;
        }
    }
}
```

While the bulk of this code is the same manager-style coding you've seen in previous chapters, there is some messaging tucked into the addEvent( ) and removeEvent( ) methods. I won't go into any detail about how JMS works, as both *Enterprise Java-Beans* and *Java Message Service* (both from O'Reilly) cover this in depth. However, you should be able to see that in both creation and deletion, notification is sent out to anyone listening on the Forethought topic.

In this example, I've chosen to use the ObjectMessage type, which allows any serializable object to be sent as the body of the message. Of course, the information map for the event class (EventInfo) is a perfect fit here, and one more reason to use these value objects. That class, in turn, contains a List of UserInfo objects, so even more information is stuffed into the message body. Additionally, some indication of what action has occurred needs to be included. Rather than putting this application-specific data into the information map, a string property of the message is set, which will be decoded by message recipients. The result is a simple yet useful message that is broadcast upon creation and deletion of events in the Forethought system. This completes the EventManager bean, and allows us to move on to a message-driven bean that will consume and use these messages.

Business Logic and Messaging Logic

As in the case of using pure JMS, described in the last section, I am not going to discuss the basics of message-driven beans. Instead, I'll simply show you a new bean for your application, the Scheduler bean, which consumes messages from the EventManager bean just created. One nice thing about message-driven beans is that they are completely server-based components. This means that no remote or home interface is required. Given that, Example 9-4 jumps straight to the implementation code for this new bean.

Example 9-4. The Scheduler Bean

```
package com.forethought.ejb.scheduler;

import java.util.Iterator;
import java.util.List;
import javax.ejb.EJBException;
import javax.ejb.MessageDrivenBean;
import javax.ejb.MessageDrivenContext;
import javax.jms.JMSException;
import javax.jms.Message;
import javax.jms.MessageListener;
import javax.jms.ObjectMessage;
import javax.jms.Session;
import javax.jms.Topic;
import javax.jms.TopicConnection;
import javax.jms.TopicConnectionFactory;
import javax.jms.TopicSession;
import javax.jms.TopicPublisher;
import javax.naming.Context;
import javax.naming.InitialContext;
import javax.naming.NamingException;

// Event bean
import com.forethought.ejb.event.EventInfo;

// User bean
import com.forethought.ejb.user.UserInfo;

public class SchedulerBean implements MessageDrivenBean {

    /** The context for the message-driven bean, set by the EJB container */
    private MessageDrivenContext messageContext;

    /** Required creation method for message-driven beans */
    public void ejbCreate() {
        // No action required for message-driven beans
    }

    /** Required removal method for message-driven beans */
    public void ejbRemove() {
        messageContext = null;
    }
```

Example 9-4. The Scheduler Bean (continued)

```java
    /** Required method for container to set context */
    public void setMessageDrivenContext(MessageDrivenContext messageContext) {
        this.messageContext = messageContext;
    }

    public void onMessage(Message message) {
        try {
            // Convert to the correct message type
            ObjectMessage objectMessage = (ObjectMessage)message;

            // Dissect message
            String action = objectMessage.getStringProperty("Action");
            EventInfo eventInfo = (EventInfo)objectMessage.getObject();

            // Dispatch
            sendEventNotification(action, eventInfo);
        } catch (JMSException e) {
            throw new EJBException(e);
        } catch (NamingException e) {
            throw new EJBException(e);
        }
    }

    private void sendEventNotification(String action, EventInfo eventInfo)
        throws JMSException, NamingException {

        // Ignore deleted events
        if (action.equalsIgnoreCase("delete")) {
            return;
        }

        // Ensure that at least one employee involved
        boolean hasEmployee = false;
        for (Iterator i = eventInfo.getAttendees().iterator(); i.hasNext(); ) {
            UserInfo userInfo = (UserInfo)i.next();
            if (userInfo.getType().equals("Employee")) {
                hasEmployee = true;
                break;
            }
        }
        if (!hasEmployee) {
            return;
        }

        // Get the client topic destination
        Context context = new InitialContext();
        TopicConnectionFactory factory =
            (TopicConnectionFactory)context.lookup(
                "java:comp/env/jms/TopicFactory");
        Topic topic = (Topic)context.lookup("java:comp/env/jms/EmployeeTopic");

        // Connect to topic
        TopicConnection connection = factory.createTopicConnection();
```

Example 9-4. The Scheduler Bean (continued)

```
        // Send off notification of this event
        TopicSession session =
            connection.createTopicSession(false, Session.AUTO_ACKNOWLEDGE);
        TopicPublisher publisher = session.createPublisher(topic);

        // Build message
        ObjectMessage message = session.createObjectMessage( );
        message.setObject(eventInfo);
        publisher.publish(message);

        // Close up
        connection.close( );
    }
}
```

As you can see, this bean does some basic data filtering but not much more. It uses the onMessage( ) method to consume any and all messages from the EventManager bean or any other publisher to the *Scheduler* topic. It then sends out new messages to the *Employee* topic (introduced for the first time here), using another ObjectMessage, through the sendEventNotification( ) method. Given that this bean does little more than resend messages, you are probably wondering why it even exists. This is a good question, and has a good answer.

The EventManager bean could have easily sent messages directly to the *Employee* topic, handling filtering on its own. However, that assumes that no other action needs to be taken. For example, a more advanced Scheduler bean might update a company-wide directory server with the event information, log the changes to a static text file, and update a scheduling database using entity beans. This logic is specific to scheduling, not simple creation and addition of events. If all of this scheduling logic were added into the EventManager component, it would quickly become unclear what code in that bean was specifically event-related, and what code was scheduling-related. In other words, the bean would quickly cease to be a simple manager/administrative component.

Further, that scenario presumes that only the EventManager takes action related to scheduling. It's plausible that other beans, Java classes, or messaging clients might also be able to update events, change attendees, or perform other scheduling-related actions. By taking all scheduling-related code and placing it in a separate bean, any additional logic can be maintained in a single place (the Scheduler bean). Finally, this design allows changes to scheduling logic to occur without having to make the Event-Manager unavailable; if this happened, the EventManager would simply be sending messages out that would be consumed at a later date (or not at all, as the case may be). In any case, it should be clear that separating your messaging logic from your data logic is critical, and explains the reasoning behind a separate Scheduler bean. Don't be fooled by the simplicity of the current Scheduler implementation; things in a real-world system would quickly become more complex than shown here.

You should now follow the appendixes' and your server's instructions to deploy these new components, including the message-driven bean. Once those resources are in place, it's time to look at writing a standalone Java client that takes these messages and does something with them.

Messaging on the Client

At this point, handling messaging from the client perspective is a piece of cake. It's simply a matter of connecting to the messaging service (through your application server's messaging middleware) and listening to a specific Topic or Queue. To ensure that you can get some sample code up and running to see how this works, I've included Example 9-5, a simple listener class.

Example 9-5. The JMSTester Class

```
package com.forethought.client;

import java.util.Date;
import javax.jms.JMSException;
import javax.jms.Message;
import javax.jms.MessageListener;
import javax.jms.ObjectMessage;
import javax.jms.Session;
import javax.jms.TextMessage;
import javax.jms.Topic;
import javax.jms.TopicConnection;
import javax.jms.TopicConnectionFactory;
import javax.jms.TopicSession;
import javax.jms.TopicSubscriber;
import javax.naming.Context;
import javax.naming.InitialContext;
import javax.naming.NamingException;

// Event bean
import com.forethought.ejb.event.EventInfo;

// User bean
import com.forethought.ejb.user.UserInfo;

public class JMSTester implements MessageListener {

    public JMSTester(String factoryName, String topicName)
        throws JMSException, NamingException {

        Context context = getInitialContext();

        // Get topic factory
        TopicConnectionFactory factory =
            (TopicConnectionFactory)context.lookup(factoryName);
        Topic topic = (Topic)context.lookup(topicName);
```

Example 9-5. The JMSTester Class (continued)

```
        // Connect to topic
        TopicConnection connection = factory.createTopicConnection( );

        // Send off notification of this event creation
        TopicSession session =
            connection.createTopicSession(false, Session.AUTO_ACKNOWLEDGE);
        TopicSubscriber subscriber = session.createSubscriber(topic);

        subscriber.setMessageListener(this);

        System.out.println("Starting connection listener on '" +
            topicName + "'...");
        connection.start( );
    }

    public void onMessage(Message message) {
        try {
            ObjectMessage objectMessage = (ObjectMessage)message;
            String action = objectMessage.getStringProperty("Action");
            if (action == null) {
                action = "NO ACTION SPECIFIED";
            }
            Object obj = objectMessage.getObject( );

            EventInfo info = (EventInfo)obj;
            String description = info.getDescription( );
            Date dateTime = info.getDateTime( );
            System.out.println("[" + action + "]");
            System.out.println("  * Description: " + description);
            System.out.println("  * Date: " + dateTime);
        } catch (JMSException e) {
            e.printStackTrace( );
        }

    }

    public static void main(String[] args) {
        try {
            new JMSTester("forethought.TopicFactory", args[0]);

            while (true) {
                Thread.sleep(1000);
            }
        } catch (Exception e) {
            e.printStackTrace( );
        }
    }

    private Context getInitialContext( ) throws NamingException {
        // Insert application-specific connection details here if needed
        return new InitialContext( );
    }
}
```

This is loosely based on code from both *Enterprise JavaBeans* and *Java Message Service*, so thanks to Richard Monson-Haefel and Dave Chappell for the good work. You can start this client up and simply specify the JNDI name of the messaging topic to listen to. You also might want to add some logic to add a few events, as shown here:

```
// Look up the EventManager bean
System.out.println("Looking up the EventManager bean.\n");
ref = context.lookup("forethought.EventManagerHome");
EventManagerHome eventManagerHome = (EventManagerHome)
    PortableRemoteObject.narrow(ref, EventManagerHome.class);
EventManager eventManager = eventManagerHome.create();

// Create an event
java.text.DateFormat formatter =
    java.text.DateFormat.getDateInstance();
List attendees = new LinkedList();
attendees.add(userManager.get("shirlbg"));
attendees.add(userManager.get("gqg10012"));
EventInfo eventInfo =
    eventManager.addEvent("Lunch Meeting",
        formatter.parse("February 1, 2002 11:30am CST"),
        attendees);
if (eventInfo != null) {
    System.out.println("Created new event (#1).\n");
} else {
    System.out.println("Could not create event #1.");
    return;
}

List clients = new LinkedList();
clients.add(userManager.get("shirlbg"));
clients.add(userManager.get("rhyner"));
clients.add(userManager.get("greggo"));
EventInfo eventInfo2 =
    eventManager.addEvent("Round Table",
        formatter.parse("March 8, 2002 1:45pm CST"),
        clients);
if (eventInfo2 != null) {
    System.out.println("Created new event (#2).\n");
} else {
    System.out.println("Could not create event #2.");
    return;
}

// Remove event
deleted = eventManager.removeEvent(eventInfo);
if (!deleted) {
    System.out.println("Could not delete event #1.");
    return;
}
System.out.println("Deleted event #1.");
```

```
    deleted = eventManager.removeEvent(eventInfo2);
    if (!deleted) {
        System.out.println("Could not delete event #2.");
        return;
    }
    System.out.println("Deleted event #2.\n");
```

Several sample classes are included with the book's downloadable code (online at *http://www.newInstance.com*), and those examples include classes that add events as shown. These events trigger messages from the EventManager bean, and those messages are then received by the Scheduler bean. In the previous example, the first event is not passed on to the *Employee* topic because it involves two clients; the second event, though, should be received by the *Employee* topic. Both deletions are ignored by the Scheduler bean and are not passed on to the *Employee* topic.

To see this code in action, open up several windows. Run the JMSTester in two, one connecting to the *forethought.EmployeeTopic* and one connecting to the *forethought. SchedulerTopic*. You can then see both sets of event notifications. Finally (in a third window or shell), run the code that creates events, as shown previously. You should see the messages appear in both shells running the listener sample application:

```
Starting connection listener on 'forethought.SchedulerTopic'...
[create]
  * Description: Lunch Meeting
  * Date: Fri Feb 01 00:00:00 CST 2002
[create]
  * Description: Round Table
  * Date: Fri Mar 08 00:00:00 CST 2002
[delete]
  * Description: Lunch Meeting
  * Date: Fri Feb 01 00:00:00 CST 2002
[delete]
  * Description: Round Table
  * Date: Fri Mar 08 00:00:00 CST 2002
```

Here's the same sample listening to a different topic:

```
C:\dev\javaentI>java com.forethought.client.JMSTester forethought.EmployeeTopic
Starting connection listener on 'forethought.EmployeeTopic'...
[NO ACTION SPECIFIED]
  * Description: Round Table
  * Date: Fri Mar 08 00:00:00 CST 2002
```

As you can see, everything is behaving just as planned. You could embed the relevant listening component of JMSTester in a calendar application, an alarm clock program, or any other desktop program that would help employees know when meetings are set and when they are about to occur. The possibilities are limited only by your own programming imagination.

Packaging

So far, I've left the details of method permissions, as well as roles and transactions, out of deployment discussions, primarily to avoid confusing an already complex set of issues. With the coding in this book done, though, it's time to circle back around and deal with these issues, as they complete the Forethought deployment descriptors.

First, realize that all these options exist within the `assembly-descriptor` element, which itself exists as a child of the root element in the descriptor, `ejb-jar`. It should follow right after the `enterprise-beans` element. This is all basic information, though, so I won't dwell on it; I assume you can use your server's tools and DTDs to determine the basics of the XML formatting. You should also realize that the entire `assembly-descriptor` element is optional in a deployment descriptor. That said, the only good reason for leaving the `assembly-descriptor` out is the case where you are developing beans, but someone else in your organization is actually deploying your beans. In other words, no application should have deployed beans (in production) without assembly descriptors for those beans.

Security Roles

The first option you have is to define one or more security roles. As is detailed in *Enterprise JavaBeans*, these roles are merely logical; there are no predefined roles in the EJB 2.0 specification that can be used. Instead, the role names used here are mapped at deployment time to actual security parameters in the application environment. Furthermore, these logical roles are most often associated with actual physical roles when the web access layer is defined. Because authentication is handled in the web tier (or web services tier) more often than not, it is often premature at this point to assume too much about security.

In the case of the Forethought application, everything defined so far is accessible by any administrator. Because I have left the Forethought business logic concerning investments, transactions, and other business-specific details out, this is the only role I define in the descriptor:

```
<assembly-descriptor>
  <security-role>
    <description>
      The Administrator role is used for any user that must perform data
        access and direct manipulation of the Forethought data. It allows
        use of the manager beans in the Forethought application.
    </description>
    <role-name>Administrator</role-name>
  </security-role>
</assembly-descriptor>
```

Method Permissions

Next, you can define one or more method permissions. These permissions use the roles defined in the security-role element, and so naturally follow the placement of those elements. This is also well covered in various EJB books, and involves simply mapping the logical roles in your application to specific bean methods:

```
<assembly-descriptor>
  <security-role>
    <description>
      The Administrator role is used for any user that must perform data
          access and direct manipulation of the Forethought data. It allows
          use of the manager beans in the Forethought application.
    </description>
    <role-name>Administrator</role-name>
  </security-role>

  <method-permission>
    <role-name>Administrator</role-name>
    <method>
      <ejb-name>UserManagerBean</ejb-name>
      <method-name>*</method-name>
    </method>
  </method-permission>
</assembly-descriptor>
```

As a warning, some application servers (including the J2EE SDK) do not handle the wildcard (*) very well, and report errors with this sort of declaration. However, these are not errors, as the EJB specification states that wildcards are acceptable values for the method-name element.

I won't spend any more time on roles or permissions, as there are no real design strategies to speak of yet. Future volumes will cover linking the web application tier and web services tier with beans, and coordinating method permissions in that respect. At this point, though, you can define as few or as many logical roles as you like to get familiar with this portion of the XML descriptor.

Container Transactions

The last option is to define one or more container transactions. For the beans detailed in this book, you should require that a transaction exist for each and every entity bean in the application. This is a fairly basic principle; you always want transaction safety in place when dealing with your database.

However, there is a little more to be worked out with regard to the various session beans in the application. First, take the Sequence bean; this bean is always used in the various entity beans' ejbCreate( ) methods. Therefore, the Supports value is sufficient. This value ensures that if a transaction exists, it will be used; however, if a non-transactional component is in use, it will not require a new transaction to be committed. This value is in use any time a component (like the Sequence bean) is operating upon application data that does not have to be kept pristine. For example, a primary key value that is one or two values too high is of no consequence. Use an entry like this for the Sequence bean:

```
<container-transaction>
  <method>
    <ejb-name>SequenceBean</ejb-name>
    <method-name>getNextValue</method-name>
  </method>
  <trans-attribute>Supports</trans-attribute>
</container-transaction>
```

All of your entity beans should also require transactions. Even if the calling component does not have a transaction in existence, one should be required for operating on business data. This is defined in a similar way as shown previously, with only a different value for the transaction attribute:

```
<container-transaction>
  <method>
    <ejb-name>UserBean</ejb-name>
    <method-name>*</method-name>
  </method>
  <trans-attribute>Required</trans-attribute>
</container-transaction>
<container-transaction>
  <method>
    <ejb-name>OfficeBean</ejb-name>
    <method-name>*</method-name>
  </method>
  <trans-attribute>Required</trans-attribute>
</container-transaction>
```

Finally, you need to decide how to manage transactions for your façade and manager beans, which expose this data to application clients. Here, you will most likely see these beans called from nontransactional components, such as servlets, Java classes, or web services. Because these beans often deal with multiple data sources (users, office, and types, for example), they should also work within transactions. Therefore, the Required transaction attribute value would seem appropriate here, as well.

However, you must decide how to handle the case in which one manager (such as AccountManager) might use another manager (such as UserManager). The two options are to use the same transaction throughout (a value of Required), or to require a new transaction for the scope of each manager (a value of RequiresNew). I prefer to have each manager executing within its own transaction. This keeps data consistency, but also allows a manager's actions to be separated from another manager's actions. My deployment entries would then look like this:

```
<container-transaction>
  <method>
    <ejb-name>UserManagerBean</ejb-name>
```

```
      <method-name>*</method-name>
    </method>
    <trans-attribute>RequiresNew</trans-attribute>
  </container-transaction>
  <container-transaction>
    <method>
      <ejb-name>AccountManagerBean</ejb-name>
      <method-name>*</method-name>
    </method>
    <trans-attribute>RequiresNew</trans-attribute>
  </container-transaction>
```

I realize that this is hardly an exhaustive discussion of transactions and security. However, these issues are either very basic (allowing or disallowing access, requiring or not requiring a transaction), or incredibly complex (manually handling rollbacks, relational data integrity, multi-phase commits). As a result, these topics must be either handled briefly, as I have done, or in depth in books focused on transactions or security. I'll leave it to you to decide if you need the additional complexity in your applications. If you do, I highly recommend *Java Security* by Scott Oaks and *Database Programming with JDBC and Java* by George Reese (both from O'Reilly), which focus extensively on these topics.

What's Next?

After adding JMS capabilities and packaging information to your application programming toolkit, you really do have the tools to build almost any Java enterprise application conceivable. While there is certainly an endless array of variables that will change in your own programming, you should feel confident that you have the knowledge and techniques required to handle those changes. From here, it's a short ride to handling application front-ends.

In the next chapter, I'll address that very issue. While this volume does not cover web applications, web services, or other front-end paradigms, I don't want to leave you without some guidance on where to go from here. Chapter 10 should give you some direction, as well as an impetus to explore more than just the application foundations discussed in this volume. I'll also include some discussion on why so many of the decisions in this book were made, answer some of those "why?" questions still floating around, and really have you ready to take on enterprise applications.

## CHAPTER 10

Beyond Architecture

You now have a solid application backbone in place. You may be expecting another five or ten chapters detailing how to write a GUI or HTML interface, servlets and JavaServer Pages for application logic, a web services interface, or any number of other layers. However, the *Building Java Enterprise Applications* series is geared at teaching you solid application design. For that reason, this chapter marks the end of this volume, and leaves discussion of application front-ends for Volumes II and III.

If this doesn't make much sense to you, consider that any application backbone, like the Forethought application used throughout the book, should be easily segregated into several discrete layers. Figure 10-1 illustrates this, and should remind you of the discussions from Chapter 2.

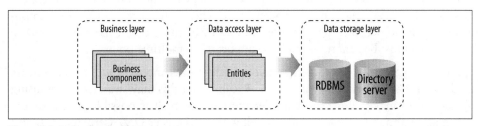

Figure 10-1. Application layering

As you can see, a web services front-end relies on the same back-end as does a traditional J2EE web application (servlets, JSP, etc.). If you design your application backbone specifically for presentation through a web application, then using that same backbone for a web application can become awkward and kludgy. By the same token, a backbone built to work specifically with a web services presentation layer can cause problems when converting or adding a web presentation layer using HTML, WML, and other markup languages. The best approach, then, is to design your application's infrastructure to be wholly independent of any specific presentation layer. That is the approach endorsed and detailed in this book, and the reasoning behind why this volume does not discuss front-end issues.

In this chapter, I'll explain further how some of the decisions made in previous chapters are critical to the layers you will add on top of the application infrastructure. I'll begin by discussing how decisions made in these "lower" application layers can improve the flexibility of your application. From there, I'll move on to some general discussion on how to determine what sort of application front-end you may want to add to your own applications. This provides a natural progression into future volumes, and some advice on how to proceed with your application programming.

Flexibility

The first thing you should always consider in developing applications is maintaining flexibility in your design. I realize that I have devoted the last nine chapters to this principle, but it's well worth repeating. I'll briefly run over the salient points in relation to application architecture here, for use in your own programming projects. You can also see these in effect in the various code samples throughout the book, as well as in Appendix E.

Data Modeling Versus Entity Modeling

The first consideration in design flexibility is in how you model your data. In the Forethought case, this refers to the way that your database and directory server expose the contained information to the rest of the application. When you are developing a single application, this detail is not as important as it is when you have multiple entry points into the application. For example, when not only servlets access the data layer but also session beans, a web service client, and possibly CORBA components, the issue becomes much more important. In these cases, the model used to expose data must be generic enough to support these multiple points of entry.

Specifically, you will need to decide if your entity beans and data access components model your data, or model your entities. I realize that this may seem like a confusing distinction to make. However, consider the User bean. It is possible to expose the information about a user as a data model, with its ID, user DN, username, first and last name, related office ID, and so forth. You can then expose offices the same way, and programmatically build the link between users and offices. In other words, you simply provide access to the data model, and then have your Java components handle any joins, links, etc. The problem here is that you have exposed data without giving it any context, allowing application components to misuse the data, interpret it incorrectly, or even provide clients with data you don't want them to have (like user passwords or database IDs).

A better approach is to provide this data as *entities*; the difference is that an entity is data with some specific context. For example, instead of getting the ID of a user's office, a client would only be able to get the actual office object (the Office bean in an EJB application). In this way, your data layer doesn't provide database IDs and the like, but instead provides entities that protect this database-specific information from users. Extending this case even further, using session beans (through the façade pattern as well as simple business objects) provides even greater insulation over your data layer. In this way, you can handle security, data integrity, and relationships between pieces of data in your application backbone; front-ends for the data layer do not have to worry about how data is interpreted, as that interpretation is handled before it ever sees the data. In retrospect, it should be obvious how this principle was applied throughout the application design in this book. Additionally, CMP in EJB 2.0 makes this even easier with persistence relationships, removing the need for entity beans to ever directly interact with other tables' IDs.*

Single Point of Access

Another important point to keep in mind is the number of access points that your application backbone will provide. By access points, I do not mean user interfaces or client interactions, but data access points. For example, a servlet front-end and a web service front-end that both use the same data layer (like the one outlined in this book) use the same access point, because they go through the same session and entity beans to get at the data. Changing the way that this access point functions affects all front-ends using it for access, which is exactly what you want.

However, when multiple access points are present, things get more complex. For example, consider the use of the Sequence session bean. This bean depends upon the PRIMARY_KEYS table, which in turn assumes that primary keys are always obtained through this table. If another access point were provided for the Forethought tables (through another set of entity beans not using the Sequence bean, direct JDBC access, or even non-Java access), the primary key values in the PRIMARY_KEYS table become stale and invalid. In fact, continuing to use the Sequence bean can then result in errors because of duplicate primary key values.

This rather sticky situation isn't the only reason to avoid multiple access points. You also introduce significant security risks; a change to access rights in one access point doesn't affect security in the others. This means that every transactional change, every security access change, and every database or directory server change must be propagated to every single access point available. Therefore, you would do well to provide a single means of data access, and then enforce that rule. This was an assumption made in the Forethought application design, and many decisions in effect in this book would be invalidated if multiple access points were to be provided.

One final note is in order, though: a single access point does not mean that you cannot mix APIs like JDBC, EJB, and even newer technologies like JDO (Java Data

---

* Actually, container-generated classes for your CMP beans may have to interact with these IDs. However, the interfaces and simple abstract classes that you write are free of these sorts of details.

Objects, not covered in this book). An access point can use any and all of these various APIs, but does so in a way that integrates, rather than segregates, methodologies. Your effort to limit access points does not limit the technologies you use; it simply limits the number of entry points provided for other application clients. Although at first glance limiting the access points might seem to decrease flexibility, you can actually allow more types of clients to access your application because you know you can maintain control and configuration over your data layer.

Standardized Access APIs

The final point I want to make in terms of providing flexibility is in your choice of APIs. I realize that because you have chosen Java for your programming, you may already have chosen standardized APIs like the J2EE API set, JAXP, WSDL, UDDI, and the like. However, for those of you who want to understand why a decision was made, or who must justify a decision to managers (and that should cover just about all of you), it's worth pointing out that by using a set of established APIs, you ensure that application clients can easily communicate with your application infrastructure.

As an example, you may want to expose a portion of your data to other companies or businesses. In the Forethought case, this might be other brokerages or financial institutions that can leverage your investment data. For this to occur, those external entities must be able to communicate with your application. Rather than expecting those clients to work with proprietary data formats, proprietary APIs, and a whole set of application-specific idioms, you can simply inform these clients that you provide (for example) session beans via RMI/IIOP for data access. Transaction levels and security rights all still apply, and it becomes fairly trivial for companies to implement cross-company communications. This is only possible through the use of standard, accepted APIs for application access.

By the same token, you would want the same convenience when your code must interact with other companies' data. Rather than having to write thousands of lines of code to interpret company- or vendor-specific paradigms, you can use the techniques in this and other Java and XML books to make these tasks simple. Just as you would prefer this sort of setup for your coding, you should take the same steps to allow others to interact with your code. Even if you never need to interact with external code, maintenance and upkeep are simplified when standard programming techniques using documented APIs are in play. Again, some rather simple (and logical) decisions early on can greatly increase the flexibility of your applications in the long run.

Decision Point

I don't want to leave you completely on your own in terms of what to program next. Obviously, you need some sort of user interface on top of the infrastructure put together so far, and of course it needs to fit in with the architecture described up to this point. The two most common application front-end paradigms, as of this writing, are the standard web application (servlets, JSP) and the web services framework (SOAP, UDDI, WSDL). I'll briefly touch on each. This will also give you some insight as to what the next volumes will cover.

Web Applications

A web application, in the context of this book, is meant to refer to a J2EE-centric application programming model. This means that servlets are used for application logic, and either provide presentation on their own or defer to some other presentation technology. Popular options in this area are JavaServer Pages (JSP), frameworks like Apache Turbine (*http://jakarta.apache.org/turbine*), and Apache Cocoon (*http://xml.apache.org/cocoon*). While these are just a few of many examples for handling content and presentation, they all build on the J2EE core APIs (usually servlets), and well-understood Java and XML APIs like SAX, DOM, and JDOM.

If you don't know what type of front-end you want to provide to the end user, this is almost certainly the best choice. It is the most common, and as a result you can easily find resources on the relevant technologies. Books like *Java Servlet Programming* and *JavaServer Pages* (both from O'Reilly) provide good introductions to these APIs, and will get you quickly up and running. Additionally, building web services and other front-ends can most easily be done upon an existing web application. And, obviously, a web application provides access through any standard web browser, as well as providing easy inroads into web-enabled phones, PDAs, and other mobile devices.

If you do decide to move into the web application world, you should employ the same principles endorsed in this book. Start with a layer for application logic, using servlets. Ensure that any content is handled independently of presentation details, so the same data can be shown to an HTML browser, an XML viewer, or a WML phone; this is in the same vein as the clean separation of data and business logic detailed in this book. From there, move into presentation technologies, and try not to code in such a way that only specifically formatted content is accepted. In other words, developing an engine for converting data into presentation is a better idea than simply taking very specific data and creating a very specific screen for viewing. I will focus on these very ideas in Volume II of this series, *Web Applications*.

Web Services

Coming in a close second to the traditional web application is the web services paradigm. I should start by saying that web services are still young enough that any predictions here or anywhere else are just that: predictions. Don't depend on them, as things could easily change a year, a month, or even a week from now. That said, it does appear that web services are going to play an important part in the next generation of web-enabled applications. The emergence of semi-standards like WSDL and full-blown standards like UDDI and SOAP offer a lot of promise to a higher degree of application interoperation than what is currently available.

If you do want to web-service-enable your application, you should probably start by adding some application logic on top of what was discussed in this book. Remember, the more context you can add to your data, the more useful it becomes to other companies. A book is more useful than a collection of titles and ISBN numbers, and a "library" (in some object form) is generally more useful than just a book. Although it is certainly possible to expose EJBs directly as web services, it is generally a better idea to add some layer of functionality on top of these beans.

You should also begin to dig into the various web services specifications, like SOAP and UDDI. You may also want to check out related books, like *Programming Web Services with SOAP* (O'Reilly), a language-independent look at web applications, and *Java & XML* (O'Reilly), which covers SOAP, WSDL, and UDDI for Java specifically. You can also find example code online at locations like *http://xml.apache.org/soap*. Many application server vendors, like BEA Weblogic and Lutris Enhydra, also offer web services "packs" or add-ons to their server products, which provide tools to aid in conversion from beans and Java classes to web services. I won't cover web services in detail until Volume III of this series, in order to let some of the glitter shake off the paradigm in favor of stability and proven techniques.

What's Next?

Despite all of the information covered, it can still be confusing to decide what to do next. With over a thousand lines of code in this book, you still do not have a complete application. And while I hope you pick up Volume II of this series when it becomes available, I certainly wouldn't advise you not to press on in the interim. So, in closing, I want to provide some suggestions on how to proceed in your enterprise application programming.

First, take some time to understand the supplemental code in Appendix E. While I didn't cover all of this in detail in the various chapters, there is quite a bit of information stuffed in between curly braces and brackets. The code (particularly when downloaded from *http://www.newInstance.com*) is loaded with comments and Javadoc, and illustrates some concepts in addition to those explicitly covered in the text of the book. You can also gain a good bit of insight about container-managed persistence in EJB 2.0, the nuts and bolts of the Java Message Service and message-driven beans, and more. I've included all of this code in printed form in Appendix E, so take advantage of the listings.

Next, try to find something at your job to apply these concepts to. Your own assignments in the enterprise application space should allow you a test bed for the concepts mentioned here and for techniques of your own. My ideas all stem from actual problems I've had to solve; you should assemble your own toolkit of similar ideas and programming idioms. In other words, practice makes perfect, and you need to do more than simply read through this book to master application programming in Java.

Finally, don't wait on a book to start building out your application. Develop a servlet front-end, code up some JSPs, or delve into web services, using either the Forethought backbone or an application of your own. This will put you ahead of those who won't venture into new territory without a roadmap, and you may find yourself teaching them before long. Future volumes of this series, or other books, may cause you to make changes down the line; however, you will have a sound understanding of what led you to these changes, and that experience is invaluable. Most of all, enjoy yourself, and I'll see you online.

SQL Scripts

This appendix contains the SQL scripts that are specific to a variety of different databases. In addition to adding enhancements that will improve performance on a specific database, these scripts omit any constructs that are not supported by a specific database (for example, the InstantDB script does not employ foreign keys, a feature still under development). If you are having trouble with the standard SQL scripts provided in Chapters 3 or 5, check to see if a script for your specific database is included here.* All of the scripts shown here are available for download online by visiting *http://www.newInstance.com.*

Additionally, many of these scripts contain information that is not SQL, but instead is an instruction set for the database. For example, the Cloudscape database needs connection information specified at the head of any SQL script run against it, and InstantDB needs information about the JDBC driver to use. For each of the databases covered here, specific deployment details are covered in Appendix B. Any additional information specified in the examples in this appendix is also used in Appendix B as part of deployment.

Finally, the scripts used to create the accounts storage assume that the scripts to create the user store have already been run. In other words, if you are using Cloudscape, you must execute the script in Example A-1 before executing the one in Example A-6. This is because the foreign key constraint on the USER_ID in the ACCOUNTS table references a column that must already exist from the USERS table. Errors will result if the user store has not already been created. Again, following the steps outlined in Appendix B will ensure these problems do not arise.

---

* If your database is not covered here, please feel free to send a working SQL script (for both the users and accounts storage) to me directly at *brett@newInstance.com.* If I can ensure that it works, I will be happy to include it online and in updated versions of this book. I welcome people helping me to support a large number of databases.

The User Store

The SQL scripts in this section duplicate the functionality of the script shown in Example 3-1, and create the storage for user information.

Cloudscape

Example A-1 is a version of the SQL script that works on the Cloudscape Java database.

Example A-1. SQL Script for Creating the User Store on Cloudscape Databases

```
-- USER_TYPES table
CREATE TABLE USER_TYPES (
        USER_TYPE_ID        INT PRIMARY KEY NOT NULL,
        USER_TYPE           VARCHAR(20) NOT NULL
);

-- OFFICES table
CREATE TABLE OFFICES (
        OFFICE_ID           INT PRIMARY KEY NOT NULL,
        CITY                VARCHAR(20) NOT NULL,
        STATE               CHAR(2) NOT NULL
);

-- USERS table
CREATE TABLE USERS (
        USER_ID             INT PRIMARY KEY NOT NULL,
        OFFICE_ID           INT NOT NULL,
        USER_DN             VARCHAR(100) NOT NULL,
        USER_TYPE_ID        INT NOT NULL,
        FIRST_NAME          VARCHAR(20) NOT NULL,
        LAST_NAME           VARCHAR(30) NOT NULL,
        CONSTRAINT OFFICE_ID_FK FOREIGN KEY (OFFICE_ID)
          REFERENCES OFFICES (OFFICE_ID),
        CONSTRAINT USER_TYPE_ID_FK FOREIGN KEY (USER_TYPE_ID)
          REFERENCES USER_TYPES (USER_TYPE_ID)
);
```

InstantDB

Example A-2 is a version of the SQL script that creates the user store for an InstantDB database, and in particular work on the version of InstantDB that ships with Lutris EAS, Version 4.1.

Example A-2. SQL Script for Creating the User Store on InstantDB Databases

```
; Load InstantDB JDBC drivers
d org.enhydra.instantdb.jdbc.idbDriver;
o jdbc:idb=forethought.prp;
```

Example A-2. SQL Script for Creating the User Store on InstantDB Databases (continued)

```
; USER_TYPES table
e CREATE TABLE USER_TYPES (
        USER_TYPE_ID        INT PRIMARY KEY NOT NULL,
        USER_TYPE           VARCHAR(20) NOT NULL
  );

; OFFICES table
e CREATE TABLE OFFICES (
        OFFICE_ID           INT PRIMARY KEY NOT NULL,
        CITY                VARCHAR(20) NOT NULL,
        STATE               CHAR(2) NOT NULL
  );

; USERS table
e CREATE TABLE USERS (
        USER_ID             INT PRIMARY KEY NOT NULL,
        OFFICE_ID           INT NOT NULL,
        USER_DN             VARCHAR(100) NOT NULL,
        USER_TYPE_ID        INT NOT NULL,
        FIRST_NAME          VARCHAR(20) NOT NULL,
        LAST_NAME           VARCHAR(30) NOT NULL
  );

; Close up
c close;
```

MySQL

Example A-3 is a version of the SQL script that creates the user store on a MySQL database.

Example A-3. SQL Script for Creating the User Store on MySQL Databases

```
-- USER_TYPES table
CREATE TABLE USER_TYPES (
      USER_TYPE_ID        INT PRIMARY KEY NOT NULL,
      USER_TYPE           VARCHAR(20) NOT NULL
);

-- OFFICES table
CREATE TABLE OFFICES (
      OFFICE_ID           INT PRIMARY KEY NOT NULL,
      CITY                VARCHAR(20) NOT NULL,
      STATE               CHAR(2) NOT NULL
);

-- USERS table
CREATE TABLE USERS (
      USER_ID             INT PRIMARY KEY NOT NULL,
      OFFICE_ID           INT NOT NULL,
      USER_DN             VARCHAR(100) NOT NULL,
```

```
        USER_TYPE_ID        INT NOT NULL,
        FIRST_NAME          VARCHAR(20) NOT NULL,
        LAST_NAME           VARCHAR(30) NOT NULL,
        CONSTRAINT OFFICE_ID_FK FOREIGN KEY (OFFICE_ID)
          REFERENCES OFFICES (OFFICE_ID),
        CONSTRAINT USER_TYPE_ID_FK FOREIGN KEY (USER_TYPE_ID)
          REFERENCES USER_TYPES (USER_TYPE_ID)
);
```

Oracle

The SQL script shown in Example A-4 creates the user store on Oracle databases, and in particular Version 8.x of the database.

Example A-4. SQL Script for Creating the User Store on Oracle Databases

```
-- USER_TYPES table
CREATE TABLE USER_TYPES (
        USER_TYPE_ID        INTEGER PRIMARY KEY NOT NULL,
        USER_TYPE           VARCHAR2(20) NOT NULL
);

-- OFFICES table
CREATE TABLE OFFICES (
        OFFICE_ID           INTEGER PRIMARY KEY NOT NULL,
        CITY                VARCHAR2(20) NOT NULL,
        STATE               CHAR(2) NOT NULL
);

-- USERS table
CREATE TABLE USERS (
        USER_ID             INTEGER PRIMARY KEY NOT NULL,
        OFFICE_ID           INTEGER NOT NULL,
        USER_DN             VARCHAR2(100) NOT NULL,
        USER_TYPE_ID        INTEGER NOT NULL,
        FIRST_NAME          VARCHAR2(20) NOT NULL,
        LAST_NAME           VARCHAR2(30) NOT NULL,
        CONSTRAINT OFFICE_ID_FK FOREIGN KEY (OFFICE_ID)
          REFERENCES OFFICES (OFFICE_ID),
        CONSTRAINT USER_TYPE_ID_FK FOREIGN KEY (USER_TYPE_ID)
          REFERENCES USER_TYPES (USER_TYPE_ID)
);
```

PostgreSQL

Example A-5 is an SQL script that creates the user store on PostgreSQL databases.

Example A-5. SQL Script for Creating the User Store on PostgreSQL Databases

```
-- USER_TYPES table
CREATE TABLE USER_TYPES (
```

```
      USER_TYPE_ID         INT PRIMARY KEY NOT NULL,
      USER_TYPE            VARCHAR(20) NOT NULL
);

-- OFFICES table
CREATE TABLE OFFICES (
      OFFICE_ID            INT PRIMARY KEY NOT NULL,
      CITY                 VARCHAR(20) NOT NULL,
      STATE                CHAR(2) NOT NULL
);

-- USERS table
CREATE TABLE USERS (
      USER_ID              INT PRIMARY KEY NOT NULL,
      OFFICE_ID            INT NOT NULL,
      USER_DN              VARCHAR(100) NOT NULL,
      USER_TYPE_ID         INT NOT NULL,
      FIRST_NAME           VARCHAR(20) NOT NULL,
      LAST_NAME            VARCHAR(30) NOT NULL,
      CONSTRAINT OFFICE_ID_FK FOREIGN KEY (OFFICE_ID)
        REFERENCES OFFICES (OFFICE_ID),
      CONSTRAINT USER_TYPE_ID_FK FOREIGN KEY (USER_TYPE_ID)
        REFERENCES USER_TYPES (USER_TYPE_ID)
);
```

The Accounts Store

The SQL scripts in this section handle the creation of the accounts store under different databases, and are equivalent to the script shown in Example 3-3 of the text.

Cloudscape

The SQL script shown in Example A-6 creates the accounts store and constraints on Cloudscape databases.

Example A-6. SQL Script for Creating the Accounts Store on Cloudscape Databases

```
-- ACCOUNT_TYPES table
CREATE TABLE ACCOUNT_TYPES (
      ACCOUNT_TYPE_ID      INT PRIMARY KEY NOT NULL,
      ACCOUNT_TYPE         VARCHAR(20) NOT NULL
);

-- ACCOUNTS table
CREATE TABLE ACCOUNTS (
      ACCOUNT_ID           INT PRIMARY KEY NOT NULL,
      USER_ID              INT NOT NULL,
      ACCOUNT_TYPE_ID      INT NOT NULL,
      BALANCE              FLOAT NOT NULL,
      CONSTRAINT USER_ID_FK FOREIGN KEY (USER_ID)
```

```
        REFERENCES USERS (USER_ID),
    CONSTRAINT ACCOUNT_TYPE_ID_FK FOREIGN KEY (ACCOUNT_TYPE_ID)
        REFERENCES ACCOUNT_TYPES (ACCOUNT_TYPE_ID)
);

-- TRANSACTIONS table
CREATE TABLE TRANSACTIONS (
        TRANSACTION_ID      INT PRIMARY KEY NOT NULL,
        ACCOUNT_ID          INT NOT NULL,
        AMOUNT              FLOAT NOT NULL,
        DATE_TIME           DATE NOT NULL,
        CONSTRAINT ACCOUNT_ID_FK FOREIGN KEY (ACCOUNT_ID)
          REFERENCES ACCOUNTS (ACCOUNT_ID)
);

-- FUNDS table
CREATE TABLE FUNDS (
        FUND_ID             INT PRIMARY KEY NOT NULL,
        NAME                VARCHAR(20) NOT NULL,
        DESCRIPTION         VARCHAR(200)
);

-- INVESTMENTS table
CREATE TABLE INVESTMENTS (
        INVESTMENT_ID       INT PRIMARY KEY NOT NULL,
        FUND_ID             INT NOT NULL,
        ACCOUNT_ID          INT NOT NULL,
        INITIAL_AMOUNT      FLOAT NOT NULL,
        YIELD               FLOAT,
        CONSTRAINT FUND_ID_FK FOREIGN KEY (FUND_ID)
          REFERENCES FUNDS (FUND_ID),
        CONSTRAINT ACCOUNT_ID_FK2 FOREIGN KEY (ACCOUNT_ID)
          REFERENCES ACCOUNTS (ACCOUNT_ID)
);
```

InstantDB

Example A-7 is an SQL script that creates the accounts store for InstantDB databases.

Example A-7. SQL Script for Creating the Accounts Store on InstantDB Databases

```
; Load InstantDB JDBC drivers
d org.enhydra.instantdb.jdbc.idbDriver;
o jdbc:idb=forethought.prp;

; ACCOUNT_TYPES table
e CREATE TABLE ACCOUNT_TYPES (
        ACCOUNT_TYPE_ID     INT PRIMARY KEY NOT NULL,
        ACCOUNT_TYPE        VARCHAR(20) NOT NULL
  );
```

Example A-7. SQL Script for Creating the Accounts Store on InstantDB Databases (continued)

```
; ACCOUNTS table
e CREATE TABLE ACCOUNTS (
        ACCOUNT_ID          INT PRIMARY KEY NOT NULL,
        USER_ID             INT NOT NULL,
        ACCOUNT_TYPE_ID     INT NOT NULL,
        BALANCE             FLOAT NOT NULL
  );

; TRANSACTIONS table
e CREATE TABLE TRANSACTIONS (
        TRANSACTION_ID      INT PRIMARY KEY NOT NULL,
        ACCOUNT_ID          INT NOT NULL,
        AMOUNT              FLOAT NOT NULL,
        DATE_TIME           DATE NOT NULL
  );

; FUNDS table
e CREATE TABLE FUNDS (
        FUND_ID             INT PRIMARY KEY NOT NULL,
        NAME                VARCHAR(20) NOT NULL,
        DESCRIPTION         VARCHAR(200)
  );

; INVESTMENTS table
CREATE TABLE INVESTMENTS (
        INVESTMENT_ID       INT PRIMARY KEY NOT NULL,
        FUND_ID             INT NOT NULL,
        ACCOUNT_ID          INT NOT NULL,
        INITIAL_AMOUNT      FLOAT NOT NULL,
        YIELD               FLOAT
);

; Close up
c close;
```

MySQL

Example A-8 is an SQL script that creates the accounts store on MySQL databases.

Example A-8. SQL Script for Creating the Accounts Store on MySQL Databases

```
-- ACCOUNT_TYPES table
CREATE TABLE ACCOUNT_TYPES (
      ACCOUNT_TYPE_ID     INT PRIMARY KEY NOT NULL,
      ACCOUNT_TYPE        VARCHAR(20) NOT NULL
);

-- ACCOUNTS table
CREATE TABLE ACCOUNTS (
      ACCOUNT_ID          INT PRIMARY KEY NOT NULL,
      USER_ID             INT NOT NULL,
      ACCOUNT_TYPE_ID     INT NOT NULL,
      BALANCE             FLOAT NOT NULL,
```

```
        CONSTRAINT USER_ID_FK FOREIGN KEY (USER_ID)
          REFERENCES USERS (USER_ID),
        CONSTRAINT ACCOUNT_TYPE_ID_FK FOREIGN KEY (ACCOUNT_TYPE_ID)
          REFERENCES ACCOUNT_TYPES (ACCOUNT_TYPE_ID)
);

-- TRANSACTIONS table
CREATE TABLE TRANSACTIONS (
        TRANSACTION_ID        INT PRIMARY KEY NOT NULL,
        ACCOUNT_ID            INT NOT NULL,
        AMOUNT                FLOAT NOT NULL,
        DATE_TIME             DATE NOT NULL,
        CONSTRAINT ACCOUNT_ID_FK FOREIGN KEY (ACCOUNT_ID)
          REFERENCES ACCOUNTS (ACCOUNT_ID)
);

-- FUNDS table
CREATE TABLE FUNDS (
        FUND_ID               INT PRIMARY KEY NOT NULL,
        NAME                  VARCHAR(20) NOT NULL,
        DESCRIPTION           VARCHAR(200)
);

-- INVESTMENTS table
CREATE TABLE INVESTMENTS (
        INVESTMENT_ID         INT PRIMARY KEY NOT NULL,
        FUND_ID               INT NOT NULL,
        ACCOUNT_ID            INT NOT NULL,
        INITIAL_AMOUNT        FLOAT NOT NULL,
        YIELD                 FLOAT,
        CONSTRAINT FUND_ID_FK FOREIGN KEY (FUND_ID)
          REFERENCES FUNDS (FUND_ID),
        CONSTRAINT ACCOUNT_ID_FK2 FOREIGN KEY (ACCOUNT_ID)
          REFERENCES ACCOUNTS (ACCOUNT_ID)
);
```

Oracle

The SQL script shown in Example A-9 creates the storage for accounts information on Oracle databases.

Example A-9. SQL Script for Creating the Accounts Store on Oracle Databases

```
-- ACCOUNT_TYPES table
CREATE TABLE ACCOUNT_TYPES (
        ACCOUNT_TYPE_ID       INTEGER PRIMARY KEY NOT NULL,
        ACCOUNT_TYPE          VARCHAR2(20) NOT NULL
);

-- ACCOUNTS table
CREATE TABLE ACCOUNTS (
        ACCOUNT_ID            INTEGER PRIMARY KEY NOT NULL,
```

```
        USER_ID                 INTEGER NOT NULL,
        ACCOUNT_TYPE_ID         INTEGER NOT NULL,
        BALANCE                 FLOAT NOT NULL,
        CONSTRAINT USER_ID_FK FOREIGN KEY (USER_ID)
          REFERENCES USERS (USER_ID),
        CONSTRAINT ACCOUNT_TYPE_ID_FK FOREIGN KEY (ACCOUNT_TYPE_ID)
          REFERENCES ACCOUNT_TYPES (ACCOUNT_TYPE_ID)
);

-- TRANSACTIONS table
CREATE TABLE TRANSACTIONS (
        TRANSACTION_ID          INTEGER PRIMARY KEY NOT NULL,
        ACCOUNT_ID              INTEGER NOT NULL,
        AMOUNT                  FLOAT NOT NULL,
        DATE_TIME               DATE NOT NULL,
        CONSTRAINT ACCOUNT_ID_FK FOREIGN KEY (ACCOUNT_ID)
          REFERENCES ACCOUNTS (ACCOUNT_ID)
);

-- FUNDS table
CREATE TABLE FUNDS (
        FUND_ID                 INTEGER PRIMARY KEY NOT NULL,
        NAME                    VARCHAR2(20) NOT NULL,
        DESCRIPTION             VARCHAR2(200)
);

-- INVESTMENTS table
CREATE TABLE INVESTMENTS (
        INVESTMENT_ID           INTEGER PRIMARY KEY NOT NULL,
        FUND_ID                 INTEGER NOT NULL,
        ACCOUNT_ID              INTEGER NOT NULL,
        INITIAL_AMOUNT          FLOAT NOT NULL,
        YIELD                   FLOAT,
        CONSTRAINT FUND_ID_FK FOREIGN KEY (FUND_ID)
          REFERENCES FUNDS (FUND_ID),
        CONSTRAINT ACCOUNT_ID_FK2 FOREIGN KEY (ACCOUNT_ID)
          REFERENCES ACCOUNTS (ACCOUNT_ID)
);
```

PostgreSQL

Example A-10 is an SQL script that creates the accounts store on PostgreSQL databases.

Example A-10. SQL Script for Creating the Accounts Store on PostgreSQL Databases

```
-- ACCOUNT_TYPES table
CREATE TABLE ACCOUNT_TYPES (
        ACCOUNT_TYPE_ID         INT PRIMARY KEY NOT NULL,
        ACCOUNT_TYPE            VARCHAR(20) NOT NULL
);
```

Example A-10. SQL Script for Creating the Accounts Store on PostgreSQL Databases (continued)

```
-- ACCOUNTS table
CREATE TABLE ACCOUNTS (
      ACCOUNT_ID            INT PRIMARY KEY NOT NULL,
      USER_ID               INT NOT NULL,
      ACCOUNT_TYPE_ID       INT NOT NULL,
      BALANCE               FLOAT NOT NULL,
      CONSTRAINT USER_ID_FK FOREIGN KEY (USER_ID)
        REFERENCES USERS (USER_ID),
      CONSTRAINT ACCOUNT_TYPE_ID_FK FOREIGN KEY (ACCOUNT_TYPE_ID)
        REFERENCES ACCOUNT_TYPES (ACCOUNT_TYPE_ID)
);

-- TRANSACTIONS table
CREATE TABLE TRANSACTIONS (
      TRANSACTION_ID        INT PRIMARY KEY NOT NULL,
      ACCOUNT_ID            INT NOT NULL,
      AMOUNT                FLOAT NOT NULL,
      DATE_TIME             DATE NOT NULL,
      CONSTRAINT ACCOUNT_ID_FK FOREIGN KEY (ACCOUNT_ID)
        REFERENCES ACCOUNTS (ACCOUNT_ID)
);

-- FUNDS table
CREATE TABLE FUNDS (
      FUND_ID               INT PRIMARY KEY NOT NULL,
      NAME                  VARCHAR(20) NOT NULL,
      DESCRIPTION           VARCHAR(200)
);

-- INVESTMENTS table
CREATE TABLE INVESTMENTS (
      INVESTMENT_ID         INT PRIMARY KEY NOT NULL,
      FUND_ID               INT NOT NULL,
      ACCOUNT_ID            INT NOT NULL,
      INITIAL_AMOUNT        FLOAT NOT NULL,
      YIELD                 FLOAT,
      CONSTRAINT FUND_ID_FK FOREIGN KEY (FUND_ID)
        REFERENCES FUNDS (FUND_ID),
      CONSTRAINT ACCOUNT_ID_FK2 FOREIGN KEY (ACCOUNT_ID)
        REFERENCES ACCOUNTS (ACCOUNT_ID)
);
```

Events and Scheduling

With the user and accounts stores in place, all that's left to add to the core database schema is the storage for events. This includes the EVENTS and ATTENDEES table. The scripts in this section are database-specific versions of the SQL script shown in Example 3-4.

Cloudscape

Example A-11 is the Cloudscape version of the SQL script that creates the events and scheduling storage.

Example A-11. SQL Script for Creating the Events Store on Cloudscape Databases

```
-- EVENTS table
CREATE TABLE EVENTS (
        EVENT_ID            INT PRIMARY KEY NOT NULL,
        DESCRIPTION         VARCHAR(50) NOT NULL,
        DATE_TIME           DATE NOT NULL
);

-- ATTENDEES table
CREATE TABLE ATTENDEES (
        USER_ID             INT NOT NULL,
        EVENT_ID            INT NOT NULL,
        CONSTRAINT AT_USER_ID_FK FOREIGN KEY (USER_ID)
          REFERENCES USERS (USER_ID),
        CONSTRAINT EVENT_ID_FK FOREIGN KEY (EVENT_ID)
          REFERENCES EVENTS (EVENT_ID)
);
```

InstantDB

The InstantDB-specific SQL for creating the events store is shown in Example A-12.

Example A-12. SQL Script for Creating the Events Store on InstantDB Databases

```
; Load InstantDB JDBC drivers
d org.enhydra.instantdb.jdbc.idbDriver;
o jdbc:idb=forethought.prp;

; EVENTS table
e CREATE TABLE EVENTS (
        EVENT_ID            INT PRIMARY KEY NOT NULL,
        DESCRIPTION         VARCHAR(50) NOT NULL,
        DATE_TIME           DATE NOT NULL
  );

; ATTENDEES table
e CREATE TABLE ATTENDEES (
        USER_ID             INT NOT NULL,
        EVENT_ID            INT NOT NULL,
        CONSTRAINT AT_USER_ID_FK FOREIGN KEY (USER_ID)
          REFERENCES USERS (USER_ID),
        CONSTRAINT EVENT_ID_FK FOREIGN KEY (EVENT_ID)
          REFERENCES EVENTS (EVENT_ID)
  );

; Close up
c close;
```

MySQL

Example A-13 is an SQL script that creates the events storage on MySQL databases.

Example A-13. SQL Script for Creating the Events Store on MySQL Databases

```
-- EVENTS table
CREATE TABLE EVENTS (
      EVENT_ID            INT PRIMARY KEY NOT NULL,
      DESCRIPTION         VARCHAR(50) NOT NULL,
      DATE_TIME           DATE NOT NULL
);

-- ATTENDEES table
CREATE TABLE ATTENDEES (
      USER_ID             INT NOT NULL,
      EVENT_ID            INT NOT NULL,
      CONSTRAINT AT_USER_ID_FK FOREIGN KEY (USER_ID)
        REFERENCES USERS (USER_ID),
      CONSTRAINT EVENT_ID_FK FOREIGN KEY (EVENT_ID)
        REFERENCES EVENTS (EVENT_ID)
);
```

Oracle

An Oracle-specific script for creating the events storage is shown in Example A-14.

Example A-14. SQL Script for Creating the Events Store on Oracle Databases

```
-- EVENTS table
CREATE TABLE EVENTS (
      EVENT_ID            INTEGER PRIMARY KEY NOT NULL,
      DESCRIPTION         VARCHAR2(50) NOT NULL,
      DATE_TIME           DATE NOT NULL
);

-- ATTENDEES table
CREATE TABLE ATTENDEES (
      USER_ID             INTEGER NOT NULL,
      EVENT_ID            INTEGER NOT NULL,
      CONSTRAINT AT_USER_ID_FK FOREIGN KEY (USER_ID)
        REFERENCES USERS (USER_ID),
      CONSTRAINT EVENT_ID_FK FOREIGN KEY (EVENT_ID)
        REFERENCES EVENTS (EVENT_ID)
);
```

PostgreSQL

The SQL script for PostgreSQL databases is shown in Example A-15.

Example A-15. SQL Script for Creating the Events Store on PostgreSQL Databases

```
-- EVENTS table
CREATE TABLE EVENTS (
      EVENT_ID              INT PRIMARY KEY NOT NULL,
      DESCRIPTION           VARCHAR(50) NOT NULL,
      DATE_TIME             DATE NOT NULL
);

-- ATTENDEES table
CREATE TABLE ATTENDEES (
      USER_ID               INT NOT NULL,
      EVENT_ID              INT NOT NULL,
      CONSTRAINT AT_USER_ID_FK FOREIGN KEY (USER_ID)
        REFERENCES USERS (USER_ID),
      CONSTRAINT EVENT_ID_FK FOREIGN KEY (EVENT_ID)
        REFERENCES EVENTS (EVENT_ID)
);
```

Starting Over

With every creation comes at least one deletion. You'll probably find that you need to clear out your database and re-create it from time to time. In an effort to make this easy for you, the scripts to perform this action are presented below. Just be careful; the data in your database will be completely wiped out by these SQL scripts, with no warning. The following scripts are database-specific analogs to Example 3-6 in the text.

Cloudscape

The SQL script shown in Example A-16 deletes all of the tables and constraints for Cloudscape databases.

Example A-16. SQL Script for Deleting All Tables on Cloudscape Databases

```
-- Drop all tables
DROP TABLE INVESTMENTS;
DROP TABLE FUNDS;
DROP TABLE TRANSACTIONS;
DROP TABLE ACCOUNTS;
DROP TABLE ACCOUNT_TYPES;
DROP TABLE USERS;
DROP TABLE USER_TYPES;
DROP TABLE OFFICES;
```

InstantDB

Example A-17 is an SQL script that deletes the user and accounts storage on InstantDB databases.

Example A-17. SQL Script for Deleting All Tables on InstantDB Databases

```
; Load InstantDB JDBC drivers
d org.enhydra.instantdb.jdbc.idbDriver;
o jdbc:idb=forethought.prp;

; Drop all tables
e DROP TABLE INVESTMENTS;
e DROP TABLE FUNDS;
e DROP TABLE TRANSACTIONS;
e DROP TABLE ACCOUNTS;
e DROP TABLE ACCOUNT_TYPES;
e DROP TABLE USERS;
e DROP TABLE USER_TYPES;
e DROP TABLE OFFICES;

; Close up
c close;
```

MySQL

Example A-18 is an SQL script that deletes the Forethought data store on MySQL databases.

Example A-18. SQL Script for Deleting All Tables on MySQL Databases

```
-- Drop all tables
DROP TABLE INVESTMENTS;
DROP TABLE FUNDS;
DROP TABLE TRANSACTIONS;
DROP TABLE ACCOUNTS;
DROP TABLE ACCOUNT_TYPES;
DROP TABLE USERS;
DROP TABLE USER_TYPES;
DROP TABLE OFFICES;
```

Oracle

The SQL script shown in Example A-19 deletes the storage for Forethought information on Oracle databases.

Example A-19. SQL Script for Deleting All Tables on Oracle Databases

```
-- Drop all tables
DROP TABLE INVESTMENTS;
DROP TABLE FUNDS;
DROP TABLE TRANSACTIONS;
DROP TABLE ACCOUNTS;
DROP TABLE ACCOUNT_TYPES;
DROP TABLE USERS;
DROP TABLE USER_TYPES;
DROP TABLE OFFICES;
```

PostgreSQL

Example A-20 is the SQL script used to delete the Forethought data store on PostgreSQL databases.

Example A-20. SQL Script for Deleting All Tables on PostgreSQL Databases

```
-- Drop all tables
DROP TABLE INVESTMENTS;
DROP TABLE FUNDS;
DROP TABLE TRANSACTIONS;
DROP TABLE ACCOUNTS;
DROP TABLE ACCOUNT_TYPES;
DROP TABLE USERS;
DROP TABLE USER_TYPES;
DROP TABLE OFFICES;
```

Primary Keys

The storage described in Chapter 5 for primary key generation requires an additional table in the database schema. The scripts in this section are product-specific versions of the SQL script shown in Example 5-1.

 Since this table is added in Chapter 5, this section is presented after the "Starting Over" section in this appendix. The scripts shown previously do not drop the table created in this section; instead, this script drops any existing table and then re-creates the storage. If you decide to use this methodology, be sure you do not rerun this script once the table it creates is in use; it effectively resets the primary key counters, and can cause duplicate keys to be added to the database. Another approach would be to write some more advanced SQL to determine the highest ID value, and then start the key values at a number greater than that found. However, this advanced SQL is beyond the scope of this book.

Cloudscape

The SQL script shown in Example A-21 creates the primary key storage table on Cloudscape databases.

Example A-21. SQL Script for Creating the Primary Key Table on Cloudscape Databases

```
-- Drop any existing PRIMARY_KEYS table
DROP TABLE PRIMARY_KEYS;

-- PRIMARY_KEYS table
CREATE TABLE PRIMARY_KEYS (
      KEY_NAME        VARCHAR(20) PRIMARY KEY NOT NULL,
      NEXT_VALUE      INT NOT NULL
);
```

Example A-21. SQL Script for Creating the Primary Key Table on Cloudscape Databases (continued)

```
-- Add initial values for each table
INSERT INTO SEQUENCES VALUES ('USER_TYPES', 1);
INSERT INTO SEQUENCES VALUES ('OFFICES', 1);
INSERT INTO SEQUENCES VALUES ('USERS', 1);
INSERT INTO SEQUENCES VALUES ('ACCOUNT_TYPES', 1);
INSERT INTO SEQUENCES VALUES ('ACCOUNTS', 1);
INSERT INTO SEQUENCES VALUES ('TRANSACTIONS', 1);
INSERT INTO SEQUENCES VALUES ('FUNDS', 1);
INSERT INTO SEQUENCES VALUES ('INVESTMENTS', 1);
```

InstantDB

Example A-22 is an SQL script that creates the primary key storage on InstantDB databases.

Example A-22. SQL Script for Creating the Primary Keys Table on InstantDB Databases

```
; Load InstantDB JDBC drivers
d org.enhydra.instantdb.jdbc.idbDriver;
o jdbc:idb=forethought.prp;

; Drop any existing PRIMARY_KEYS table
e DROP TABLE PRIMARY_KEYS;

; PRIMARY_KEYS table
e CREATE TABLE PRIMARY_KEYS (
        KEY_NAME        VARCHAR(20) PRIMARY KEY NOT NULL,
        NEXT_VALUE      INT NOT NULL
  );

; Add initial values for each table
e INSERT INTO SEQUENCES VALUES ('USER_TYPES', 1);
e INSERT INTO SEQUENCES VALUES ('OFFICES', 1);
e INSERT INTO SEQUENCES VALUES ('USERS', 1);
e INSERT INTO SEQUENCES VALUES ('ACCOUNT_TYPES', 1);
e INSERT INTO SEQUENCES VALUES ('ACCOUNTS', 1);
e INSERT INTO SEQUENCES VALUES ('TRANSACTIONS', 1);
e INSERT INTO SEQUENCES VALUES ('FUNDS', 1);
e INSERT INTO SEQUENCES VALUES ('INVESTMENTS', 1);

; Close up
c close;
```

MySQL

Example A-23 is an SQL script that creates primary key value storage on MySQL databases.

Example A-23. SQL Script for Creating the Primary Key Table on MySQL Databases

```
-- Drop any existing PRIMARY_KEYS table
DROP TABLE PRIMARY_KEYS;

-- PRIMARY_KEYS table
CREATE TABLE PRIMARY_KEYS (
      KEY_NAME        VARCHAR(20) PRIMARY KEY NOT NULL,
      NEXT_VALUE      INT NOT NULL
);

-- Add initial values for each table
INSERT INTO SEQUENCES VALUES ('USER_TYPES', 1);
INSERT INTO SEQUENCES VALUES ('OFFICES', 1);
INSERT INTO SEQUENCES VALUES ('USERS', 1);
INSERT INTO SEQUENCES VALUES ('ACCOUNT_TYPES', 1);
INSERT INTO SEQUENCES VALUES ('ACCOUNTS', 1);
INSERT INTO SEQUENCES VALUES ('TRANSACTIONS', 1);
INSERT INTO SEQUENCES VALUES ('FUNDS', 1);
INSERT INTO SEQUENCES VALUES ('INVESTMENTS', 1);
```

Oracle

The SQL script shown in Example A-24 creates the storage for Forethought primary keys on Oracle databases.

Example A-24. SQL Script for Creating the Primary Key Table on Oracle Databases

```
-- Drop any existing PRIMARY_KEYS table
DROP TABLE PRIMARY_KEYS;

-- PRIMARY_KEYS table
CREATE TABLE PRIMARY_KEYS (
      KEY_NAME        VARCHAR2(20) PRIMARY KEY NOT NULL,
      NEXT_VALUE      INTEGER NOT NULL
);

-- Add initial values for each table
INSERT INTO SEQUENCES VALUES ('USER_TYPES', 1);
INSERT INTO SEQUENCES VALUES ('OFFICES', 1);
INSERT INTO SEQUENCES VALUES ('USERS', 1);
INSERT INTO SEQUENCES VALUES ('ACCOUNT_TYPES', 1);
INSERT INTO SEQUENCES VALUES ('ACCOUNTS', 1);
INSERT INTO SEQUENCES VALUES ('TRANSACTIONS', 1);
INSERT INTO SEQUENCES VALUES ('FUNDS', 1);
INSERT INTO SEQUENCES VALUES ('INVESTMENTS', 1);
```

PostgreSQL

Example A-25 is an SQL script that creates the Forethought primary key store on PostgreSQL databases.

Example A-25. SQL Script for Creating the Primary Key Table on PostgreSQL Databases

```
-- Drop any existing PRIMARY_KEYS table
DROP TABLE PRIMARY_KEYS;

-- PRIMARY_KEYS table
CREATE TABLE PRIMARY_KEYS (
      KEY_NAME          VARCHAR(20) PRIMARY KEY NOT NULL,
      NEXT_VALUE        INT NOT NULL
);

-- Add initial values for each table
INSERT INTO SEQUENCES VALUES ('USER_TYPES', 1);
INSERT INTO SEQUENCES VALUES ('OFFICES', 1);
INSERT INTO SEQUENCES VALUES ('USERS', 1);
INSERT INTO SEQUENCES VALUES ('ACCOUNT_TYPES', 1);
INSERT INTO SEQUENCES VALUES ('ACCOUNTS', 1);
INSERT INTO SEQUENCES VALUES ('TRANSACTIONS', 1);
INSERT INTO SEQUENCES VALUES ('FUNDS', 1);
INSERT INTO SEQUENCES VALUES ('INVESTMENTS', 1);
```

Creating Types

Chapter 7 detailed using SQL to populate the various "type" tables (USER_TYPES and ACCOUNT_TYPES). As explained in the text, this was necessary because only local interfaces were available for the relevant entity beans. This section provides the SQL scripts for that task on various databases.

Cloudscape

The SQL script shown in Example A-26 creates the user and account type data on Cloudscape databases.

Example A-26. SQL Script for Creating Type Data on Cloudscape Databases

```
-- Create User Types
INSERT INTO USER_TYPES VALUES (1, 'Client');
INSERT INTO USER_TYPES VALUES (2, 'Employee');

-- Create Account Types
INSERT INTO ACCOUNT_TYPES VALUES (1, 'Everyday');
INSERT INTO ACCOUNT_TYPES VALUES (2, 'Investment');
INSERT INTO ACCOUNT_TYPES VALUES (3, 'Investment Plus');
INSERT INTO ACCOUNT_TYPES VALUES (4, 'Money Market');
INSERT INTO ACCOUNT_TYPES VALUES (5, 'Savings');
```

InstantDB

Example A-27 is an SQL script that creates types on InstantDB databases.

Example A-27. SQL Script for Creating Type Data on InstantDB Databases

```
; Load InstantDB JDBC drivers
d org.enhydra.instantdb.jdbc.idbDriver;
o jdbc:idb=forethought.prp;

; Create User Types
e INSERT INTO USER_TYPES VALUES (1, 'Client');
e INSERT INTO USER_TYPES VALUES (2, 'Employee');

; Create Account Types
e INSERT INTO ACCOUNT_TYPES VALUES (1, 'Everyday');
e INSERT INTO ACCOUNT_TYPES VALUES (2, 'Investment');
e INSERT INTO ACCOUNT_TYPES VALUES (3, 'Investment Plus');
e INSERT INTO ACCOUNT_TYPES VALUES (4, 'Money Market');
e INSERT INTO ACCOUNT_TYPES VALUES (5, 'Savings');
```

MySQL

Example A-28 is an SQL script that creates type data on MySQL databases.

Example A-28. SQL Script for Creating Type Data on MySQL Databases

```
-- Create User Types
INSERT INTO USER_TYPES VALUES (1, 'Client');
INSERT INTO USER_TYPES VALUES (2, 'Employee');

-- Create Account Types
INSERT INTO ACCOUNT_TYPES VALUES (1, 'Everyday');
INSERT INTO ACCOUNT_TYPES VALUES (2, 'Investment');
INSERT INTO ACCOUNT_TYPES VALUES (3, 'Investment Plus');
INSERT INTO ACCOUNT_TYPES VALUES (4, 'Money Market');
INSERT INTO ACCOUNT_TYPES VALUES (5, 'Savings');
```

Oracle

The SQL script shown in Example A-29 creates the storage for Forethought types on Oracle databases.

Example A-29. SQL Script for Creating Type Data on Oracle Databases

```
-- Create User Types
INSERT INTO USER_TYPES VALUES (1, 'Client');
INSERT INTO USER_TYPES VALUES (2, 'Employee');

-- Create Account Types
INSERT INTO ACCOUNT_TYPES VALUES (1, 'Everyday');
INSERT INTO ACCOUNT_TYPES VALUES (2, 'Investment');
INSERT INTO ACCOUNT_TYPES VALUES (3, 'Investment Plus');
INSERT INTO ACCOUNT_TYPES VALUES (4, 'Money Market');
INSERT INTO ACCOUNT_TYPES VALUES (5, 'Savings');
```

PostgreSQL

Example A-30 is an SQL script used to create user and account types on PostgreSQL databases.

Example A-30. SQL Script for Creating the Type Data on PostgreSQL Databases

```
-- Create User Types
INSERT INTO USER_TYPES VALUES (1, 'Client');
INSERT INTO USER_TYPES VALUES (2, 'Employee');

-- Create Account Types
INSERT INTO ACCOUNT_TYPES VALUES (1, 'Everyday');
INSERT INTO ACCOUNT_TYPES VALUES (2, 'Investment');
INSERT INTO ACCOUNT_TYPES VALUES (3, 'Investment Plus');
INSERT INTO ACCOUNT_TYPES VALUES (4, 'Money Market');
INSERT INTO ACCOUNT_TYPES VALUES (5, 'Savings');
```

SQL Deployment

This appendix contains deployment details about specific databases. If you are having trouble executing the SQL scripts covered in Chapters 3 or 5 or in Appendix A, this appendix can be used as a helpful reference. The instructions in this chapter are supplied merely as a convenience, and are only one of many ways that SQL can be executed against databases. You should consult the vendor documentation for your database to see alternatives to the methods provided here.

The instructions in each section cover a means of deploying SQL scripts into a database. In this context, *deployment* refers simply to executing the SQL against the database so that tables, columns, and relationships are generated. If you are following along with the examples (and hopefully you are!), you will want to execute the SQL for your database (from Appendix A) against your instance. Once this is done, the entity beans and other code that utilize the database are ready to be used. As in the other appendixes, new versions of these products are always appearing; these may cause small inconsistencies in the instructions provided here. Please be tolerant of these mistakes; if major problems arise, I'll attempt to correct them in later revisions and editions. I also welcome you letting me know about problems you find via the email addresses listed in the Preface; if you have a different database, you can also send me instructions on deployment for that product, and I'll test it and seek to include it in future editions.

Cloudscape

Cloudscape was initially released by Informix as free for development, testing, and use. More recently, IBM acquired Cloudscape, and unfortunately removed free downloads from the Cloudscape web site. As a result, you'll have to get Cloudscape in one of the various application servers that include it for sample usage, such as BEA Weblogic or the J2EE reference implementation. If you have an older version from a previous download, I'd recommend using MySQL or PostgreSQL instead, as opposed to sticking with an old copy of the free version of Cloudscape.

To create and set up the Forethought database, I highly recommend using the Cloudview graphical tool bundled with Cloudscape. You can start this tool by setting your classpath to include *cloudscape.jar* and *tools.jar* from the Cloudscape release, and executing the following command:

```
C:\dev\javaentI\appB\cloudscape>java COM.cloudscape.tools.cview
```

Once the tool has started, you should use the File → New → Database... menu option to create the database. Enter in the directory you wish to use; for Weblogic users, I'd recommend selecting the same directory in which the preconfigured databases exist. This is generally *$WL_HOME/samples/eval/cloudscape/data*. Append to this the name of the database, ForethoughtDB, as shown in Figure B-1.

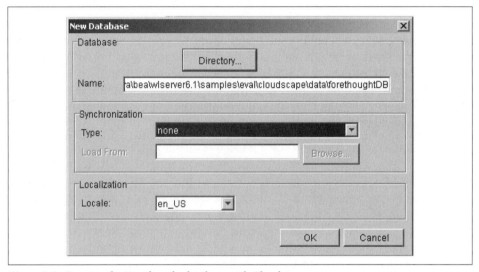

Figure B-1. Creating the Forethought database with Cloudview

After some whirring on your hard drive, you'll be placed on the main database screen. The right pane allows you to type in SQL statements and execute those statements against the database. You can also load an SQL script from disk, which is exactly what you should choose, by clicking the notepad icon. Load the Cloudscape version of the *database_schema_users.sql* script. Click the lightning bolt icon, which will execute this script, creating several tables. Repeat this process for the other database scripts from the various database-related chapters.

 Some versions of Cloudscape "choke" on the *database_schema_keys. sql* script if the PRIMARY_KEYS table does not already exist, as the first line of that script tries to drop this table. If this happens, simply comment out that line and rerun the script, and things will work normally. You can then uncomment the DROP line so that future executions create the PRIMARY_KEYS table from scratch.

You can verify that tables have been created by clicking the Tables option on the left window pane, and viewing the various names and columns. Your view of the new database should look similar to that shown in Figure B-2.

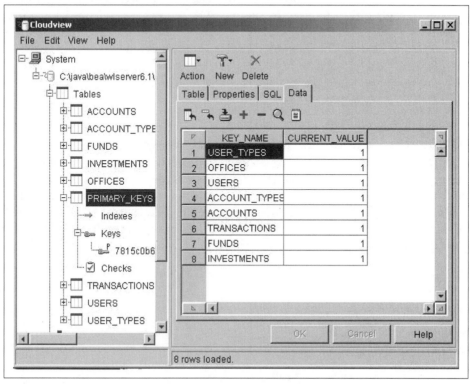

Figure B-2. Viewing the Forethought database in Cloudview

Once you're satisfied that all these tables have been created, you're ready to continue with the code examples in the book.

 I show Cloudscape running on Windows; of course, the same goes for Unix platforms, and shouldn't cause those users any trouble. Just use the equivalent scripts for your platform, and create your database using Cloudview in the same fashion.

InstantDB

Once InstantDB has been downloaded and installed (it is available online at *http://instantdb.enhydra.org*), you need to add the InstantDB libraries to your Java classpath. Because InstantDB is 100% Java, this is literally all it takes to get the database ready for use. The relevant library files are contained within *idb.jar* and *idbf.jar*, both located in the *classes* subdirectory of the InstantDB installation. InstantDB also requires the Java JTA classes, as well as the JDBC standard extensions. These two JAR files, *jta-spec1_0_1.jar* and *jdbc2_0-stdext.jar*, can be downloaded from Sun's web site at *http://java.sun.com/products/jta* and *http://java.sun.com/products/jdbc*, respectively. Add these two libraries to your classpath as well. Finally, the various utilities, including the one used to execute SQL scripts, are contained in another InstantDB archive, *idbexmpl.jar*, which is also in the *classes* subdirectory of the InstantDB installation. The resulting classpath is shown as follows:

```
/java/instantdb (bmclaugh)> echo $CLASSPATH
/java/instantdb/classes/idb.jar:/java/instantdb/classes/idbf.jar:
/java/instantdb/classes/idbf.jar:
/java/instantdb/classes/jta-spec1_0_1.jar:
/java/instantdb/classes/jdbc2_0-stdext.jar
```

The Java class used to execute SQL scripts is `org.enhydra.instantdb.ScriptTool`. This program takes an SQL script (slightly modified with some InstantDB-specific instructions, as seen in Appendix A) and a properties file, and echoes the results out to the console. First, though, you need to create this properties file, which specifies options such as temporary directories and where the database files should be stored. A sample properties file, referenced in the SQL scripts in Appendix A, is shown in Example B-1.

Example B-1. Forethought Properties File

```
! Path where index tables are held.
indexPath=./indexes

! Path where system tables are held.
systemPath=./system

! Path where database tables are held.
tablePath=./tables

! Path where results set tables are held.
tmpPath=./tmp

! Non-zero means paths are relative to the properties file.
relativeToProperties=1

! The amount of each column to cache.
cacheAmount=512

! Determines whether to cache columns in tables based on an
! absolute number of rows, or the percentage number of rows in the table.
cacheCondition=CACHE_ROWS

! Percentage of free space in an index that must be present before
! the index reorganizes itself.
indexLoad=5

! Number of rows to read into the disk read ahead buffer.
```

```
rowCacheSize=128

! Non-zero means trace output also directed to console.
traceConsole=1

! Relative or absolute path where exporting and tracing goes.
traceFile=./trace.log

! Bitmap of various items that can be traced.
traceLevel=2
```

With this in place, create a directory for the Forethought database and associated files; for example, */java/InstantDB/forethought*. Ensure that the two SQL scripts (*database_schema_users.sql* and *database_schema_accounts.sql*) and the Forethought properties file (*forethought.prp*) are in this directory. Then execute the ScriptTool class with the SQL script as the argument:

```
/java/instantdb (bmclaugh)> java org.enhydra.instantdb.ScriptTool
                            database_schema_users.sql
Enhydra InstantDB - Version 3.20 beta 1
The Initial Developer of the Original Code is Lutris Technologies Inc.
Portions created by Lutris are Copyright (C) 1997-2000 Lutris
  Technologies, Inc.

All Rights Reserved.

Connected to jdbc:idb:forethought.prp
Driver   InstantDB JDBC Driver
Version  Version 3.20

...

Database forethought is shutting down...
Database forethought shutdown complete.
```

Note that you did not have to explicitly create the Forethought database; the directory and properties file provide the only required information needed, and then scripts can be executed against that database. Now, execute the same command for the accounts script (*database_schema_accounts.sql*), and you are ready to go. InstantDB also provides a tool for graphical browsing of the database, the org. enhydra.instantdb.DBBrowser class. This allows you to select a properties file (*forethought.prp* in our case) and then browse the database structure.

Once you move through Chapters 5 and 7, you will need to follow the same instructions. Run the ScriptTool on the *database_schema_keys.sql* script to create the primary key value table, and the *database_schema_createTypes.sql* script to create the type data.

MySQL

To use MySQL, download the package from *http://www.mysql.org* and install it. I've got a mysql user with access to the scripts, and the */usr/local/mysql/bin* directory in that user's path. I've also set my root MySQL user's password to a non-empty password; you should do this too, with the command mysqladmin -u root password [new password]. You can then create the Forethought database with the following command:

```
[localhost:~] mysql% mysqladmin -u root -p create forethought
Enter password:
```

You won't get any visible output, but don't be concerned; this does create the database. You're now ready to connect to the database and run the SQL scripts. Use the mysql command for this, as shown:

```
[localhost:~] mysql% mysql -u root -p forethought
Enter password:
Welcome to the MySQL monitor.  Commands end with ; or \g.
Your MySQL connection id is 16 to server version: 3.23.37

Type 'help;' or '\h' for help. Type '\c' to clear the buffer

mysql> source database_schema_users.sql
Query OK, 0 rows affected (0.00 sec)

Query OK, 0 rows affected (0.01 sec)

Query OK, 0 rows affected (0.00 sec)

Query OK, 1 row affected (0.01 sec)

mysql> source database_schema_accounts.sql
Query OK, 0 rows affected (0.01 sec)

Query OK, 0 rows affected (0.00 sec)

Query OK, 0 rows affected (0.01 sec)

Query OK, 0 rows affected (0.00 sec)

Query OK, 0 rows affected (0.01 sec)

mysql> exit
Bye
```

In the same manner, you can use the source command to execute the keys script, the data types script, and the script that drops tables. In my example, the scripts are in the same directory that I ran the mysql command from; you'll need to modify the path to the script if this isn't the case in your setup.

Oracle

Unlike many of the databases in this appendix, particularly the Java-based ones such as InstantDB and Cloudscape, creating a new database with Oracle is not such a trivial matter. In fact, entire books have been written about configuration and maintenance of Oracle databases! So in this section, the assumption is made that the database has already been created and set up. The global name of the database is *ftht.middleearth.com* ("ftht" instead of "forethought" because there is an eight-character limit on global names, and "middleearth.com" because it's my home network's domain), and the SID is *FTHT*. Other than these basic parameters, specific configuration items like rollback sizes and TEMP tablespaces are left to you or your DBA.

Additionally, the examples shown assume that a user has been created in the database, with the username "forethought" and the password "forethought". This user (for simplicity's sake) has been given the role *DBA*. This makes connecting, creating tables, and other administrative duties possible without explicitly granting many permissions (like *CREATE SESSION, ALTER ANY TABLE*, etc.).

Deployment and execution of SQL scripts in Oracle is usually done through the use of the Oracle SQL*Plus tool, with the database to modify up and running. You connect as the user able to administrate the database schema; here the user "forethought" is used. You should be in the directory where the SQL scripts you want to execute are located.

Each SQL script can be run by prepending the name of the script with the @ symbol. Creating the database schema, then, can be done as shown here:

```
SQL*Plus: Release 8.1.6.0.0 - Production on Tue Sep 19 20:42:35 2000

(c) Copyright 1999 Oracle Corporation.  All rights reserved.

Enter user-name: forethought
Enter password:

Connected to:
Oracle8i Enterprise Edition Release 8.1.6.0.0 - Production
With the Partitioning option
JServer Release 8.1.6.0.0 - Production

SQL> @database_schema_users.sql

Table created.


Table created.


Table created.
```

```
SQL> @database_schema_accounts.sql

Table created.


Table created.


Table created.


Table created.


Table created.

SQL>
```

This rather uninteresting output is a sign that things went correctly. The same principles can be followed for the Oracle SQL scripts outlined throughout the rest of the book.

There is one note to make regarding *database_schema_keys.sql* and *database_schema_createTypes.sql*. Because both of these scripts cause rows to be inserted, you will need to issue an explicit database commit (Oracle does not, by default, auto-commit). Here's how to handle the keys script, as an example:

```
C:\projects\javaapps\oracle>sqlplus forethought/forethought@forethought

SQL*Plus: Release 8.1.6.0.0 - Production on Fri Sep 29 10:31:11 2000

(c) Copyright 1999 Oracle Corporation.  All rights reserved.


Connected to:
Oracle8i Enterprise Edition Release 8.1.6.0.0 - Production
With the Partitioning option
JServer Release 8.1.6.0.0 - Production

SQL> @database_schema_keys.sql
DROP TABLE PRIMARY_KEYS
           *
ERROR at line 1:
ORA-00942: table or view does not exist



Table created.


1 row created.
```

```
1 row created.


1 row created.


1 row created.


1 row created.


1 row created.


1 row created.


1 row created.

SQL> commit;

Commit complete.

SQL> exit
Disconnected from Oracle8i Enterprise Edition Release 8.1.6.0.0 -
  Production With the Partitioning option
JServer Release 8.1.6.0.0 - Production

C:\projects\javaapps\oracle>
```

PostgreSQL

PostgreSQL, along with mySQL, is a popular open source option for Unix-flavored systems like Linux, Solaris, and my own Mac OS X. You can download the distribution from *http://www.postgresql.org* (for U.S. users, the best mirror site is *http://www3.us.postgresql.org*). Installation instructions are included in the distribution and are also available at the web site. Install the database and then start it as shown here:

```
[localhost:~] postgres% /usr/local/pgsql/bin/postmaster -D /usr/local/pqsql/data
```

Once you've got the database running, presumably with the "postgres" user (as the installation instructions recommend), you need to create the Forethought database:

```
[localhost:~] postgres% /usr/local/pgsql/bin/createdb forethought
CREATE DATABASE
```

The next step is to connect to the database and run your SQL scripts against it. This is done with the psql tool, a handy utility for just this purpose. Run this script, specifying the database to connect to and the file with SQL to execute:

```
[localhost:~] postgres% psql -f database_schema_users.sql forethought
NOTICE:  CREATE TABLE/PRIMARY KEY will create implicit index 'user_types_pkey' for
table 'user_types'
psql:database_schema_users.sql:5: NOTICE:  CREATE TABLE/PRIMARY KEY will create
implicit index 'user_types_pkey' for table 'user_types'
CREATE
NOTICE:  CREATE TABLE/PRIMARY KEY will create implicit index 'offices_pkey' for
table 'offices'
psql:database_schema_users.sql:12: NOTICE:  CREATE TABLE/PRIMARY KEY will create
 implicit index 'offices_pkey' for table 'offices'
CREATE
NOTICE:  CREATE TABLE/PRIMARY KEY will create implicit index 'users_pkey' for table
'users'
NOTICE:  CREATE TABLE will create implicit trigger(s) for FOREIGN KEY check(s)
psql:database_schema_users.sql:26: NOTICE:  CREATE TABLE/PRIMARY KEY will create
 implicit index 'users_pkey' for table 'users'
psql:database_schema_users.sql:26: NOTICE:  CREATE TABLE will create implicit
trigger(s) for FOREIGN KEY check(s)
CREATE
INSERT 18781 1
```

Your input should look similar. This lets you know exactly what is going on at the database level. Repeat the process for the accounts SQL (from Chapter 3), the keys SQL (from Chapter 5), and the types data (Chapter 7). You're now set for the rest of the book's examples.

Directory Server Setup

This appendix covers deployment of LDAP directory servers from several vendors. Although there are not nearly as many varieties of directory servers as there are databases, there is a huge degree of difference between creating and administrating a directory server schema on each vendor's product. The most common vendors are included here;* if you don't have a license for the commercial products, you can use the free, open source OpenLDAP product in your applications.

For each product, an arbitrary platform is chosen. This is often the most appropriate platform (for example, OpenLDAP is most commonly run on Linux, Solaris, or other Unix-flavored platforms); however, in some cases (such as iPlanet), the platform is simply a matter of convenience. In cases where a Windows installation and configuration is shown, you should be able to easily convert the instructions to Unix. For Unix installs, you will need to consult the documentation to see if the product will run on Windows; you also may need to download a Unix-style shell for Windows, such as the Cygnus tools, located at *http://www.cygwin.com*. These tools often allow you to execute Unix programs on Windows platforms.

Installation for each product is briefly described. If specific parts of the installation involve configuration used in the book's example, those steps are highlighted. For example, in installing the iPlanet Directory Server, the organization of the server must be set (*o=forethought.com*); in such cases, the needed installation points are highlighted. In all other cases, you should use the overview given here as well as the product's documentation to perform an appropriate installation on your platform.

---

* If your directory server is not covered here, please feel free to send instructions for creating users, groups, and permissions to me directly at *brett@newInstance.com*. If I can ensure that it works, I will be happy to include it online and in updated versions of this book.

iPlanet

iPlanet's Directory Server product is the most popular commercial solution for LDAP services, and it provides a simple administration console that makes configuration much easier than in many other products (such as OpenLDAP, which works off of textual LDIF files). It also has strong integration if other iPlanet products are being used (such as the iPlanet web server or iPlanet application server). It has versions for Windows and most popular Unix platforms, including Linux.

Installation

Installing the iPlanet directory server on Unix and on Windows is an almost identical process.* The primary difference is in launching the install. On Windows, simply clicking the downloaded executable (named *d50diu.exe* or something similar, depending on the version; some versions also come zipped instead of as an executable) starts the GUI install. On Unix, expanding the archive (named *d50diu.tar.gz* or something similar) results in a directory with a binary to start the install. Running this binary will start the graphical installation.

When walking through the prompts, be sure to select both the server and the console tools in the setup type screen. Once you have installed the server, you may want to install just the console on any remote administration machines. With the console, you can use the graphical tools to administrate the server from any machine with a TCP/IP connection to the directory server.

You will need to select a directory and set of features to install; ensuring that only the root user on Unix systems has access to the directory server is a very good idea. If this is your first directory server on your network, you will need to set up this instance as the *configuration directory server*. The configuration directory server will hold information about all iPlanet and Netscape server products across your network. If you already have an existing directory server functioning in this capacity, you should enter its access information at this point, as shown in Figure C-1.

You can also select another directory server in which to store user and group information. However, you probably want this server (and any replicants you might set up) to store the application information, so be sure to select "Store data in this directory server" at that prompt.

Finally, you will need to set the hostname, port, and organization of this new server instance. As discussed in Chapter 3, you should use the default port of 389 unless

---

* This assumes that you are either on a local Unix machine or have X Windows access to the machine; in these cases, you can use the supplied GUI for installation. While it is highly recommended that you not install programs that require root access without local access to the machine, the installation program does have a text mode. You can simply follow the prompts, as it mirrors the graphical install.

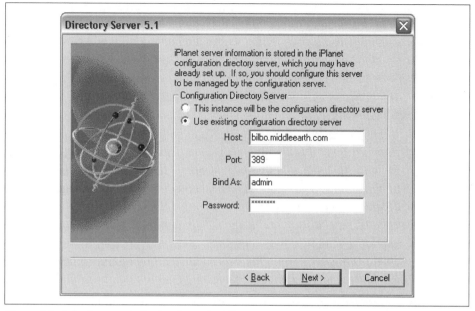

Figure C-1. Selecting an existing configuration directory server

you have a good reason not to.* Finally, set the organization of the instance to Fore-thought's domain, *forethought.com*, by using *o=forethought.com* as the directory server suffix.

You will need to select an administration password, the domain you are administrat-ing (if you selected the instance as the configuration directory server), and the pass-word for the directory manager. Be sure to take note of the passwords used, especially for the directory manager (*cn=Directory Manager*); you will need it for the sample code. To follow along with the book, use the password "forethought" for this instance. Next, select the options that do not import any sample data for the server instance. Finally, select a port for the administration services to run on (port 9999 is used in the examples in the book). With all these options set, you can finish up the installation of your iPlanet directory server.

Once installation has completed (assuming that no errors have occurred), you should start up the directory server and administration server. On Windows, this will be set to happen automatically at startup, and will also occur after installation is complete (of course, like most Microsoft programs, you will need to restart your computer first). You can manually control the services through the Services program under the

---

* Two such reasons come to mind. First, using SSL over LDAP typically is accomplished by using port 636 for communication. Second, using nonstandard ports is sometimes considered a security enhancement for many applications. If you do choose to change the port here, you will need to make this change in all the code examples throughout the rest of the book to match the port used here.

Control Panel. For Unix systems, you can run *ns-slapd* and *admind* to start the directory server instance and administration server, respectively; you should consider adding these commands to a startup script so the directory service will run every time your machine reboots.* Once these services have been started, you are ready to add your application-specific configuration items.

Object Class Hierarchy

The iPlanet directory server boasts the easiest-to-use configuration manager. Making the changes to the LDAP schema described in Chapter 3 is very simple using this interface. First, launch the iPlanet Console (mine is Version 5.0). You will need to enter in the hostname and port of the directory server you want to manage, and then enter in the admin user's password.

Once logged in, expand the server tree of the machine you are connecting to; you should see entries for both Administration Server and Directory Server under *<hostname>/Server Group*. Double-clicking on the Directory Server entry will open up the directory server management console.

In the directory server management tool, click on the Configuration tab; you should see the Schema folder in the tree view on the left. Click on this folder, and you are ready to add new object classes to the LDAP schema.

The forethoughtPermission object class

Since the *inetOrgPerson* object class is used as-is, the first task is to create the *forethoughtPermission* object class described in the text. Clicking the Create... button will open up the Create Object Class dialog. Here, you can enter all the information for the new object class. Type in the name of the new class (*forethoughtPermission*), and leave the default parent of *top*. In addition to the required attribute of *objectClass*, you should add cn, which will store the name of the permission. Then add the description attribute to the allowed attributes, so a human-readable description of the permission can be entered. This is in addition to the aci attribute, inherited from the *top* object class. With these tasks done, you are ready to add the new class to the LDAP schema by clicking the OK button; your dialog box should now look like Figure C-2.

Once this is in place, you are ready to create the *groupOfForethoughtNames* class and its related attributes.

---

* While this technique is useful for development (starting up both the directory server and administration server on reboot), you should strongly consider *not* starting the administration server automatically once you move the server into production. Always running the administration server is an open invitation for hackers to try and crack your directory server instance. It is recommended that you automatically start only the directory server itself in these situations. The same practice is a good idea on Windows machines, as well.

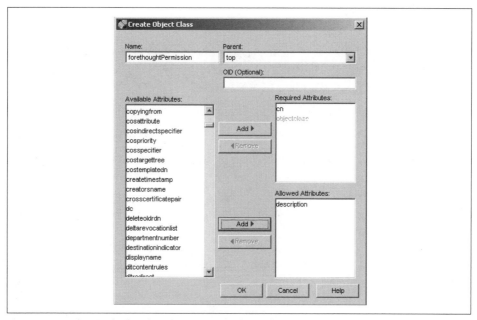

Figure C-2. Creating the forethoughtPermission object class

The groupOfForethoughtNames object class

The first task in creating the *groupOfForethoughtNames* object class is to add the uniquePermission attribute to the LDAP schema. From the screen where you clicked Create... to create a new object class, click the Attributes tab up top, and then click the Create... button here. Enter the name of the new attribute (*uniquePermission*), and then select DN for the Syntax option. This will ensure that a DN is supplied in a valid format, which will of course refer to an instance of our *forethoughtPermission* object class. You should also check the box allowing multiple values, so multiple permissions can be linked to each group. Your screen should now be similar to Figure C-3.

Once you've set all the options, clicking OK will add the attribute to your LDAP schema. This also gets you ready to perform your original task, creating the new object class for user groups (or roles).

The process of creating the *groupOfForethoughtNames* object class is identical to that of creating the *forethoughtPermission* object class. Go back to the Object Classes tab in the configuration section of the manager tool. Click the Create... button, and enter in the information about the new object class: the name, *groupOfForethoughtNames*; the parent, *groupOfUniqueNames*; and the additional optional attribute, *uniquePermission*. Then OK the changes, and your LDAP schema is ready for use. Figure C-4 shows this final step in schema modification.

After following all the steps outlined here, you are ready to add the extra organizational units required in the Forethought application.

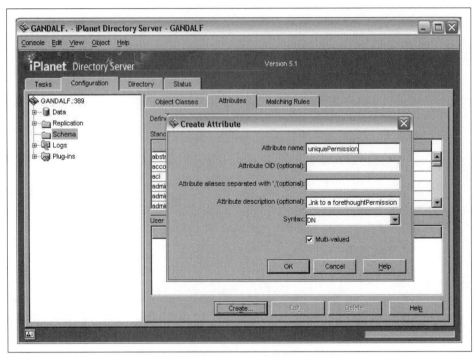

Figure C-3. Adding the uniquePermission attribute to the LDAP schema

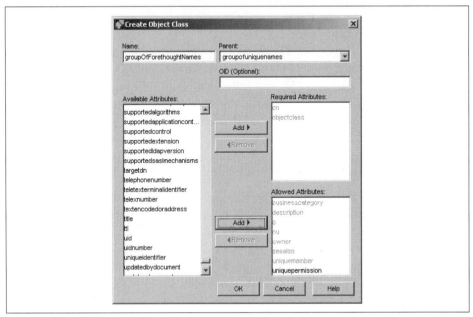

Figure C-4. Creating the groupOfForethoughtNames object class

Directory Hierarchy

The iPlanet directory server does not have any of the organizational units detailed in Chapter 3 set up by default. To view the hierarchy currently in place for your server, click on the Directory tab in the top-left section of the manager tool. This will move you from configuration to the directory structure itself. You will see several iPlanet-specific objects (*NetscapeRoot*, *schema*, etc.), but it is the first entry, *forethought.com*, that you are concerned with. Expand the organization, and you will see any existing organizational units that are in place.

Right-clicking on the *forethought.com* organization icon will open up a pop-up window; selecting "New >" will open up a submenu; finally, select "Organizational Unit...". Here, enter the information for the first new unit, *People*: the name and, optionally, a description. Figure C-5 shows the completed dialog. Finally, click OK, and you should see the new organization unit added to the directory browser.

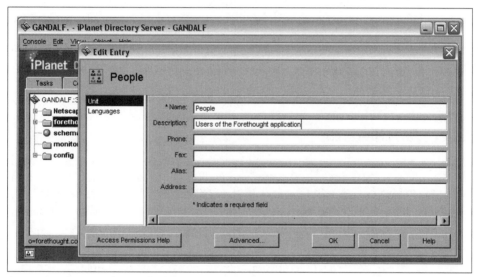

Figure C-5. Creating the People organization unit

Repeat this process for the *Groups* and *Permissions* organizational units. Once that is done, you are ready for the programmatic tasks detailed in Chapters 4 and 5.

OpenLDAP

You can get openLDAP from *http://www.openldap.org*. It's both free and open source, so licensing and deployment are non-issues with this software. As of this writing, the latest version for general use is 2.0.18. Once you've downloaded the archive, expand it into a directory like *openldap-2.0.18/*.

Installation

Installation is detailed in the *INSTALL* document included in the source distribution. Basically, you'll need to execute these commands (output is not shown):

```
[localhost:~/openldap-2.0.17] bmclaugh% ./configure

[localhost:~/openldap-2.0.17] bmclaugh% make depend

[localhost:~/openldap-2.0.17] bmclaugh% make

[localhost:~/openldap-2.0.17] bmclaugh% make test

[localhost:~/openldap-2.0.17] bmclaugh% su root -c 'make install'
```

Note that this last step requires root access; this is typical for all installations of software like this (as well as the databases detailed in Appendix B). Once this is done, you should have a ready-to-run LDAP directory server.

You should then modify the *slapd.conf* file to use Forethought-specific names. This file is located in the root directory of your installation. Modify it to have this entry:

```
database ldbm
suffix "dc=forethought,dc=com"
rootdn "cn=Manager,dc=forethought,dc=com"
rootpw secret
```

Object Class Hierarchy

You now need to create the Forethought-specific object classes and attributes. While iPlanet offers a GUI for these tasks, you will need to dive into LDIF and the openLDAP configuration file formats by hand. This is a little more complex, but offers you more control over your directory server's object class and data hierarchies.

The forethoughtPermission object class

First, create the *forethoughtPermission* object class; this is simple, as no new attributes are required. You should start by creating a new file; I suggest calling it *forethought.schema*, as it will add Forethought extensions to the openLDAP default schema definitions. Add to this new file the following definition:

```
objectclass ( 2.1.1.1.1 NAME 'forethoughtPermission'
              DESC 'Forethought application permission objects'
              SUP top
              MUST ( 'cn' )
              MAY 'description' )
```

The objectclass keyword defines the type of object that you are creating. The rest of the entry details this new class. First, a unique identifier should be provided. I picked an arbitrary number that is probably not in use in your own openLDAP installation. Then, the name of the class is supplied. I've also added a description for use by other administrators. SUP indicates the superclass for the object class; MUST defines required attributes; and MAY defines optional attributes. The values for each of these attributes are fairly self-explanatory; additionally, longer explanations can be found in the relevant sections of the chapters and in the earlier sections on iPlanet configuration. In a nutshell, you want a required name and optional description for this new object class.

The groupOfForethoughtNames object class

Creating the *groupOfForethoughtNames* object class follows the same general outlines. First, though, you need to add a new attribute, uniquePermission. This will reference the *forethoughtPermission* object class you just created. Add this entry to the schema configuration file you just created:

```
attributetype ( 2.1.1.1.2 NAME 'uniquePermission'
                DESC 'Link to a forethoughtPermission object'
                SYNTAX 1.3.6.1.4.1.1466.115.121.1.12 )
```

As in the case of defining an object class, a unique object identifier is supplied, as well as the name of the new attribute. The DESC is obviously a description. You then just need to supply the syntax (type) of the attribute. You can see how this lengthy number relates to a syntax by viewing Table 6-3 in the openLDAP administration guide, online at *http://www.openldap.org/doc/admin/schema.html#Extending%20Schema*. In this case, the syntax refers to a distinguished name (DN). This will link to the DN of an instance of the *forethoughtPermission* object class.

With this attribute in place, you can create the *groupOfForethoughtNames* object class:

```
objectclass ( 2.1.1.1.3 NAME 'groupOfForethoughtNames'
              DESC 'Forethought application group objects'
              SUP groupofuniquenames
              MAY 'uniquePermission' )
```

This should be self-explanatory. The one important point is that when declaring a superclass (in this case, *groupOfUniqueNames*), you automatically get all the required and optional attributes from that class. So the MUST and MAY keywords only supplement this existing set of attributes. For this reason, you only need to add the new attribute to the definition for the uniquePermission attribute.

With these three entries, add a reference to your new schema configuration file into the openLDAP *slapd.conf* file. Look for an entry like this:

```
# include schema
        include /usr/local/openldap/schema/core.schema
        include /usr/local/openldap/schema/cosine.schema
        include /usr/local/openldap/schema/inetorgperson.schema
```

Add to it your filename:

```
# include schema
        include /usr/local/openldap/schema/core.schema
```

```
        include /usr/local/openldap/schema/cosine.schema
        include /usr/local/openldap/schema/inetorgperson.schema
# Forethought schema definitions
        include /usr/local/openldap/schema/forethought.schema
```

Start your directory server, and the new Forethought objects and attributes will be available for use.

Directory Hierarchy

You will need to create three organizational units in your directory to match the Forethought structure: *Groups*, *People*, and *Permissions*. This is a trivial task in openLDAP; it simply requires that you define a file with these entries using the LDIF format. Here is just such a file:

```
# People organizational unit
        dn: ou=People,dc=forethought,dc=com
        cn: People
        objectClass: organizationalUnit

# Groups organizational unit
        dn: ou=Groups,dc=forethought,dc=com
        cn: Groups
        objectClass: organizationalUnit

# Permissions organizational unit
        dn: ou=Permissions,dc=forethought,dc=com
        cn: Permissions
        objectClass: organizationalUnit
```

You can then use the ldapadd command to add the entries in your LDIF file to your (running) directory server:

```
[localhost:~/openldap-2.0.17] bmclaugh% ldapadd -f forethought.ldif -x
    -D "cn=Manager,dc=forethought,dc=com" -w [password]
```

You now have both the required object classes and directory hierarchy to proceed with the Forethought application.

Application Server Setup

This appendix covers deployment of EJB components into EJB containers. For the sake of keeping this book under 1000 pages, I've detailed the setup of only the BEA Weblogic application server. This is the most prevalent production application server, and is also valuable because the way it handles vendor-specific deployment descriptors is representative of how most application servers operate.

BEA Weblogic

Installation of Weblogic is covered by the vendor's very thorough online and printed documentation. I've had no problem installing Weblogic on Windows, Linux, and Solaris, and found the process simple on all three platforms.

Configuration

Once you have an installation, you will need to set up the JDBC and JMS connections for use by code throughout the book. While Weblogic offers a web-based administration console, I find it easier to simply modify the server configuration file directly. You can find this file in the configuration directory for your specific server installation domain.

For example, I created a domain called middleearth. This resulted in a *middleearth* directory under the configuration root: *[Installation Root]/bea/wlserver6.1/config/middleearth*. Within this directory, the *config.xml* file controls the server configuration. You will need to make several additions to this file. I've highlighted the portions of my own configuration file that you will need to duplicate:

```
<?xml version="1.0" encoding="UTF-8"?>

<Domain Name="middleearth">
    <Application Deployed="true" Name="certificate"
                Path=".\config\middleearth\applications">
        <WebAppComponent Name="certificate" Targets="frodoWL" URI="certificate.war"/>
```

```
</Application>
<Log FileName="config/middleearth/logs/wl-domain.log" Name="middleearth"/>
<Application Deployed="true" Name="DefaultWebApp"
            Path=".\config\middleearth\applications">
  <WebAppComponent Name="DefaultWebApp" Targets="frodoWL" URI="DefaultWebApp"/>
</Application>
<Application Deployed="true" Name="forethoughtEntities"
            Path=".\config\middleearth\applications">
  <EJBComponent Name="forethoughtEntities" Targets="frodoWL"
                URI="forethoughtEntities.jar"/>
</Application>
<JTA Name="middleearth"/>
<SNMPAgent Name="middleearth"/>
<PasswordPolicy Name="wl_default_password_policy"/>
<JDBCDataSource JNDIName="jdbc.forethoughtDB" Name="ForethoughtDB"
                PoolName="forethoughtPool" Targets="frodoWL"/>
<Realm FileRealm="wl_default_file_realm" Name="wl_default_realm"/>

<!-- CustomRealm elements left out for brevity -->

<Server ListenPort="7001" Name="frodoWL" NativeIOEnabled="true"
        TransactionLogFilePrefix="config/middleearth/logs/">
    <KernelDebug Name="frodoWL"/>
    <WebServer DefaultWebApp="DefaultWebApp"
        LogFileName="./config/middleearth/logs/access.log"
        LoggingEnabled="true" Name="frodoWL"/>
    <ExecuteQueue Name="default" ThreadCount="15"/>
    <Log FileName="config/middleearth/logs/weblogic.log" Name="frodoWL"/>
    <ServerStart Name="frodoWL"/>
    <ServerDebug Name="frodoWL"/>
    <SSL Enabled="true" ListenPort="7002" Name="frodoWL"
        ServerCertificateChainFileName="config/middleearth/ca.pem"
        ServerCertificateFileName="config/middleearth/democert.pem"
        ServerKeyFileName="config/middleearth/demokey.pem"/>
</Server>

<!-- CustomRealm elements left out for brevity -->

<JDBCConnectionPool CapacityIncrement="5"
    DriverName="COM.cloudscape.core.JDBCDriver" InitialCapacity="15"
    MaxCapacity="50" Name="forethoughtPool"
    Properties="user=none;password=none;server=none"
    Targets="frodoWL" TestTableName="OFFICES"
    URL="jdbc:cloudscape:forethoughtDB"/>
<ApplicationManager Name="middleearth"/>
<JMSServer Name="ForethoughtJMSServer"
    Store="ForethoughtJMSFileStore" Targets="frodoWL">
    <JMSTopic JNDIName="forethought.EmployeeTopic" Name="Employee Topic"/>
    <JMSTopic JNDIName="forethought.SchedulerTopic" Name="Scheduler Topic"/>
</JMSServer>
<Security GuestDisabled="false" Name="middleearth"
    PasswordPolicy="wl_default_password_policy" Realm="wl_default_realm"/>
<FileRealm Name="wl_default_file_realm"/>
<JMSFileStore Directory="./config/middleearth/jmsStore"
```

```
                Name="ForethoughtJMSFileStore"/>
      <JMSConnectionFactory JNDIName="forethought.TopicFactory"
        Name="Forethought Topic Factory" Targets="frodoWL"
        UserTransactionsEnabled="true"/>

      <!-- CustomRealm elements left out for brevity -->
    </Domain>
```

You can see the JMS and JDBC stores. You need to define the store, and then link it with the name of the server you want it available for. In my setup, the server is named *frodoWL*.

Be sure to make these changes offline, as any changes to this file are lost at the next startup when the server is running.

Deployment Descriptors

BEA Weblogic requires a *weblogic-ejb-jar.xml* descriptor for every *ejb-jar.xml* descriptor in a deployed unit. This essentially "decodes" the *ejb-jar.xml*, providing vendor-specific details for the container. Additionally, another descriptor is required for beans that use container-managed persistence. This is typically called *weblogic-cmp-rdbms-jar.xml*, although you can override this name if you choose. So, for a given JAR file, you may have as many as three deployment descriptors specifically related to your beans.

However, these descriptors are extremely verbose (XML generally is), and the value of reprinting them in this appendix is limited. You can view and download these descriptors, as well as the standard *ejb-jar.xml* descriptor (discussed in Appendix E), online at *http://www.newInstance.com*. They are fairly self-explanatory, and have all been extensively tested with the 6.x family of BEA Weblogic products.

Supplemental Code Listings

Code listings that are mentioned, but not included, in the text of this book are included in this appendix. All the code in this appendix, as well as in the body of the book, can also be downloaded from the book's web site at *http://www.newInstance. com*. The code in this appendix is vendor-neutral, and should be compileable by following steps in the chapters and other appendixes. The code listings are organized by topic; while this usually corresponds to chapters, each section specifies the areas of the text where the code fits in.

Additionally, this book commonly makes modifications to code shown earlier to facilitate later needs. For example, while Chapters 4 and 5 detail the Forethought entity beans, later chapters modify these same beans. It becomes difficult, at best, to track these changes in an appendix. To simplify things, then, the code in this appendix is always the *final* version of the code. In other words, a User entity bean listed here in reference to Chapter 4 or 5 actually includes any changes made in later chapters. For this reason, you may find yourself looking at code referred to by an early chapter, but which has modifications from later chapters that are beyond your current understanding. Don't worry about it; the later chapters in the book ensure that you have a complete grasp of what is going on in all classes. If you want to see the code as it develops, chapter by chapter, you can download the code from *http://www. newInstance.com*, where the classes are made available on a chapter-by-chapter basis.

Entity Beans

The following entity beans complete the set of Forethought entities begun in Chapters 4 and 5. You should also notice that the deployment descriptor, *ejb-jar.xml*, contains entries for all Forethought entity beans; this includes those beans discussed in Chapters 4 and 5, including the Office entity bean and the Sequence session bean. Thus, you will need these classes, as well as the EntityAdapter and SessionAdapter classes, to compile these beans.

The UserType Bean

Example E-1 is the local interface for the UserType entity bean. Since this bean is never directly exposed to the client, it has only local interfaces, accessed by the User bean.

Example E-1. The UserTypeLocal Interface

```
package com.forethought.ejb.userType;

import javax.ejb.EJBException;
import javax.ejb.EJBLocalObject;

public interface UserTypeLocal extends EJBLocalObject {

    public Integer getId( ) throws EJBException;

    public String getType( ) throws EJBException;
    public void setType(String type) throws EJBException;
}
```

Example E-2 is the local home interface for the UserType entity bean. It defines a finder for user types by the type (the USER_TYPE column), as well as the primary key value.

Example E-2. The UserTypeLocalHome Interface

```
package com.forethought.ejb.userType;

import javax.ejb.CreateException;
import javax.ejb.EJBException;
import javax.ejb.EJBLocalHome;
import javax.ejb.FinderException;

public interface UserTypeLocalHome extends EJBLocalHome {

    public UserTypeLocal create(String type)
        throws CreateException, EJBException;

    public UserTypeLocal findByPrimaryKey(Integer userTypeID)
        throws FinderException, EJBException;

    public UserTypeLocal findByType(String type)
        throws FinderException, EJBException;
}
```

Example E-3 is the implementation class for the UserType entity bean.

Example E-3. The UserTypeBean Implementation Class

```
package com.forethought.ejb.userType;

import javax.ejb.CreateException;
```

Example E-3. The UserTypeBean Implementation Class (continued)

```java
import javax.naming.Context;
import javax.naming.InitialContext;
import javax.naming.NamingException;

import com.forethought.ejb.sequence.SequenceException;
import com.forethought.ejb.sequence.SequenceLocal;
import com.forethought.ejb.sequence.SequenceLocalHome;
import com.forethought.ejb.util.EntityAdapter;

public abstract class UserTypeBean extends EntityAdapter {

    public Integer ejbCreate(String type) throws CreateException {
        // Get the next primary key value
        try {
            Context context = new InitialContext();

            // Note that RMI-IIOP narrowing is not required
            SequenceLocalHome home = (SequenceLocalHome)
                context.lookup("java:comp/env/ejb/SequenceLocalHome");
            SequenceLocal sequence = home.create();
            String userTypeKey =
                (String)context.lookup("java:comp/env/constants/UserTypeKey");
            Integer id = sequence.getNextValue(userTypeKey);

            // Set values
            setId(id);
            setType(type);

            return null;
        } catch (NamingException e) {
            throw new CreateException("Could not obtain an " +
                "InitialContext.");
        } catch (SequenceException e) {
            throw new CreateException("Error getting primary key value: " +
                e.getMessage());
        }
    }

    public void ejbPostCreate(String type) {
        // Empty implementation
    }

    public abstract Integer getId();
    public abstract void setId(Integer id);

    public abstract String getType();
    public abstract void setType(String type);
}
```

The User Bean

Example E-4 is the remote interface for the User entity bean. Note how the user's office is exposed. The office is represented by an Office bean and is a relationship field. You cannot expose a relationship field directly because it deals with local interfaces and not remote ones. Instead, the office is set through the office's remote interface. You can check out the code in the bean implementation that translates these values into local interface calls on the Office bean implementation in Example E-9. The same principles also apply to the user's UserType relationship.

Example E-4. The User Remote Interface

```
package com.forethought.ejb.user;

import java.rmi.RemoteException;
import javax.ejb.EJBObject;

// Office bean
import com.forethought.ejb.office.Office;
import com.forethought.ejb.office.OfficeInfo;

// UserType bean
import com.forethought.ejb.userType.UnknownUserTypeException;

public interface User extends EJBObject {

    public UserInfo getInfo() throws RemoteException;
    public void setInfo(UserInfo userInfo)
        throws RemoteException, UnknownUserTypeException;

    public Integer getId() throws RemoteException;

    public String getUserDn() throws RemoteException;
    public void setUserDn(String userDn) throws RemoteException;

    public Office getOffice() throws RemoteException;
    public void setOffice(Office office) throws RemoteException;

    public String getType() throws RemoteException;
    public void setType(String type)
        throws RemoteException, UnknownUserTypeException;

    public String getFirstName() throws RemoteException;
    public void setFirstName(String firstName) throws RemoteException;

    public String getLastName() throws RemoteException;
    public void setLastName(String lastName) throws RemoteException;
}
```

Example E-5 is a local interface for the User bean. Just as the Office bean provides local interfaces for use by the User bean in persistence relationships, this bean provides local interfaces for use by the Account bean in persistence relationships.

Example E-5. The UserLocal Interface

```
package com.forethought.ejb.user;

import javax.ejb.EJBException;
import javax.ejb.EJBLocalObject;

// Office bean
import com.forethought.ejb.office.OfficeLocal;

// UserType bean
import com.forethought.ejb.userType.UnknownUserTypeException;

public interface UserLocal extends EJBLocalObject {

    public Integer getId( ) throws EJBException;

    public String getUserDn( ) throws EJBException;
    public void setUserDn(String userDN) throws EJBException;

    public OfficeLocal getOfficeLocal( ) throws EJBException;
    public void setOfficeLocal(OfficeLocal officeLocal) throws EJBException;

    public String getType( ) throws EJBException;
    public void setType(String type)
        throws EJBException, UnknownUserTypeException;

    public String getFirstName( ) throws EJBException;
    public void setFirstName(String firstName) throws EJBException;

    public String getLastName( ) throws EJBException;
    public void setLastName(String lastName) throws EJBException;
}
```

Example E-6 is the information map for the User entity bean, used by both the local and remote interfaces.

Example E-6. The UserInfo Class

```
package com.forethought.ejb.user;

import java.io.Serializable;

// Office bean
import com.forethought.ejb.office.OfficeInfo;

public class UserInfo implements Serializable {

    private int id;
```

```java
    private String officeCity;
    private String officeState;
    private String type;
    private String userDn;
    private String firstName;
    private String lastName;

    UserInfo(int id, String userDn, String type,
            String firstName, String lastName, OfficeInfo officeInfo) {

        this.id = id;
        this.userDn = userDn;
        this.type = type;
        this.firstName = firstName;
        this.lastName = lastName;
        this.officeCity = officeInfo.getCity();
        this.officeState = officeInfo.getState();
    }

    public int getId() {
        return id;
    }

    public String getUserDn() {
        return userDn;
    }

    public void setUserDn(String userDn) {
        this.userDn = userDn;
    }

    public String getOfficeCity() {
        return officeCity;
    }

    public void setOfficeCity(String officeCity) {
        this.officeCity = officeCity;
    }

    public String getOfficeState() {
        return officeState;
    }

    public void setOfficeState(String officeState) {
        this.officeState = officeState;
    }

    public String getType() {
        return type;
    }

    public void setType(String type) {
```

Example E-6. The UserInfo Class (continued)

```
            this.type = type;
    }

    public String getFirstName( ) {
        return firstName;
    }

    public void setFirstName(String firstName) {
        this.firstName = firstName;
    }

    public String getLastName( ) {
        return lastName;
    }

    public void setLastName(String lastName) {
        this.lastName = lastName;
    }
}
```

Example E-7 is the home interface for the User entity bean.

Example E-7. The UserHome Interface

```
package com.forethought.ejb.user;

import java.rmi.RemoteException;
import javax.ejb.CreateException;
import javax.ejb.EJBHome;
import javax.ejb.FinderException;

// Office bean
import com.forethought.ejb.office.Office;

// UserType bean
import com.forethought.ejb.userType.UnknownUserTypeException;

public interface UserHome extends EJBHome {

    public User create(String userDn, String type,
                        String firstName, String lastName, Office office)
        throws CreateException, RemoteException, UnknownUserTypeException;

    public User findByPrimaryKey(Integer userID)
        throws FinderException, RemoteException;

    public User findByUserDn(String userDn)
        throws FinderException, RemoteException;

    public User findByName(String firstName, String lastName)
```

```
        throws FinderException, RemoteException;
}
```

Example E-8 is the local home interface for the User bean. See the description for Example E-5 if you aren't clear on why this is needed.

Example E-8. The UserLocalHome Interface

```java
package com.forethought.ejb.user;

import javax.ejb.CreateException;
import javax.ejb.EJBException;
import javax.ejb.EJBLocalHome;
import javax.ejb.FinderException;

// Office bean
import com.forethought.ejb.office.Office;

// UserType bean
import com.forethought.ejb.userType.UnknownUserTypeException;

public interface UserLocalHome extends EJBLocalHome {

    public UserLocal create(String userDN, String type,
                            String firstName, String lastName, Office office)
        throws CreateException, EJBException, UnknownUserTypeException;

    public UserLocal findByPrimaryKey(Integer userID)
        throws FinderException, EJBException;

    public UserLocal findByUserDn(String userDn)
        throws FinderException, EJBException;

    public UserLocal findByName(String firstName, String lastName)
        throws FinderException, EJBException;
}
```

Example E-9 is the implementation class for the User entity bean.

Example E-9. The UserBean Implementation Class

```java
package com.forethought.ejb.user;

import java.rmi.RemoteException;
import javax.ejb.CreateException;
import javax.ejb.EJBException;
import javax.ejb.FinderException;
import javax.naming.Context;
import javax.naming.InitialContext;
import javax.naming.NamingException;
import javax.rmi.PortableRemoteObject;
```

Example E-9. The UserBean Implementation Class (continued)

```java
import com.forethought.ejb.util.EntityAdapter;

// Sequence bean
import com.forethought.ejb.sequence.SequenceException;
import com.forethought.ejb.sequence.SequenceLocal;
import com.forethought.ejb.sequence.SequenceLocalHome;

// Office bean
import com.forethought.ejb.office.Office;
import com.forethought.ejb.office.OfficeHome;
import com.forethought.ejb.office.OfficeLocal;
import com.forethought.ejb.office.OfficeLocalHome;

// UserType bean
import com.forethought.ejb.userType.UnknownUserTypeException;
import com.forethought.ejb.userType.UserTypeLocal;
import com.forethought.ejb.userType.UserTypeLocalHome;

public abstract class UserBean extends EntityAdapter {

    public Integer ejbCreate(String userDn, String type,
                             String firstName, String lastName, Office office)
        throws CreateException, UnknownUserTypeException {

        // Get the next primary key value
        try {
            Context context = new InitialContext();
            // Note that RMI-IIOP narrowing is not required
            SequenceLocalHome home = (SequenceLocalHome)
                context.lookup("java:comp/env/ejb/SequenceLocalHome");
            SequenceLocal sequence = home.create();
            String userKey =
                (String)context.lookup("java:comp/env/constants/UserKey");
            Integer id = sequence.getNextValue(userKey);

            // Set values
            setId(id);
            setUserDn(userDn);
            setFirstName(firstName);
            setLastName(lastName);

            return null;
        } catch (NamingException e) {
            throw new CreateException("Could not obtain an " +
                "InitialContext: " + e.getMessage());
        } catch (SequenceException e) {
            throw new CreateException("Error getting primary key value: " +
                e.getMessage());
        }
    }
```

```java
public void ejbPostCreate(String userDn, String type,
                          String firstName, String lastName,
                          Office office)
    throws CreateException, UnknownUserTypeException {

    // Handle CMP relationships
    setOffice(office);
    setType(type);
}

public UserInfo getInfo( ) throws RemoteException {
    OfficeInfo officeInfo = null;
    Office office = getOffice( );
    if (office != null) {
        officeInfo = office.getInfo( );
    }

    UserInfo userInfo =
        new UserInfo(getId().intValue(), getUserDn( ),
                     getUserTypeLocal().getType( ),
                     getFirstName( ), getLastName( ),
                     officeInfo);

    return userInfo;
}

public void setInfo(UserInfo userInfo) throws UnknownUserTypeException {
    setUserDn(userInfo.getUserDn( ));
    setFirstName(userInfo.getFirstName( ));
    setLastName(userInfo.getLastName( ));
    setType(userInfo.getType( ));
}

public String getType( ) {
    return getUserTypeLocal().getType( );
}

public void setType(String type) throws UnknownUserTypeException {
    try {
        Context context = new InitialContext( );
        UserTypeLocalHome userTypeLocalHome =
            (UserTypeLocalHome)context.lookup(
                    "java:comp/env/ejb/UserTypeLocalHome");
        UserTypeLocal userTypeLocal =
            userTypeLocalHome.findByType(type);
        setUserTypeLocal(userTypeLocal);
    } catch (NamingException e) {
        throw new EJBException("Error looking up UserType bean: " +
            e.getMessage( ));
    } catch (FinderException e) {
        // Couldn't find supplied type
        throw new UnknownUserTypeException(type);
```

Example E-9. The UserBean Implementation Class (continued)

```
        }
    }

    public Office getOffice( ) {
        OfficeLocal officeLocal = getOfficeLocal( );
        if (officeLocal == null) {
            return null;
        }

        // Construct primary key for this office
        Integer officeID = getOfficeLocal().getId( );

        try {
            // Find the remote interface for this office
            Context context = new InitialContext( );
            OfficeHome officeHome =
                (OfficeHome)context.lookup(
                    "java:comp/env/ejb/OfficeHome");
            Office office = officeHome.findByPrimaryKey(officeID);
            return office;
        } catch (NamingException e) {
            throw new EJBException("Error looking up Office bean: " +
                e.getMessage( ));
        } catch (RemoteException e) {
            throw new EJBException("Error looking up Office bean: " +
                e.getMessage( ));
        } catch (FinderException shouldNeverHappen) {
            // This should never happen; the ID from an office's remote
            // interface should match an office's ID in a local interface
            throw new EJBException("Error matching remote Office to " +
                "local Office: " + shouldNeverHappen.getMessage( ));
        }
    }

    public void setOffice(Office office) {
        try {
            // Handle case where no office supplied
            if (office == null) {
                setOfficeLocal(null);
                return;
            }

            // Construct primary key for this office
            Integer officeID = office.getId( );

            // Find the local interface for this office
            Context context = new InitialContext( );
            OfficeLocalHome officeLocalHome =
                (OfficeLocalHome)context.lookup(
                    "java:comp/env/ejb/OfficeLocalHome");
            OfficeLocal officeLocal =
                officeLocalHome.findByPrimaryKey(officeID);
```

Example E-9. The UserBean Implementation Class (continued)

```
            setOfficeLocal(officeLocal);
        } catch (NamingException e) {
            throw new EJBException("Error looking up Office bean: " +
                e.getMessage( ));
        } catch (RemoteException e) {
            throw new EJBException("Error looking up Office bean: " +
                e.getMessage( ));
        } catch (FinderException shouldNeverHappen) {
            // This should never happen; the ID from an office's remote
            // interface should match an office's ID in a local interface
            throw new EJBException("Error matching remote Office to " +
                "local Office: " + shouldNeverHappen.getMessage( ));
        }
    }

    public abstract Integer getId( );
    public abstract void setId(Integer id);

    public abstract String getUserDn( );
    public abstract void setUserDn(String userDn);

    public abstract UserTypeLocal getUserTypeLocal( );
    public abstract void setUserTypeLocal(UserTypeLocal userTypeLocal);

    public abstract OfficeLocal getOfficeLocal( );
    public abstract void setOfficeLocal(OfficeLocal officeLocal);

    public abstract String getFirstName( );
    public abstract void setFirstName(String firstName);

    public abstract String getLastName( );
    public abstract void setLastName(String lastName);
}
```

The User bean is the first bean to use CMP relationships so far. CMP relationships are well documented in various EJB books, and turn out to be simple to understand. Several other beans in this appendix use these relationships as well, so you should be able to pick things up by following the examples.

You should also note that for the first time in this book, the ejbPostCreate( ) method is used in this bean. The EJB 2.0 specification dictates that CMP relationships cannot be dealt with in the ejbCreate( ) method; instead, they must be handled by the ejbPostCreate( ) method. This allows the container to make some assumptions about what classes and resources must be available for each method invocation. As a result, the two relationship-based methods, (setOffice( ) and setUserType( ), are invoked by the ejbPostCreate( ) method in this bean.

The AccountType Bean

Example E-10 is the AccountType entity bean's local interface. Like the UserType bean, it also has only local interfaces exposed.

Example E-10. The AccountTypeLocal Interface

```
package com.forethought.ejb.accountType;

import javax.ejb.EJBException;
import javax.ejb.EJBLocalObject;

public interface AccountTypeLocal extends EJBLocalObject {

    public Integer getId( ) throws EJBException;

    public String getType( ) throws EJBException;
    public void setType(String type) throws EJBException;
}
```

The local home interface for the AccountType bean is shown in Example E-11.

Example E-11. The AccountTypeLocalHome Interface

```
package com.forethought.ejb.accountType;

import javax.ejb.CreateException;
import javax.ejb.EJBException;
import javax.ejb.EJBLocalHome;
import javax.ejb.FinderException;

public interface AccountTypeLocalHome extends EJBLocalHome {

    public AccountTypeLocal create(String type)
        throws CreateException, EJBException;

    public AccountTypeLocal findByPrimaryKey(Integer accountTypeID)
        throws FinderException, EJBException;

    public AccountTypeLocal findByType(String type)
        throws FinderException, EJBException;
}
```

Example E-12 is the implementation class for the AccountType bean.

Example E-12. The AccountTypeBean Implementation Class

```
package com.forethought.ejb.accountType;

import javax.ejb.CreateException;
import javax.naming.Context;
import javax.naming.InitialContext;
import javax.naming.NamingException;
```

```java
import com.forethought.ejb.sequence.SequenceException;
import com.forethought.ejb.sequence.SequenceLocal;
import com.forethought.ejb.sequence.SequenceLocalHome;
import com.forethought.ejb.util.EntityAdapter;

public abstract class AccountTypeBean extends EntityAdapter {

    public Integer ejbCreate(String type) throws CreateException {
        // Get the next primary key value
        try {
            Context context = new InitialContext();

            // Note that RMI-IIOP narrowing is not required
            SequenceLocalHome home = (SequenceLocalHome)
                context.lookup("java:comp/env/ejb/SequenceLocalHome");
            SequenceLocal sequence = home.create();
            String accountTypeKey =
                (String)context.lookup(
                    "java:comp/env/constants/AccountTypeKey");
            Integer id = sequence.getNextValue(accountTypeKey);

            // Set values
            setId(id);
            setType(type);

            return null;
        } catch (NamingException e) {
            throw new CreateException("Could not obtain an " +
                "InitialContext.");
        } catch (SequenceException e) {
            throw new CreateException("Error getting primary key value: " +
                e.getMessage());
        }
    }

    public void ejbPostCreate(String type) {
        // Empty implementation
    }

    public abstract void setId(Integer id);
    public abstract Integer getId();

    public abstract String getType();
    public abstract void setType(String type);
}
```

The Fund Bean

Example E-13 is the remote interface for the Fund entity bean.

Example E-13. The Fund Remote Interface

```
package com.forethought.ejb.fund;

import java.rmi.RemoteException;
import javax.ejb.EJBObject;

public interface Fund extends EJBObject {

    public FundInfo getInfo() throws RemoteException;
    public void setInfo(FundInfo fundInfo) throws RemoteException;

    public Integer getId() throws RemoteException;

    public String getName() throws RemoteException;
    public void setName(String name) throws RemoteException;

    public String getDescription() throws RemoteException;
    public void setDescription(String description)
        throws RemoteException;
}
```

Example E-14 is the local interface for the Fund bean, and is used in container-managed relationships.

Example E-14. The Fund Local Interface

```
package com.forethought.ejb.fund;

import javax.ejb.EJBException;
import javax.ejb.EJBLocalObject;

public interface FundLocal extends EJBLocalObject {

    public Integer getId() throws EJBException;

    public String getName() throws EJBException;
    public void setName(String name) throws EJBException;

    public String getDescription() throws EJBException;
    public void setDescription(String description)
        throws EJBException;
}
```

Example E-15 shows the information class (FundInfo) for the Fund entity bean.

Example E-15. The FundInfo Class

```
package com.forethought.ejb.fund;

import java.io.Serializable;
```

Example E-15. The FundInfo Class (continued)

```java
public class FundInfo implements Serializable {

    private int id;
    private String name;
    private String description;

    protected FundInfo(int id, String name, String description) {
        this.id = id;
        this.name = name;
        this.description = description;
    }

    public int getId( ) {
        return id;
    }

    public String getName( ) {
        return name;
    }

    public void setName(String name) {
        this.name = name;
    }

    public String getDescription( ) {
        return description;
    }

    public void setDescription(String description) {
        this.description = description;
    }
}
```

The home interface for the Fund entity bean is shown in Example E-16.

Example E-16. The FundHome Interface

```java
package com.forethought.ejb.fund;

import java.rmi.RemoteException;
import javax.ejb.CreateException;
import javax.ejb.EJBHome;
import javax.ejb.FinderException;

public interface FundHome extends EJBHome {

    public Fund create(String name, String description)
        throws CreateException, RemoteException;

    public Fund findByPrimaryKey(Integer fundID)
        throws FinderException, RemoteException;
```

```
    public Fund findByName(String name)
        throws FinderException, RemoteException;
}
```

The local home interface for the Fund bean is shown in Example E-17.

Example E-17. The FundLocalHome Interface

```
package com.forethought.ejb.fund;

import javax.ejb.CreateException;
import javax.ejb.EJBException;
import javax.ejb.EJBLocalHome;
import javax.ejb.FinderException;

public interface FundLocalHome extends EJBLocalHome {

    public FundLocal create(String name, String description)
        throws CreateException, EJBException;

    public FundLocal findByPrimaryKey(Integer fundID)
        throws FinderException, EJBException;

    public FundLocal findByName(String name)
        throws FinderException, EJBException;
}
```

Example E-18 is the Fund bean's implementation class.

Example E-18. The FundBean Implementation Class

```
package com.forethought.ejb.fund;

import javax.ejb.CreateException;
import javax.naming.Context;
import javax.naming.InitialContext;
import javax.naming.NamingException;

import com.forethought.ejb.sequence.SequenceException;
import com.forethought.ejb.sequence.SequenceLocal;
import com.forethought.ejb.sequence.SequenceLocalHome;
import com.forethought.ejb.util.EntityAdapter;

public abstract class FundBean extends EntityAdapter {

    public Integer ejbCreate(String name, String description)
        throws CreateException {
        // Get the next primary key value
        try {
            Context context = new InitialContext();
```

```
            // Note that RMI-IIOP narrowing is not required
            SequenceLocalHome home = (SequenceLocalHome)
                context.lookup("java:comp/env/ejb/SequenceLocalHome");
            SequenceLocal sequence = home.create();
            String fundKey =
                (String)context.lookup(
                    "java:comp/env/constants/FundKey");
            Integer id = sequence.getNextValue(fundKey);

            // Set values
            setId(id);
            setName(name);
            setDescription(description);

            return null;
        } catch (NamingException e) {
            throw new CreateException("Could not obtain an " +
                "InitialContext.");
        } catch (SequenceException e) {
            throw new CreateException("Error getting primary key value: " +
                e.getMessage());
        }
    }

    public void ejbPostCreate(String name, String description) {
        // Empty implementation
    }

    public FundInfo getInfo() {
        FundInfo fundInfo =
            new FundInfo(getId().intValue(), getName(), getDescription());
        return fundInfo;
    }

    public void setInfo(FundInfo fundInfo) {
        setName(fundInfo.getName());
        setDescription(fundInfo.getDescription());
    }

    public abstract Integer getId();
    public abstract void setId(Integer id);

    public abstract String getName();
    public abstract void setName(String name);

    public abstract String getDescription();
    public abstract void setDescription(String description);
}
```

The Account Bean

Example E-19 is the Account bean's remote interface.

Example E-19. The Account Remote Interface

```
package com.forethought.ejb.account;

import java.rmi.RemoteException;
import javax.ejb.EJBObject;

// AccountType bean
import com.forethought.ejb.accountType.UnknownAccountTypeException;

// User bean
import com.forethought.ejb.user.User;

public interface Account extends EJBObject {

    public AccountInfo getInfo() throws RemoteException;
    public void setInfo(AccountInfo accountInfo)
        throws RemoteException, UnknownAccountTypeException;

    public Integer getId() throws RemoteException;

    public User getUser() throws RemoteException;
    public void setUser(User user) throws RemoteException;

    public String getType() throws RemoteException;
    public void setType(String type)
        throws RemoteException, UnknownAccountTypeException;

    public float getBalance() throws RemoteException;
    public void setBalance(float balance) throws RemoteException;
}
```

Example E-20 is the local interface for the Account bean, used in CMP relationships.

Example E-20. The AccountLocal Interface

```
package com.forethought.ejb.account;

import javax.ejb.EJBException;
import javax.ejb.EJBLocalObject;

// AccountType bean
import com.forethought.ejb.accountType.UnknownAccountTypeException;

// User bean
import com.forethought.ejb.user.UserLocal;

public interface AccountLocal extends EJBLocalObject {

    public Integer getId() throws EJBException;
```

```
    public UserLocal getUserLocal( ) throws EJBException;
    public void setUserLocal(UserLocal userLocal) throws EJBException;

    public String getType( ) throws EJBException;
    public void setType(String type)
        throws EJBException, UnknownAccountTypeException;

    public float getBalance( ) throws EJBException;
    public void setBalance(float balance) throws EJBException;
}
```

The information map for the Account bean is shown in Example E-21.

Example E-21. The AccountInfo Class

```
package com.forethought.ejb.account;

import java.io.Serializable;

// User bean
import com.forethought.ejb.user.UserInfo;

public class AccountInfo implements Serializable {

    private int id;
    private UserInfo userInfo;
    private String type;
    private float balance;

    AccountInfo(int id, String type, float balance, UserInfo userInfo) {

        this.id = id;
        this.type = type;
        this.balance = balance;
        this.userInfo = userInfo;
    }

    public int getId( ) {
        return id;
    }

    public UserInfo getUserInfo( ) {
        return userInfo;
    }

    public void setUserInfo(UserInfo userInfo) {
        this.userInfo = userInfo;
    }

    public String getType( ) {
        return type;
    }
```

Example E-21. The AccountInfo Class (continued)

```
    public void setType(String type) {
        this.type = type;
    }

    public float getBalance( ) {
        return balance;
    }

    public void setBalance(float balance) {
        this.balance = balance;
    }
}
```

The home interface for the Account bean is shown in Example E-22.

Example E-22. The AccountHome Interface

```
package com.forethought.ejb.account;

import java.rmi.RemoteException;
import java.util.Collection;
import javax.ejb.CreateException;
import javax.ejb.EJBHome;
import javax.ejb.FinderException;

// AccountType bean
import com.forethought.ejb.accountType.UnknownAccountTypeException;

// User bean
import com.forethought.ejb.user.User;

public interface AccountHome extends EJBHome {

    public Account create(String type, float balance, User user)
        throws CreateException, RemoteException, UnknownAccountTypeException;

    public Account findByPrimaryKey(Integer accountID)
        throws FinderException, RemoteException;

    public Collection findByBalance(float minBalance, float maxBalance)
        throws FinderException, RemoteException;
}
```

Example E-23 shows the Account bean's local home interface.

Example E-23. The AccountLocalHome Interface

```
package com.forethought.ejb.account;

import java.util.Collection;
import javax.ejb.CreateException;
import javax.ejb.EJBException;
import javax.ejb.EJBLocalHome;
```

Example E-23. The AccountLocalHome Interface (continued)

```java
import javax.ejb.FinderException;

// User bean
import com.forethought.ejb.user.User;

// AccountType bean
import com.forethought.ejb.accountType.UnknownAccountTypeException;

public interface AccountLocalHome extends EJBLocalHome {

    public AccountLocal create(String type, float balance, User user)
        throws CreateException, EJBException, UnknownAccountTypeException;

    public AccountLocal findByPrimaryKey(Integer accountID)
        throws FinderException, EJBException;

    public Collection findByBalance(float minBalance, float maxBalance)
        throws FinderException, EJBException;
}
```

Example E-24 is the implementation class for the Account bean.

Example E-24. The AccountBean Implementation Class

```java
package com.forethought.ejb.account;

import java.rmi.RemoteException;
import javax.ejb.CreateException;
import javax.ejb.EJBException;
import javax.ejb.FinderException;
import javax.naming.Context;
import javax.naming.InitialContext;
import javax.naming.NamingException;
import javax.rmi.PortableRemoteObject;

import com.forethought.ejb.util.EntityAdapter;

// Sequence bean
import com.forethought.ejb.sequence.SequenceException;
import com.forethought.ejb.sequence.SequenceLocal;
import com.forethought.ejb.sequence.SequenceLocalHome;

// AccountType bean
import com.forethought.ejb.accountType.AccountTypeLocal;
import com.forethought.ejb.accountType.AccountTypeLocalHome;
import com.forethought.ejb.accountType.UnknownAccountTypeException;

// User bean
import com.forethought.ejb.user.User;
import com.forethought.ejb.user.UserInfo;
import com.forethought.ejb.user.UserLocal;
import com.forethought.ejb.user.UserLocalHome;
```

Example E-24. The AccountBean Implementation Class (continued)

```java
import com.forethought.ejb.user.UserHome;

public abstract class AccountBean extends EntityAdapter {

    public Integer ejbCreate(String type, float balance, User user)
        throws CreateException, UnknownAccountTypeException {

        // Get the next primary key value
        try {
            Context context = new InitialContext();
            // Note that RMI-IIOP narrowing is not required
            SequenceLocalHome home = (SequenceLocalHome)
                context.lookup("java:comp/env/ejb/SequenceLocalHome");
            SequenceLocal sequence = home.create();
            String accountKey =
                (String)context.lookup("java:comp/env/constants/AccountKey");
            Integer id = sequence.getNextValue(accountKey);

            // Set values
            setId(id);
            setBalance(balance);

            return null;
        } catch (NamingException e) {
            throw new CreateException("Could not obtain an " +
                "InitialContext: " + e.getMessage());
        } catch (SequenceException e) {
            throw new CreateException("Error getting primary key value: " +
                e.getMessage());
        }
    }

    public void ejbPostCreate(String type, float balance, User user)
        throws UnknownAccountTypeException {

        // Handle CMP relationships
        setType(type);
        setUser(user);
    }

    public AccountInfo getInfo() throws RemoteException {
        AccountInfo accountInfo =
            new AccountInfo(getId().intValue(), getAccountTypeLocal().getType(),
                            getBalance(), getUser().getInfo());

        return accountInfo;
    }

    public void setInfo(AccountInfo accountInfo)
        throws UnknownAccountTypeException {

        setType(accountInfo.getType());
```

```
        setBalance(accountInfo.getBalance( ));
        setUser(accountInfo.getUserInfo( ));
    }

    public void setType(String type) throws UnknownAccountTypeException {
        try {
            Context context = new InitialContext( );
            AccountTypeLocalHome accountTypeLocalHome =
                (AccountTypeLocalHome)context.lookup(
                    "java:comp/env/ejb/AccountTypeLocalHome");
            AccountTypeLocal accountTypeLocal =
                accountTypeLocalHome.findByType(type);
            setAccountTypeLocal(accountTypeLocal);
        } catch (NamingException e) {
            throw new EJBException("Error looking up AccountType bean: " +
                e.getMessage( ));
        } catch (FinderException e) {
            // Couldn't find supplied type
            throw new UnknownAccountTypeException(type);
        }
    }

    public String getType( ) {
        return getAccountTypeLocal().getType( );
    }

    public void setUser(User user) {
        try {
            // Construct primary key for this user
            Integer userID = user.getId( );

            // Find the local interface for this office
            Context context = new InitialContext( );
            UserLocalHome userLocalHome =
                (UserLocalHome)context.lookup(
                    "java:comp/env/ejb/UserLocalHome");
            UserLocal userLocal =
                userLocalHome.findByPrimaryKey(userID);
            setUserLocal(userLocal);
        } catch (NamingException e) {
            throw new EJBException("Error looking up User bean: " +
                e.getMessage( ));
        } catch (RemoteException e) {
            throw new EJBException("Error looking up User bean: " +
                e.getMessage( ));
        } catch (FinderException shouldNeverHappen) {
            // This should never happen; the ID from an office's remote
            //   interface should match an office's ID in a local interface
            throw new EJBException("Error matching remote User to " +
                "local User: " + shouldNeverHappen.getMessage( ));
        }
    }
```

Example E-24. The AccountBean Implementation Class (continued)

```java
private void setUser(UserInfo userInfo) {
    try {
        // Construct primary key for this user
        Integer userID = new Integer(userInfo.getId());

        // Find the local interface for this office
        Context context = new InitialContext();
        UserLocalHome userLocalHome =
            (UserLocalHome)context.lookup(
                "java:comp/env/ejb/UserLocalHome");
        UserLocal userLocal =
            userLocalHome.findByPrimaryKey(userID);
        setUserLocal(userLocal);
    } catch (NamingException e) {
        throw new EJBException("Error looking up User bean: " +
            e.getMessage());
    } catch (FinderException shouldNeverHappen) {
        // This should never happen; the ID from an office's remote
        // interface should match an office's ID in a local interface
        throw new EJBException("Error matching remote User to " +
            "local User: " + shouldNeverHappen.getMessage());
    }
}

public User getUser() {
    // Construct primary key for this office
    Integer userID = getUserLocal().getId();

    try {
        // Find the remote interface for this office
        Context context = new InitialContext();
        UserHome userHome =
            (UserHome)context.lookup(
                "java:comp/env/ejb/UserHome");
        User user = userHome.findByPrimaryKey(userID);
        return user;
    } catch (NamingException e) {
        throw new EJBException("Error looking up User bean: " +
            e.getMessage());
    } catch (RemoteException e) {
        throw new EJBException("Error looking up User bean: " +
            e.getMessage());
    } catch (FinderException shouldNeverHappen) {
        // This should never happen; the ID from a user's remote
        // interface should match a user's ID in a local interface
        throw new EJBException("Error matching remote User to " +
            "local User: " + shouldNeverHappen.getMessage());
    }
}

public abstract Integer getId();
public abstract void setId(Integer id);
```

```
    public abstract UserLocal getUserLocal( );
    public abstract void setUserLocal(UserLocal userLocal);

    public abstract AccountTypeLocal getAccountTypeLocal( );
    public abstract void setAccountTypeLocal(AccountTypeLocal accountTypeLocal);

    public abstract float getBalance( );
    public abstract void setBalance(float balance);
}
```

The Transaction Bean

The remote interface for the Transaction bean is shown in Example E-25.

Example E-25. The Transaction Remote Interface

```
package com.forethought.ejb.transaction;

import java.rmi.RemoteException;
import java.util.Date;
import javax.ejb.EJBObject;

// Account bean
import com.forethought.ejb.account.Account;

public interface Transaction extends EJBObject {

    public TransactionInfo getInfo( ) throws RemoteException;
    public void setInfo(TransactionInfo transactionInfo)
        throws RemoteException;

    public Integer getId( ) throws RemoteException;

    public Account getAccount( ) throws RemoteException;
    public void setAccount(Account account) throws RemoteException;

    public float getAmount( ) throws RemoteException;
    public void setAmount(float amount) throws RemoteException;

    public Date getDateTime( ) throws RemoteException;
    public void setDateTime(Date dateTime) throws RemoteException;
}
```

Example E-26 is the Transaction bean's information/value class.

Example E-26. The TransactionInfo Class

```
package com.forethought.ejb.transaction;

import java.io.Serializable;
import java.util.Date;
```

Example E-26. The TransactionInfo Class (continued)

```java
// Account bean
import com.forethought.ejb.account.AccountInfo;

public class TransactionInfo implements Serializable {

    private int id;
    private AccountInfo accountInfo;
    private float amount;
    private Date dateTime;

    TransactionInfo(int id, float amount, Date dateTime,
                    AccountInfo accountInfo) {
        this.id = id;
        this.amount = amount;
        this.dateTime = dateTime;
        this.accountInfo = accountInfo;
    }

    public int getId( ) {
        return id;
    }

    public AccountInfo getAccountInfo( ) {
        return accountInfo;
    }

    public void setAccountInfo(AccountInfo accountInfo) {
        this.accountInfo = accountInfo;
    }

    public float getAmount( ) {
        return amount;
    }

    public void setAmount(float amount) {
        this.amount = amount;
    }

    public Date getDateTime( ) {
        return dateTime;
    }

    public void setDateTime(Date dateTime) {
        this.dateTime = dateTime;
    }
}
```

Example E-27 shows the home interface for the Transaction bean.

Example E-27. The TransactionHome Interface

```
package com.forethought.ejb.transaction;

import java.rmi.RemoteException;
import java.util.Date;
import java.util.Collection;
import javax.ejb.CreateException;
import javax.ejb.EJBHome;
import javax.ejb.FinderException;

// Account bean
import com.forethought.ejb.account.Account;

public interface TransactionHome extends EJBHome {

    public Transaction create(float amount, Date dateTime, Account account)
        throws CreateException, RemoteException;

    public Transaction findByPrimaryKey(Integer transactionID)
        throws FinderException, RemoteException;

    public Collection findByAmount(float minAmount, float maxAmount)
        throws FinderException, RemoteException;
}
```

Example E-28 is the Transaction bean's implementation class.

Example E-28. The TransactionBean Implementation Class

```
package com.forethought.ejb.transaction;

import java.rmi.RemoteException;
import java.util.Date;
import javax.ejb.CreateException;
import javax.ejb.EJBException;
import javax.ejb.FinderException;
import javax.naming.Context;
import javax.naming.InitialContext;
import javax.naming.NamingException;
import javax.rmi.PortableRemoteObject;

import com.forethought.ejb.util.EntityAdapter;

// Sequence bean
import com.forethought.ejb.sequence.SequenceException;
import com.forethought.ejb.sequence.SequenceLocal;
import com.forethought.ejb.sequence.SequenceLocalHome;

// Account bean
import com.forethought.ejb.account.Account;
import com.forethought.ejb.account.AccountHome;
```

Example E-28. The TransactionBean Implementation Class (continued)

```java
import com.forethought.ejb.account.AccountInfo;
import com.forethought.ejb.account.AccountLocal;
import com.forethought.ejb.account.AccountLocalHome;

public abstract class TransactionBean extends EntityAdapter {

    public Integer ejbCreate(float amount, Date dateTime, Account account)
        throws CreateException {

        // Get the next primary key value
        try {
            Context context = new InitialContext( );
            // Note that RMI-IIOP narrowing is not required
            SequenceLocalHome home = (SequenceLocalHome)
                context.lookup("java:comp/env/ejb/SequenceLocalHome");
            SequenceLocal sequence = home.create( );
            String transactionKey =
                (String)context.lookup(
                    "java:comp/env/constants/TransactionKey");
            Integer id = sequence.getNextValue(transactionKey);

            // Set values
            setId(id);
            setAmount(amount);
            setDateTime(dateTime);

            return null;
        } catch (NamingException e) {
            throw new CreateException("Could not obtain an " +
                "InitialContext: " + e.getMessage( ));
        } catch (SequenceException e) {
            throw new CreateException("Error getting primary key value: " +
                e.getMessage( ));
        }
    }

    public void ejbPostCreate(float amount, Date dateTime, Account account) {
        // Handle CMP relationships
        setAccount(account);
    }

    public TransactionInfo getInfo( ) throws RemoteException {
        TransactionInfo transactionInfo =
            new TransactionInfo(getId().intValue(), getAmount(), getDateTime( ),
                                getAccount().getInfo( ));
        return transactionInfo;
    }

    public void setInfo(TransactionInfo transactionInfo) {
        setAmount(transactionInfo.getAmount( ));
        setDateTime(transactionInfo.getDateTime( ));
        setAccount(transactionInfo.getAccountInfo( ));
```

```java
    }

    public Account getAccount( ) throws RemoteException {
        // Construct primary key for this account
        Integer accountID = getAccountLocal().getId( );

        try {
            // Find the remote interface for this account
            Context context = new InitialContext( );
            AccountHome accountHome =
                (AccountHome)context.lookup(
                    "java:comp/env/ejb/AccountHome");
            Account account = accountHome.findByPrimaryKey(accountID);
            return account;
        } catch (NamingException e) {
            throw new EJBException("Error looking up Account bean: " +
                e.getMessage( ));
        } catch (RemoteException e) {
            throw new EJBException("Error looking up Account bean: " +
                e.getMessage( ));
        } catch (FinderException shouldNeverHappen) {
            // This should never happen; the ID from an account's remote
            // interface should match an account's ID in a local interface
            throw new EJBException("Error matching remote Account to " +
                "local Account: " + shouldNeverHappen.getMessage( ));
        }
    }

    public void setAccount(Account account) {
        try {
            // Construct primary key for this account
            Integer accountID = account.getId( );

            // Find the local interface for this account
            Context context = new InitialContext( );
            AccountLocalHome accountLocalHome =
                (AccountLocalHome)context.lookup(
                    "java:comp/env/ejb/AccountLocalHome");
            AccountLocal accountLocal =
                accountLocalHome.findByPrimaryKey(accountID);
            setAccountLocal(accountLocal);
        } catch (NamingException e) {
            throw new EJBException("Error looking up Account bean: " +
                e.getMessage( ));
        } catch (RemoteException e) {
            throw new EJBException("Error looking up Account bean: " +
                e.getMessage( ));
        } catch (FinderException shouldNeverHappen) {
            // This should never happen; the ID from an account's remote
            // interface should match an account's ID in a local interface
            throw new EJBException("Error matching remote Account to " +
                "local Account: " + shouldNeverHappen.getMessage( ));
```

Example E-28. The TransactionBean Implementation Class (continued)

```
        }
    }

    public void setAccount(AccountInfo accountInfo) {
        try {
            // Construct primary key for this account
            Integer accountID = new Integer(accountInfo.getId());

            // Find the local interface for this account
            Context context = new InitialContext();
            AccountLocalHome accountLocalHome =
                (AccountLocalHome)context.lookup(
                    "java:comp/env/ejb/AccountLocalHome");
            AccountLocal accountLocal =
                accountLocalHome.findByPrimaryKey(accountID);
            setAccountLocal(accountLocal);
        } catch (NamingException e) {
            throw new EJBException("Error looking up Account bean: " +
                e.getMessage());
        } catch (FinderException shouldNeverHappen) {
            // This should never happen; the ID from an account's remote
            // interface should match an account's ID in a local interface
            throw new EJBException("Error matching remote Account to " +
                "local Account: " + shouldNeverHappen.getMessage());
        }
    }

    public abstract Integer getId();
    public abstract void setId(Integer id);

    public abstract AccountLocal getAccountLocal();
    public abstract void setAccountLocal(AccountLocal accountLocal);

    public abstract float getAmount();
    public abstract void setAmount(float amount);

    public abstract Date getDateTime();
    public abstract void setDateTime(Date dateTime);
}
```

The Investment Bean

Example E-29 is the Investment bean's remote interface.

Example E-29. The Investment Remote Interface

```
package com.forethought.ejb.investment;

import java.rmi.RemoteException;
import javax.ejb.EJBObject;

// Account bean
```

```
import com.forethought.ejb.account.Account;

// Fund bean
import com.forethought.ejb.fund.Fund;

public interface Investment extends EJBObject {

    public InvestmentInfo getInfo( ) throws RemoteException;
    public void setInfo(InvestmentInfo investmentInfo) throws RemoteException;

    public Integer getId( ) throws RemoteException;

    public Fund getFund( ) throws RemoteException;
    public void setFund(Fund fund) throws RemoteException;

    public Account getAccount( ) throws RemoteException;
    public void setAccount(Account account)
        throws RemoteException;

    public float getInitialAmount( ) throws RemoteException;
    public void setInitialAmount(float initialAmount)
        throws RemoteException;

    public float getYield( ) throws RemoteException;
    public void setYield(float yield) throws RemoteException;
}
```

Example E-30 is the Investment bean's information class.

Example E-30. The InvestmentInfo Class

```
package com.forethought.ejb.investment;

import java.io.Serializable;

// Account bean
import com.forethought.ejb.account.AccountInfo;

// Fund bean
import com.forethought.ejb.fund.FundInfo;

public class InvestmentInfo implements Serializable {

    private int id;
    private FundInfo fundInfo;
    private AccountInfo accountInfo;
    private float initialAmount;
    private float yield;

    protected InvestmentInfo(int id, float initialAmount, float yield,
                             AccountInfo accountInfo, FundInfo fundInfo) {
```

```java
        this.id = id;
        this.initialAmount = initialAmount;
        this.yield = yield;
        this.accountInfo = accountInfo;
        this.fundInfo = fundInfo;
    }

    public int getId( ) {
        return id;
    }

    public FundInfo getFundInfo( ) {
        return fundInfo;
    }

    public void setFundInfo(FundInfo fundInfo) {
        this.fundInfo = fundInfo;
    }

    public AccountInfo getAccountInfo( ) {
        return accountInfo;
    }

    public void setAccountInfo(AccountInfo accountInfo) {
        this.accountInfo = accountInfo;
    }

    public float getInitialAmount( ) {
        return initialAmount;
    }

    public void setInitialAmount(float initialAmount) {
        this.initialAmount = initialAmount;
    }

    public float getYield( ) {
        return yield;
    }

    public void setYield(float yield) {
        this.yield = yield;
    }
}
```

The home interface for the Investment bean is shown in Example E-31.

Example E-31. The InvestmentHome Interface

```java
package com.forethought.ejb.investment;

import java.rmi.RemoteException;
import java.util.Collection;
```

Example E-31. The InvestmentHome Interface (continued)

```java
import javax.ejb.CreateException;
import javax.ejb.EJBHome;
import javax.ejb.FinderException;

// Account bean
import com.forethought.ejb.account.Account;

// Fund bean
import com.forethought.ejb.fund.Fund;

public interface InvestmentHome extends EJBHome {

    public Investment create(float initialAmount, Account account, Fund fund)
        throws CreateException, RemoteException;

    public Investment findByPrimaryKey(Integer investmentID)
        throws FinderException, RemoteException;

    public Collection findByInitialAmount(float minAmount, float maxAmount)
        throws FinderException, RemoteException;

    public Collection findByYield(float minYield, float maxYield)
        throws FinderException, RemoteException;
}
```

Example E-32 shows the Investment bean's implementation class.

Example E-32. The InvestmentBean Implementation Class

```java
package com.forethought.ejb.investment;

import java.rmi.RemoteException;
import javax.ejb.CreateException;
import javax.ejb.EJBException;
import javax.ejb.FinderException;
import javax.naming.Context;
import javax.naming.InitialContext;
import javax.naming.NamingException;
import javax.rmi.PortableRemoteObject;

import com.forethought.ejb.util.EntityAdapter;

// Sequence bean
import com.forethought.ejb.sequence.SequenceException;
import com.forethought.ejb.sequence.SequenceLocal;
import com.forethought.ejb.sequence.SequenceLocalHome;

// Account bean
import com.forethought.ejb.account.Account;
import com.forethought.ejb.account.AccountHome;
import com.forethought.ejb.account.AccountInfo;
import com.forethought.ejb.account.AccountLocal;
```

Example E-32. The InvestmentBean Implementation Class (continued)

```
import com.forethought.ejb.account.AccountLocalHome;

// Fund bean
import com.forethought.ejb.fund.Fund;
import com.forethought.ejb.fund.FundHome;
import com.forethought.ejb.fund.FundInfo;
import com.forethought.ejb.fund.FundLocal;
import com.forethought.ejb.fund.FundLocalHome;

public abstract class InvestmentBean extends EntityAdapter {

    public Integer ejbCreate(float initialAmount, Account account, Fund fund)
        throws CreateException {

        // Get the next primary key value
        try {
            Context context = new InitialContext();
            // Note that RMI-IIOP narrowing is not required
            SequenceLocalHome home = (SequenceLocalHome)
                context.lookup("java:comp/env/ejb/SequenceLocalHome");
            SequenceLocal sequence = home.create();
            String investmentKey =
                (String)context.lookup("java:comp/env/constants/InvestmentKey");
            Integer id = sequence.getNextValue(investmentKey);

            // Set values
            setId(id);
            setInitialAmount(initialAmount);

            // Initial yield is always 1.0
            setYield(1);

            return null;
        } catch (NamingException e) {
            throw new CreateException("Could not obtain an " +
                "InitialContext: " + e.getMessage());
        } catch (SequenceException e) {
            throw new CreateException("Error getting primary key value: " +
                e.getMessage());
        }
    }

    public void ejbPostCreate(float initialAmount, Account account, Fund fund)
        throws CreateException {

        // Handle CMP relationships
        setAccount(account);
        setFund(fund);
    }

    public InvestmentInfo getInfo() throws RemoteException {
        InvestmentInfo investmentInfo =
```

```
              new InvestmentInfo(getId().intValue(), getInitialAmount(),
                            getYield(), getAccount().getInfo(),
                            getFund().getInfo());

     return investmentInfo;
}

public void setInfo(InvestmentInfo investmentInfo) {
    setInitialAmount(investmentInfo.getInitialAmount());
    setYield(investmentInfo.getYield());
    setAccount(investmentInfo.getAccountInfo());
    setFund(investmentInfo.getFundInfo());
}

public Account getAccount() throws RemoteException {
    // Construct primary key for this account
    Integer accountID = getAccountLocal().getId();

    try {
        // Find the remote interface for this office
        Context context = new InitialContext();
        AccountHome accountHome =
            (AccountHome)context.lookup(
                "java:comp/env/ejb/AccountHome");
        Account account = accountHome.findByPrimaryKey(accountID);
        return account;
    } catch (NamingException e) {
        throw new EJBException("Error looking up Account bean: " +
            e.getMessage());
    } catch (RemoteException e) {
        throw new EJBException("Error looking up Account bean: " +
            e.getMessage());
    } catch (FinderException shouldNeverHappen) {
        // This should never happen; the ID from an account's remote
        // interface should match an account's ID in a local interface
        throw new EJBException("Error matching remote Account to " +
            "local Account: " + shouldNeverHappen.getMessage());
    }
}

public void setAccount(Account account) {
    try {
        // Construct primary key for this account
        Integer accountID = account.getId();

        // Find the local interface for this account
        Context context = new InitialContext();
        AccountLocalHome accountLocalHome =
            (AccountLocalHome)context.lookup(
                "java:comp/env/ejb/AccountLocalHome");
        AccountLocal accountLocal =
            accountLocalHome.findByPrimaryKey(accountID);
```

Example E-32. The InvestmentBean Implementation Class (continued)

```
                setAccountLocal(accountLocal);
        } catch (NamingException e) {
            throw new EJBException("Error looking up Account bean: " +
                e.getMessage());
        } catch (RemoteException e) {
            throw new EJBException("Error looking up Account bean: " +
                e.getMessage());
        } catch (FinderException shouldNeverHappen) {
            // This should never happen; the ID from an account's remote
            // interface should match an account's ID in a local interface
            throw new EJBException("Error matching remote Account to " +
                "local Account: " + shouldNeverHappen.getMessage());
        }
    }

    public void setAccount(AccountInfo accountInfo) {
        try {
            // Construct primary key for this account
            Integer accountID = new Integer(accountInfo.getId());

            // Find the local interface for this account
            Context context = new InitialContext();
            AccountLocalHome accountLocalHome =
                (AccountLocalHome)context.lookup(
                    "java:comp/env/ejb/AccountLocalHome");
            AccountLocal accountLocal =
                accountLocalHome.findByPrimaryKey(accountID);
            setAccountLocal(accountLocal);
        } catch (NamingException e) {
            throw new EJBException("Error looking up Account bean: " +
                e.getMessage());
        } catch (FinderException shouldNeverHappen) {
            // This should never happen; the ID from an account's remote
            // interface should match an account's ID in a local interface
            throw new EJBException("Error matching remote Account to " +
                "local Account: " + shouldNeverHappen.getMessage());
        }
    }

    public Fund getFund() throws RemoteException {
        // Construct primary key for this fund
        Integer fundID = getFundLocal().getId();

        try {
            // Find the remote interface for this fund
            Context context = new InitialContext();
            FundHome fundHome =
                (FundHome)context.lookup("java:comp/env/ejb/FundHome");
            Fund fund = fundHome.findByPrimaryKey(fundID);
            return fund;
        } catch (NamingException e) {
            throw new EJBException("Error looking up Fund bean: " +
```

```
                    e.getMessage( ));
        } catch (RemoteException e) {
            throw new EJBException("Error looking up Fund bean: " +
                e.getMessage( ));
        } catch (FinderException shouldNeverHappen) {
            // This should never happen; the ID from a fund's remote
            //   interface should match a fund's ID in a local interface
            throw new EJBException("Error matching remote Fund to " +
                "local Fund: " + shouldNeverHappen.getMessage( ));
        }
    }

    public void setFund(Fund fund) {
        try {
            // Construct primary key for this fund
            Integer fundID = fund.getId( );

            // Find the local interface for this fund
            Context context = new InitialContext( );
            FundLocalHome fundLocalHome =
                (FundLocalHome)context.lookup(
                    "java:comp/env/ejb/FundLocalHome");
            FundLocal fundLocal =
                fundLocalHome.findByPrimaryKey(fundID);
            setFundLocal(fundLocal);
        } catch (NamingException e) {
            throw new EJBException("Error looking up Fund bean: " +
                e.getMessage( ));
        } catch (RemoteException e) {
            throw new EJBException("Error looking up Fund bean: " +
                e.getMessage( ));
        } catch (FinderException shouldNeverHappen) {
            // This should never happen; the ID from a fund's remote
            //   interface should match a fund's ID in a local interface
            throw new EJBException("Error matching remote Fund to " +
                "local Fund: " + shouldNeverHappen.getMessage( ));
        }
    }

    public void setFund(FundInfo fundInfo) {
        try {
            // Construct primary key for this fund
            Integer fundID = new Integer(fundInfo.getId( ));

            // Find the local interface for this fund
            Context context = new InitialContext( );
            FundLocalHome fundLocalHome =
                (FundLocalHome)context.lookup(
                    "java:comp/env/ejb/FundLocalHome");
            FundLocal fundLocal =
                fundLocalHome.findByPrimaryKey(fundID);
            setFundLocal(fundLocal);
```

Example E-32. The InvestmentBean Implementation Class (continued)

```
        } catch (NamingException e) {
            throw new EJBException("Error looking up Fund bean: " +
                e.getMessage( ));
        } catch (FinderException shouldNeverHappen) {
            // This should never happen; the ID from a fund's remote
            //   interface should match a fund's ID in a local interface
            throw new EJBException("Error matching remote Fund to " +
                "local Fund: " + shouldNeverHappen.getMessage( ));
        }
    }

    public abstract Integer getId( );
    public abstract void setId(Integer id);

    public abstract FundLocal getFundLocal( );
    public abstract void setFundLocal(FundLocal fundLocal);

    public abstract AccountLocal getAccountLocal( );
    public abstract void setAccountLocal(AccountLocal accountLocal);

    public abstract float getInitialAmount( );
    public abstract void setInitialAmount(float initialAmount);

    public abstract float getYield( );
    public abstract void setYield(float yield);
}
```

The Event Bean

Example E-33 is the remote interface for the Event bean.

Example E-33. The Event Remote Interface

```
package com.forethought.ejb.event;

import java.rmi.RemoteException;
import java.util.Collection;
import java.util.Date;
import javax.ejb.EJBObject;

public interface Event extends EJBObject {

    public EventInfo getInfo( ) throws RemoteException;
    public void setInfo(EventInfo eventInfo) throws RemoteException;

    public Integer getId( ) throws RemoteException;

    public String getDescription( ) throws RemoteException;
    public void setDescription(String description)
        throws RemoteException;

    public Date getDateTime( ) throws RemoteException;
```

```
    public void setDateTime(Date dateTime) throws RemoteException;

    public Collection getAttendees( ) throws RemoteException;
    public void setAttendees(Collection attendees) throws RemoteException;
}
```

Example E-34 is the information map for the Event bean.

Example E-34. The EventInfo Class

```
package com.forethought.ejb.event;

import java.io.Serializable;
import java.rmi.RemoteException;
import java.util.Collection;
import java.util.Date;
import java.util.Iterator;
import java.util.LinkedList;

// User bean
import com.forethought.ejb.user.User;
import com.forethought.ejb.user.UserInfo;

public class EventInfo implements Serializable {

    private int id;
    private String description;
    private Date dateTime;
    private Collection attendees;

    protected EventInfo(int id, String description, Date dateTime,
                        Collection attendees) throws RemoteException {
        this.id = id;
        this.description = description;
        this.dateTime = dateTime;

        // Convert attendees to correct type
        this.attendees = new LinkedList( );
        for (Iterator i = attendees.iterator(); i.hasNext( ); ) {
            Object obj = i.next( );
            User user = (User)obj;
            this.attendees.add(user.getInfo( ));
        }
    }

    public int getId( ) {
        return id;
    }

    public String getDescription( ) {
        return description;
    }
```

Example E-34. The EventInfo Class (continued)

```java
    public void setDescription(String description) {
        this.description = description;
    }

    public Date getDateTime() {
        return dateTime;
    }

    public void setDateTime(Date dateTime) {
        this.dateTime = dateTime;
    }

    public Collection getAttendees() {
        return attendees;
    }

    public void setAttendees(Collection attendees) {
        this.attendees = attendees;
    }

    public void addAttendee(UserInfo userInfo) {
        if (attendees == null) {
            attendees = new LinkedList();
        }
        if (attendees.contains(userInfo)) {
            return;
        }
        attendees.add(userInfo);
    }

    public void removeAttendee(UserInfo userInfo) {
        if (attendees == null) {
            return;
        }
        attendees.remove(userInfo);
    }
}
```

Example E-35 is the home interface for the Event bean.

Example E-35. The EventHome Interface

```java
package com.forethought.ejb.event;

import java.rmi.RemoteException;
import java.util.Collection;
import java.util.Date;
import javax.ejb.CreateException;
import javax.ejb.EJBHome;
import javax.ejb.FinderException;

public interface EventHome extends EJBHome {
```

```
    public Event create(String description, Date dateTime, Collection attendees)
        throws CreateException, RemoteException;

    public Event findByPrimaryKey(Integer eventID)
        throws FinderException, RemoteException;

    public Collection findByDescription(String description)
        throws FinderException, RemoteException;
}
```

Finally, Example E-36 shows the bean implementation class for handling events.

Example E-36. The EventBean Implementation Class

```
package com.forethought.ejb.event;

import java.rmi.RemoteException;
import java.util.Collection;
import java.util.Date;
import java.util.Iterator;
import java.util.LinkedList;
import javax.ejb.CreateException;
import javax.ejb.EJBException;
import javax.ejb.FinderException;
import javax.naming.Context;
import javax.naming.InitialContext;
import javax.naming.NamingException;

import com.forethought.ejb.sequence.SequenceException;
import com.forethought.ejb.sequence.SequenceLocal;
import com.forethought.ejb.sequence.SequenceLocalHome;
import com.forethought.ejb.util.EntityAdapter;

// User bean
import com.forethought.ejb.user.User;
import com.forethought.ejb.user.UserHome;
import com.forethought.ejb.user.UserInfo;
import com.forethought.ejb.user.UserLocal;
import com.forethought.ejb.user.UserLocalHome;

public abstract class EventBean extends EntityAdapter {

    public Integer ejbCreate(String description, Date dateTime,
                             Collection attendees)
        throws CreateException {
        // Get the next primary key value
        try {
            Context context = new InitialContext();

            // Note that RMI-IIOP narrowing is not required
            SequenceLocalHome home = (SequenceLocalHome)
                context.lookup("java:comp/env/ejb/SequenceLocalHome");
```

```
            SequenceLocal sequence = home.create( );
            String eventKey =
                (String)context.lookup(
                    "java:comp/env/constants/EventKey");
            Integer id = sequence.getNextValue(eventKey);

            // Set values
            setId(id);
            setDescription(description);
            setDateTime(dateTime);

            return null;
        } catch (NamingException e) {
            throw new CreateException("Could not obtain an " +
                "InitialContext.");
        } catch (SequenceException e) {
            throw new CreateException("Error getting primary key value: " +
                e.getMessage( ));
        }
    }

    public void ejbPostCreate(String description, Date dateTime,
                             Collection attendees) {
        // Handle CMP relationships
        setAttendees(attendees);
    }

    public EventInfo getInfo( ) throws RemoteException {
        EventInfo eventInfo =
            new EventInfo(getId().intValue(), getDescription(), getDateTime( ),
                         getAttendees( ));
        return eventInfo;
    }

    public void setInfo(EventInfo eventInfo) {
        setDescription(eventInfo.getDescription( ));
        setDateTime(eventInfo.getDateTime( ));
        setAttendees(eventInfo.getAttendees( ));
    }

    public Collection getAttendees( ) {
        try {
            Collection attendeesLocal = getAttendeesLocal( );
            Collection attendees = new LinkedList( );

            // Get the UserHome interface
            Context context = new InitialContext( );
            UserHome userHome =
                (UserHome)context.lookup(
                    "java:comp/env/ejb/UserHome");
```

```
                // Convert each local User into a remote User
                for (Iterator i = attendeesLocal.iterator(); i.hasNext(); ) {
                    UserLocal userLocal = (UserLocal)i.next();

                    // Construct primary key for this office
                    Integer userID = userLocal.getId();

                    User user = userHome.findByPrimaryKey(userID);
                    attendees.add(user);
                }

                return attendees;
            } catch (NamingException e) {
                throw new EJBException("Error looking up User bean: " +
                    e.getMessage());
            } catch (RemoteException e) {
                throw new EJBException("Error looking up User bean: " +
                    e.getMessage());
            } catch (FinderException shouldNeverHappen) {
                // This should never happen; the ID from a user's remote
                // interface should match a user's ID in a local interface
                throw new EJBException("Error matching remote User to " +
                    "local User: " + shouldNeverHappen.getMessage());
            }
        }

    public void setAttendees(Collection attendees) {
        try {
            // Handle case where no attendees supplied
            if (attendees == null) {
                setAttendeesLocal(null);
                return;
            }

            // Get the local User home interface
            Context context = new InitialContext();
            UserLocalHome userLocalHome =
                (UserLocalHome)context.lookup(
                    "java:comp/env/ejb/UserLocalHome");

            Collection attendeesLocal = new LinkedList();
            // Convert each remote User to a local User
            for (Iterator i = attendees.iterator(); i.hasNext(); ) {
                // Construct primary key for this office
                Integer userID;
                Object obj = i.next();

                if (obj instanceof User) {
                    userID = ((User)obj).getId();
                } else if (obj instanceof UserInfo) {
                    userID = new Integer(((UserInfo)obj).getId());
```

Example E-36. The EventBean Implementation Class (continued)

```
                } else {
                    throw new EJBException("Invalid object type in attendee " +
                        "list.");
                }

                // Find the local interface for this user
                UserLocal userLocal =
                    userLocalHome.findByPrimaryKey(userID);
                attendeesLocal.add(userLocal);
            }

            setAttendeesLocal(attendeesLocal);

        } catch (NamingException e) {
            throw new EJBException("Error looking up User bean: " +
                e.getMessage());
        } catch (RemoteException e) {
            throw new EJBException("Error looking up User bean: " +
                e.getMessage());
        } catch (FinderException shouldNeverHappen) {
            // This should never happen; the ID from a user's remote
            // interface should match a user's ID in a local interface
            throw new EJBException("Error matching remote User to " +
                "local User: " + shouldNeverHappen.getMessage());
        }
    }

    public abstract Integer getId();
    public abstract void setId(Integer id);

    public abstract String getDescription();
    public abstract void setDescription(String description);

    public abstract Date getDateTime();
    public abstract void setDateTime(Date dateTime);

    public abstract Collection getAttendeesLocal();
    public abstract void setAttendeesLocal(Collection attendeesLocal);
}
```

Deployment Descriptors

The *ejb-jar.xml* deployment descriptor is required for packaging of enterprise beans. There are three deployment units detailed in this book: *forethoughtEntities.jar*, *forethoughtLogic.jar*, and *forethoughtScheduling.jar*. Each of these has its own *ejb-jar. xml*. However, deployment descriptors are both boring and verbose (they take a lot of space), so I am not reprinting those descriptors here. The chapters discuss fragments of these, and you can download and view the complete descriptors from the book's web site, *http://www.newInstance.com*.

Application Exceptions

Here are some additional exceptions that extend the ForethoughtException class, which was defined in Chapter 5. Session beans and other components throughout the rest of the book use these exceptions.

Entity Exceptions

The exceptions in the following code listings are all used in reporting the specific problem associated with a specified entity (an office, user, account, and so forth) to session bean clients. Example E-37 is the exception for reporting that a fund being searched for cannot be located.

Example E-37. The FundNotFoundException Class

```
package com.forethought.ejb.fund;

import com.forethought.ForethoughtException;

public class FundNotFoundException extends ForethoughtException {

    /** The fund name that was not found */
    private String fundName;

    public FundNotFoundException(String fundName) {
        super("A fund with the name " + fundName +
            " could not be found.");
        this.fundName = fundName;
    }

    public String getFundName( ) {
        return fundName;
    }
}
```

Example E-38 is the exception reported when an unknown user type is specified.

Example E-38. The UnknownUserTypeException Class

```
package com.forethought.ejb.userType;

import com.forethought.ForethoughtException;

public class UnknownUserTypeException extends ForethoughtException {

    /** The user type specified */
    private String userType;

    public UnknownUserTypeException(String userType) {
        super("There is no user type called " + userType +
            " in the Forethought application.");
```

Example E-38. The UnknownUserTypeException Class (continued)

```
        this.userType = userType;
    }

    public String getUserType( ) {
        return userType;
    }
}
```

Example E-39 is the exception for reporting invalid account types.

Example E-39. The UnknownAccountTypeException Class

```
package com.forethought.ejb.accountType;

import com.forethought.ForethoughtException;

public class UnknownAccountTypeException extends ForethoughtException {

    /** The account type specified */
    private String accountType;

    public UnknownAccountTypeException(String accountType) {
        super("There is no account type called " + accountType +
            " in the Forethought application.");
        this.accountType = accountType;
    }

    public String getAccountType( ) {
        return accountType;
    }
}
```

Index

We'd like to hear your suggestions for improving our indexes. Send email to *index@oreilly.com*.

configuration directory, 236
directory, setup, 235–244
messaging on, 180–189
    EventManager bean and, 181–185
multiple directory, 136–138
services framework, 15
Services with SOAP (book), 202
servlets, 14, 16
session beans
    accessing entity beans, 60
    adapters and, 79
    façade patterns and, 150
    ID, creating, 77
    managers, 102
SessionAdapter class, 79
setCity( ) method, 157
setId( ) method, 70
setPassword( ) method, 162
Simple API for XML (SAX), 12
sn attribute for BasicAttribute class, 114
SOAP, 26
source transparency, 158
SQL Navigator, 7, 38
SQL (Structured Query Language), 5, 38
    accounts store, 209–214
    deletions and, 217–219
    deployment, 225–234
    events and scheduling, 214–217
    primary keys and, 219–222
    scripts, 205–224
    user store, 206–209
SQL*net, 19
state design, 167–179
stateful beans, 22, 168–173
stateless beans, 22, 174–179
storage of user data, 38–43
    accounts, 43–45
structural constraints, 53
Structured Query Language (see SQL)
structures (data), 30
Sun (web site for downloads), 6
Sybase, 17
synchronization, 136
synchronous processing, 180

T

tables, 28, 37, 77
    naming columns, 65
    scheduling and events storage, 45
    user storage and, 39
technologies, choosing for
        applications, 10–13

tools, 7
transaction isolations (EBJ), 77
transactions for accounts, 28, 35
types, creating, 222–224

U

uid attribute for BasicAttribute class, 114
UID (user ID), 52
unique keys, 31
uniqueMember attribute, verifying group
        memberships, 124
Unix platforms, setting up directory
        servers, 235
update( ) method, 103, 157
user data, 28–32
    data constraints, 29
    passwords and, 52–53
    permissions, 32–34
    storage, 38–43
    types, 30
    unique keys, characters, and IDs, 31
User entity beans, 100
user ID (UID), 52
user store, 206–209
    Cloudscape Java databases and, 206
    InstantDB, 206
    MySQL, 207
    Oracle, 208
    PostgreSQL, 208
userInGroup( ) method, 130
    verifying group memberships, 124
UserManager component, 158–167
    format transparency, 159
    source transparency, 158
usernames, 28
userPassword attribute for BasicAttribute
        class, 114
users
    adding and deleting, 114
    addition and removal of, 122
    authenticating, 116
    credentials check, 139
    LDAP managers, 112
utilities, 7

V

value patterns, 95
VARCHAR data type, 39, 41, 43
    columns in database tables and, 39
VARCHAR2 data type, 41
vi editor, 7

W

W3C (World Wide Web Consortium), 12
WAP (Wireless Application Protocol), 12
web applications, 201
web services, 201
web, using Java and J2EE, 13
Weblogic, 62
wildcards (*), 126, 194
Windows
    databases and, 17
    setting up directory servers, 235
Wireless Application Protocol (WAP), 12

wireless devices, supporting, 12, 14
wordpad, 7
World Wide Web Consortium (W3C), 12
writing Enterprise JavaBeans and, 59

X

XML (Extensible Markup Language), 7, 14,
        25
    beans, deploying, 91
    deployment descriptor, creating, 71
XMLSpy, 7
XSL (Extensible Stylesheet Language), 14, 25

About the Author

Brett McLaughlin is one of the leading authorities on Java, XML, enterprise applications, and open source software. He works as the Enhydra strategist at Lutris Technologies and is responsible for the direction and strategy for the Enhydra application server. In addition, he is the founder or co-founder of numerous other open source projects, such as JDOM (currently in JSR at Sun), ApacheTurbine (a servlet-based web applications framework), and Enhydra Zeus (an XML data binding framework). He is a committer on OpenEJB, jBoss, and Apache Cocoon as well, placing him in the middle of Java and XML innovation.

In addition to his technology contributions, Brett is a prolific writer; he is the author of *Java & XML* (O'Reilly), the moderator of IBM's Java and XML tools and technologies newgroup, flashline.com's biweekly component columnist, and has written dozens of articles for IBM Developer Works, JavaWorld, and oreilly.com.

Colophon

Our look is the result of reader comments, our own experimentation, and feedback from distribution channels. Distinctive covers complement our distinctive approach to technical topics, breathing personality and life into potentially dry subjects.

The animal on the cover of *Building Java Enterprise Applications Volume I: Architecture* is a kangaroo rat. There are about 20 species of kangaroo rat (genus *Dipodomys*, family *Heteromyidae*) found in western North America. Some of these species are endangered. These small mammals are equipped with long, narrow feet that enable them to get about with long, strong hops. They can travel as far as two meters per hop. Their tufted tails, which are approximately as long as their bodies, are used as rudders. The forearms of kangaroo rats are so short that they often disappear within their fur. Most kangaroo rats have a color similar to the sand or soil of their environment, with black or white facial markings and two stripes running down the back. Albino kangaroo rats do occasionally appear. Like all of their relatives in the *Heteromyidae* family, kangaroo rats have large, fur-lined pouches in their cheeks into which they stuff food to carry back to their nests. They eat grass, plant greenery, and seeds. It is not uncommon to find evidence of a visit by a kangaroo rat in vegetable gardens. Remarkably, they are able to obtain all the water they need from the food that they eat. Kangaroo rats are able to live their entire lives without ever drinking water.

Kangaroo rats are nocturnal animals. They tend to be antisocial and belligerent. Kangaroo rat fights frequently occur. During these fights they jump in the air and kick at each other with their powerful legs. Kicking, in this case kicking sand, also comes in handy when cornered by enemies such as rattlesnakes or coyotes. While the enemy has sand in its eyes, the kangaroo rat makes his hopping getaway.

Kangaroo rats build their subterranean nests beneath small bushes or trees. They line the nests with leaves or grass, and build in numerous tunnels and escape outlets.

Emily Quill was the production editor and copyeditor for *Building Java Enterprise Applications Volume I: Architecture*. Jane Ellin was the proofreader, and Catherine Morris provided quality control. Sue Willing and Philip Dangler provided production assistance. Joe Wizda wrote the index.

Hanna Dyer designed the cover of this book, based on a series design by Edie Freedman. The cover image is a 19th-century engraving from the Dover Pictorial Archive. Emma Colby produced the cover layout with QuarkXPress 4.1 using Adobe's ITC Garamond font.

Melanie Wang designed the interior layout, based on a series design by David Futato. Neil Walls converted the files from Microsoft Word to FrameMaker 5.5.6 using tools created by Mike Sierra. The text font is Linotype Birka; the heading font is Adobe Myriad Condensed; and the code font is LucasFont's TheSans Mono Condensed. The illustrations that appear in the book were produced by Robert Romano and Jessamyn Read using Macromedia FreeHand 9 and Adobe Photoshop 6. The tip and warning icons were drawn by Christopher Bing. This colophon was written by Clairemarie Fisher O'Leary.

How to stay in touch with O'Reilly

1. Visit Our Award-Winning Web Site

http://www.oreilly.com/

★ "Top 100 Sites on the Web" —PC Magazine
★ CIO Magazine's Web Business 50 Awards

Our web site contains a library of comprehensive product information (including book excerpts and tables of contents), downloadable software, background articles, interviews with technology leaders, links to relevant sites, book cover art, and more. File us in your bookmarks or favorites!

2. Join Our Email Mailing Lists

Sign up to get email announcements of new books and conferences, special offers, and O'Reilly Network technology newsletters at:
elists.oreilly.com.
It's easy to customize your free elists subscription so you'll get exactly the O'Reilly news you want.

3. Get Examples from Our Books

To find example files for a book, go to:
http://www.oreilly.com/catalog
select the book, and follow the "Examples" link.

4. Contact Us via Email

order@oreilly.com
For answers to problems regarding your order or our products. To place a book order online visit:
http://www.oreilly.com/order_new/

catalog@oreilly.com
To request a copy of our latest catalog.

booktech@oreilly.com
For book content technical questions or corrections.

proposals@oreilly.com
To submit new book proposals to our editors and product managers.

international@oreilly.com
For information about our international distributors or translation queries. For a list of our distributors outside of North America check out:
http://international.oreilly.com/distributors.html

5. Work with Us

Check out our web site for current employment opportunites:
http://jobs.oreilly.com/

6. Register your book

Register your book at:
http://register.oreilly.com

O'Reilly & Associates, Inc.
1005 Gravenstein Hwy North
Sebastopol, CA 95472 USA
TEL   707-827-7000 or 800-998-9938
       (6am to 5pm PST)
FAX   707-829-0104

International Distributors

http://international.oreilly.com/distributors.html • *international@oreilly.com*

UK, EUROPE, MIDDLE EAST, AND AFRICA (EXCEPT FRANCE, GERMANY, AUSTRIA, SWITZERLAND, LUXEMBOURG, AND LIECHTENSTEIN)

INQUIRIES
O'Reilly UK Limited
4 Castle Street
Farnham
Surrey, GU9 7HS
United Kingdom
Telephone: 44-1252-711776
Fax: 44-1252-734211
Email: information@oreilly.co.uk

ORDERS
Wiley Distribution Services Ltd.
1 Oldlands Way
Bognor Regis
West Sussex PO22 9SA
United Kingdom
Telephone: 44-1243-843294
UK Freephone: 0800-243207
Fax: 44-1243-843302 (Europe/EU orders)
or 44-1243-843274 (Middle East/Africa)
Email: cs-books@wiley.co.uk

FRANCE

INQUIRIES & ORDERS
Éditions O'Reilly
18 rue Séguier
75006 Paris, France
Tel: 33-1-40-51-71-89
Fax: 33-1-40-51-72-26
Email: france@oreilly.fr

GERMANY, SWITZERLAND, AUSTRIA, LUXEMBOURG, AND LIECHTENSTEIN

INQUIRIES & ORDERS
O'Reilly Verlag
Balthasarstr. 81
D-50670 Köln, Germany
Telephone: 49-221-973160-91
Fax: 49-221-973160-8
Email: anfragen@oreilly.de (inquiries)
Email: order@oreilly.de (orders)

CANADA

(FRENCH LANGUAGE BOOKS)
Les Éditions Flammarion ltée
375, Avenue Laurier Ouest
Montréal, QC H2V 2K3 Canada
Tel: 1-514-277-8807
Fax: 1-514-278-2085
Email: info@flammarion.qc.ca

HONG KONG

City Discount Subscription Service, Ltd.
Unit A, 6th Floor, Yan's Tower
27 Wong Chuk Hang Road
Aberdeen, Hong Kong
Tel: 852-2580-3539
Fax: 852-2580-6463
Email: citydis@ppn.com.hk

KOREA

Hanbit Media, Inc.
Chungmu Bldg. 210
Yonnam-dong 568-33
Mapo-gu
Seoul, Korea
Tel: 822-325-0397
Fax: 822-325-9697
Email: hant93@chollian.dacom.co.kr

PHILIPPINES

Global Publishing
G/F Benavides Garden
1186 Benavides Street
Manila, Philippines
Tel: 632-254-8949/632-252-2582
Fax: 632-734-5060/632-252-2733
Email: globalp@pacific.net.ph

TAIWAN

O'Reilly Taiwan
1st Floor, No. 21, Lane 295
Section 1, Fu-Shing South Road
Taipei, 106 Taiwan
Tel: 886-2-27099669
Fax: 886-2-27038802
Email: mori@oreilly.com

INDIA

Shroff Publishers & Distributors PVT. LTD.
C-103, MIDC, TTC Pawane
Navi Mumbai 400 701
India
Tel: (91-22) 763 4290, 763 4293
Fax: (91-22) 768 3337
Email: spdorders@shroffpublishers.com

CHINA

O'Reilly Beijing
SIGMA Building, Suite B809
No. 49 Zhichun Road
Haidian District
Beijing, China PR 100080
Tel: 86-10-8809-7475
Fax: 86-10-8809-7463
Email: beijing@oreilly.com

JAPAN

O'Reilly Japan, Inc.
Yotsuya Y's Building
7 Banch 6, Honshio-cho
Shinjuku-ku
Tokyo 160-0003 Japan
Tel: 81-3-3356-5227
Fax: 81-3-3356-5261
Email: japan@oreilly.com

SINGAPORE, INDONESIA, MALAYSIA, AND THAILAND

TransQuest Publishers Pte Ltd
30 Old Toh Tuck Road #05-02
Sembawang Kimtrans Logistics Centre
Singapore 597654
Tel: 65-4623112
Fax: 65-4625761
Email: wendiw@transquest.com.sg

AUSTRALIA

Woodslane Pty., Ltd.
7/5 Vuko Place
Warriewood NSW 2102
Australia
Tel: 61-2-9970-5111
Fax: 61-2-9970-5002
Email: info@woodslane.com.au

NEW ZEALAND

Woodslane New Zealand, Ltd.
21 Cooks Street (P.O. Box 575)
Waganui, New Zealand
Tel: 64-6-347-6543
Fax: 64-6-345-4840
Email: info@woodslane.com.au

ARGENTINA

Distribuidora Cuspide
Suipacha 764
1008 Buenos Aires
Argentina
Phone: 54-11-4322-8868
Fax: 54-11-4322-3456
Email: libros@cuspide.com

ALL OTHER COUNTRIES

O'Reilly & Associates, Inc.
1005 Gravenstein Hwy North
Sebastopol, CA 95472 USA
Tel: 707-827-7000
Fax: 707-829-0104
Email: order@oreilly.com

O'REILLY®

TO ORDER: **800-998-9938** • **order@oreilly.com** • **www.oreilly.com**
ONLINE EDITIONS OF MOST O'REILLY TITLES ARE AVAILABLE BY SUBSCRIPTION AT **safari.oreilly.com**
ALSO AVAILABLE AT MOST RETAIL AND ONLINE BOOKSTORES